THE STATES AND THE NATION SERIES, of which this volume is a part, is designed to assist the American people in a serious look at the ideals they have espoused and the experiences they have undergone in the history of the nation. The content of every volume represents the scholarship, experience, and opinions of its author. The costs of writing and editing were met mainly by grants from the National Endowment for the Humanities, a federal agency. The project was administered by the American Association for State and Local History, a nonprofit learned society, working with an Editorial Board of distinguished editors, authors, and historians, whose names are listed below.

Delaware

A Bicentennial History

Carol E. Hoffecker

W. W. Norton & Company, Inc.
New York

American Association for State and Local History
Nashville

Author and publishers make grateful acknowledgment to the following for permission to quote from archival materials and previously published works:

Elizabeth Godwin Goggin, for permission to quote from "The History of Poor-Relief Administration in Delaware," by Elizabeth Godwin Goggin, master's thesis prepared for the University of Chicago School of Social Service Administration in 1938.

The University of Delaware and Helen B. Stewart, for permission to quote from "The Negro in Delaware to 1829," by Helen B. Stewart, master's thesis prepared for the University of Delaware in 1940.

The University of Delaware and John Gary Dean, for permission to quote from "The Free Negro in Delaware," by John Gary Dean, master's thesis prepared for the University of Delaware in 1970.

The University of Delaware, College of Marine Studies, for permission to quote from "Economic and Social Aspects of Delaware's Coastal Zone," by Joel M. Goodwin, from vol. 8 of the Delaware Bay Report Series (10 vols.), edited by Dennis F. Polis and produced (mimeographed) by the College of Marine Studies, University of Delaware.

Marion B. Reed, for permission to quote from "Readings in Delaware History: Economic Development," edited by H. Clay Reed and produced (mimeographed) in 1939 by the Department of History and Political Science, University of Delaware.

The Historical Society of Delaware, for permission to quote from Thomas Rodney's "Essay on Negroes," from the Rodney Collection.

Jessica I. Terry, for permission to quote from the papers of Charles L. Terry in "Messages of the Governors," Morris Library, University of Delaware.

Published and distributed by
W. W. Norton & Company, Inc.
500 Fifth Avenue
New York, New York 10036

Library of Congress Cataloguing-in-Publication Data

Hoffecker, Carol E
  Delaware: a Bicentennial history.

  (The States and the Nation series)
  Bibliography: p.
  Includes index.
  1. Delaware—History. I. Series.
F164.H62   975.1   76-53844
ISBN 0-393-05620-1

Printed in the United States of America
1 2 3 4 5 6 7 8 9 0

To the memory of my grandparents

Marie F. and Elmer Zebley

and

Florence C. and Charles W. Hoffecker,

all native Delawareans

Contents

Illustrations

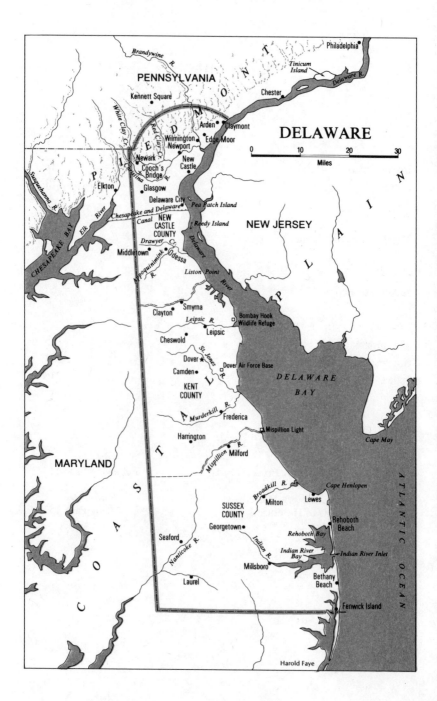

PENNSYLVANIA

Brandywine

Philadelphia

Tinicum Island

Kennett Square

Chester

Delaware R.

DELAWARE

Arden
Claymont

White Clay Cr.

Red Clay Cr.

Wilmington
Newport
Edge Moor

0   10   20   30
Miles

Newark
Cooch's
Bridge
New
Castle

Christina

Elkton

Glasgow

NEW JERSEY

Delaware City
Pea Patch Island

Susquehanna R.

Chesapeake and Delaware Canal

NEW
CASTLE
COUNTY

Reedy Island

CHESAPEAKE BAY

Elk River

Middletown

Drawyer Cr.

Odessa

Appoquinimink R.

Liston Point

Delaware River

COASTAL

Clayton

Smyrna

Leipsic R.

Leipsic

Bombay Hook
Wildlife Refuge

Cheswold

DELAWARE
BAY

St. Jones R.

Dover
Dover Air Force Base

Camden

KENT
COUNTY

Murderkill R.

Frederica

Harrington

Mispillion Light

PLAIN

Cape May

Mispillion R.

Milford

MARYLAND

Broadkill R.

Cape Henlopen

SUSSEX
COUNTY

Milton

Lewes

Georgetown

Rehoboth
Beach

Seaford

Rehoboth Bay

Nanticoke R.

Indian R.

Indian River Bay

Indian River Inlet

Millsboro

Laurel

Bethany
Beach

ATLANTIC OCEAN

Fenwick Island

Harold Faye

Invitation to the Reader

IN 1807, former President John Adams argued that a complete history of the American Revolution could not be written until the history of change in each state was known, because the principles of the Revolution were as various as the states that went through it. Two hundred years after the Declaration of Independence, the American nation has spread over a continent and beyond. The states have grown in number from thirteen to fifty. And democratic principles have been interpreted differently in every one of them.

We therefore invite you to consider that the history of your state may have more to do with the bicentennial review of the American Revolution than does the story of Bunker Hill or Valley Forge. The Revolution has continued as Americans extended liberty and democracy over a vast territory. John Adams was right: the states are part of that story, and the story is incomplete without an account of their diversity.

The Declaration of Independence stressed life, liberty, and the pursuit of happiness; accordingly, it shattered the notion of holding new territories in the subordinate status of colonies. The Northwest Ordinance of 1787 set forth a procedure for new states to enter the Union on an equal footing with the old. The Federal Constitution shortly confirmed this novel means of building a nation out of equal states. The step-by-step process through which territories have achieved self-government and national representation is among the most important of the Founding Fathers' legacies.

The method of state-making reconciled the ancient conflict between liberty and empire, resulting in what Thomas Jefferson called an empire for liberty. The system has worked and remains unaltered, despite enormous changes that have taken

ix

place in the nation. The country's extent and variety now sur-
pass anything the patriots of '76 could likely have imagined.
The United States has changed from an agrarian republic into a
highly industrial and urban democracy, from a fledgling nation
into a major world power. As Oliver Wendell Holmes remarked
in 1920, the creators of the nation could not have seen completely how it and its constitution and its states would develop.
Any meaningful review in the bicentennial era must consider
what the country has become, as well as what it was.

The new nation of equal states took as its motto *E Pluribus
Unum*—"out of many, one." But just as many peoples have
become Americans without complete loss of ethnic and cultural
identities, so have the states retained differences of character.
Some have been superficial, expressed in stereotyped images—
big, boastful Texas, "sophisticated" New York, "hillbilly"
Arkansas. Other differences have been more real, sometimes instructively, sometimes amusingly; democracy has embraced
Huey Long's Louisiana, bilingual New Mexico, unicameral Ne-
braska, and a Texas that once taxed fortunetellers and spawned
politicians called "Woodpecker Republicans" and "Skunk
Democrats." Some differences have been profound, as when
South Carolina secessionists led other states out of the Union in
opposition to abolitionists in Massachusetts and Ohio. The result was a bitter Civil War.

The Revolution's first shots may have sounded in Lexington
and Concord; but fights over what democracy should mean and
who should have independence have erupted from Pennsylvania's Gettysburg to the "Bleeding Kansas" of John Brown,
from the Alamo in Texas to the Indian battles at Montana's
Little Bighorn. Utah Mormons have known the strain of isolation; Hawaiians at Pearl Harbor, the terror of attack; Georgians
during Sherman's march, the sadness of defeat and devastation.
Each state's experience differs instructively; each adds understanding to the whole.

The purpose of this series of books is to make that kind of understanding accessible, in a way that will last in value far
beyond the bicentennial fireworks. The series offers a volume
on every state, plus the District of Columbia—fifty-one, in all.

Each book contains, besides the text, a view of the state through eyes other than the author's—a "photographer's essay," in which a skilled photographer presents his own personal perceptions of the state's contemporary flavor.

We have asked authors not for comprehensive chronicles, nor for research monographs or new data for scholars. Bibliographies and footnotes are minimal. We have asked each author for a summing up—interpretive, sensitive, thoughtful, individual, even personal—of what seems significant about his or her state's history. What distinguishes it? What has mattered about it, to its own people and to the rest of the nation? What has it come to now?

To interpret the states in all their variety, we have sought a variety of backgrounds in authors themselves and have encouraged variety in the approaches they take. They have in common only these things: historical knowledge, writing skill, and strong personal feelings about a particular state. Each has wide latitude for the use of the short space. And if each succeeds, it will be by offering you, in your capacity as a *citizen* of a state *and* of a nation, stimulating insights to test against your own.

James Morton Smith
General Editor

Preface

*T*HOMAS Jefferson described Delaware, the first state to ratify the Constitution, as a diamond because, although small, it had great value. Despite its diminutive size, the second-smallest state has had a long, complex history that exhibits many of the major themes in the economic, social, and political development of the nation. Like the United States as a whole, this tiny border state has its own rural South and industrial North, accompanied by marked geographical, ethnic, and cultural differences.

It is most amazing that Delaware emerged from the colonial period intact. Through a series of historic accidents, a part of the peninsula that separates Delaware Bay and Delaware River from the Chesapeake was conquered by or traded from the Swedes to the Dutch to the English, finally becoming the "Three Lower Counties on the Delaware" of William Penn's Quaker colony. It was largely through the self-identification of the counties' people as a community separate from either Maryland or Pennsylvania that the area became in 1776 "The Delaware State," a distinct political unit in the new United States. The rod that connects the counties of that state is the Delaware bay and river. New York has the Hudson; Arkansas and Louisiana, the Mississippi; but only in Delaware is no part of the state farther than a mere thirty-five miles from the coastline. It was the river itself, rather than any central town or market center, that gave Delaware its existence as well as its name.

Delaware's diverse geography, from the flat coastal plain to the hilly piedmont along the Pennsylvania border, offers a vividly concentrated beauty that pleases visitors and has inspired writers and artists. The most famous and influential of these was Howard Pyle, the late-nineteenth-century illustrator and author of children's books, who was a lifelong Wilmingtonian and creator of the still-famous Brandywine school of artists. The woods in the Brandywine Valley between Wilmington and Pyle's summer home at Chadds Ford, just over the Pennsylvania line, became, in his imagination, Sherwood Forest, while the coast below Cape Henlopen framed his settings for the rendezvous of pirates. Generations of American children have entered into Pyle's glorious dream world of medieval fancy and colonial escapades through pictures set among the woods and beaches of the Diamond State.

In addition to its varied scenery, Delaware possesses a fine heritage of handsome old towns and buildings. New Castle and Odessa, to name only the best-known, are veritable storehouses of colonial and early-nineteenth-century homes and churches laid out along quiet, shaded streets. Other examples of our ancestors' building arts can be found all over the state in towns and cities and among farmhouses and rural churches. Throughout this book, I have drawn attention to the best-known or most typical remnants of Delaware's architectural heritage as symbols of the various stages of the tiny state's historic development.

I have done most of my research and writing at the Eleutherian Mills Historical Library, within walking distance of the original powder mills built by Eleuthère Irénée du Pont[1] in the early days of the nineteenth century. In that beautiful setting along the Brandywine, I have tried to elucidate the major forces that have shaped Delaware's history. In recent years, critics have called Delaware the "State of Du Pont" because of the great influence that the du Pont family and their chemical empire have exerted over virtually every aspect of the life of the state. In the years since World War I, Du Pont has become the sun around which Delaware and especially Wilmington have revolved. The company and the family that the du Pont name evokes have been at the vortex of wealth and power in Delaware. Although I could not undertake an exhaustive analysis of the Du Pont influence in these pages, I have tried to write about the most important and controversial questions raised by Du Pont power as knowledgeably and fairly as I could.

1. Capitalization of the du Pont name can be confusing. The members of the family mentioned in this book use a small *d*—du Pont—while the company uses a capital *D*—Du Pont.

Every historian, whether he is aware of it or not, approaches his subject within the context of the priorities and problems of his own time. This volume speaks to the complicated issues that confront us today, during the bicentennial period. Delaware, in many ways a microcosm of the United States, exhibits many problems and issues of national concern. One such issue is that of environment versus materialism. Our generation is called upon to find a balance between the industrial production necessary to employ our people and sustain a decent way of life without creating an asphalt desert cluttered with rusting cars facing onto oil-drenched seas. Delaware's most enduring social problem continues to be race relations. In spite of a Supreme Court decision that is now twenty-one years old, our state and nation are still in the midst of a whirlwind of dispute over school integration. Yet another major concern centers around defining the proper relationship between popular democratic control and the power of wealth and big industry.

The pages that follow are intended to show how the historic development of the First State sheds light upon these major concerns of the present day. Part I deals with the land and its use in the economy. Part II tells of the many peoples and cultures who have contributed to the state's social history, while the final segment describes the growth of the political basis for Delaware's society. I hope that readers can find here some background understanding that will aid us all toward realization of the "life, liberty, and pursuit of happiness" promised two hundred years ago.

Several people have aided me substantially in the preparation of this manuscript. Richmond D. Williams, in his capacity as president of the American Association for State and Local History, introduced me to the project, while, as director of the Eleutherian Mills Historical Library, he supplied me with a pleasant, quiet office in which to work. The staff members of the Eleutherian Mills Historical Library were, as always, my most helpful aides in research. Barbara E. Benson of the Eleutherian Mills-Hagley Foundation Publications Department typed most of the first draft, read the manuscript, and made innumerable suggestions for its improvement; and Ella Phillips, another Eleutherian Mills-Hagley Foundation employee and friend, typed

xvi   *Preface*

the final version. Professors James Newton of the University of Delaware and Harold B. Hancock of Otterbein College graciously lent me a draft of their forthcoming anthology on the history of black Delawareans. Gerald George, managing editor of the Bicentennial State Histories series, was unfailingly helpful; and Martha Strayhorn, copy editor, made a number of excellent suggestions that improved the felicity as well as the sense of the manuscript. I also owe a great debt of gratitude to my colleague at the University of Delaware, John A. Munroe, a truly distinguished scholar and writer in the field of Delaware history, who read and commented on the manuscript. Edward F. Heite, Historic Registrar of the Delaware Division of Historical and Cultural Affairs, and William P. Frank, a notable local journalist, also saved me from egregious errors. For any mistakes that remain, either of fact or interpretation, I must claim sole responsibility.

Part I

The Land by the Water

$\mathcal{A}$MONG Delawareans, there is an old saying that their little state consists of three counties at low tide but at high tide, only two. In terms of Delaware's origins in geological time, the joke errs on the side of conservatism, for many millions of years ago, all but 6 percent of Delaware's 1,978 square miles of land mass was submerged in ocean waters.[1] The northern highlands of Delaware are part of the Appalachian piedmont province, while the remaining 94 percent of the state belongs to the Atlantic coastal plain, which extends from New Jersey through Florida. The northern foothills were formed more than two hundred million years ago, when the shifting of the planet's surface pushed upward the Appalachian Mountains, producing the hard crystalline rocks that are exposed in the piedmont. Millions of years later, after mammals had appeared on the earth, the sea, interacting with the rise and fall of the polar ice cap and with the movement of the earth's underwater foundations, consecutively washed up and fell back along the coast, silting over much of the piedmont rock with a wedge of unconsolidated sands, gravels, and clays to form the coastal plain. The furthermost thrust of the sea into Delaware was to a fall line that separates the state's two geological regions—a line roughly paralleling the Kirkwood Highway between Wilmington and Newark. When the glacier to the north melted for the last time, water and huge chunks of ice expanded the Delaware River and its pied-

1. Figures for the total land area of Delaware in square miles appear variously as 1,965 square miles, 2,057 square miles, and 1,982 square miles, as well as the figure used here, which appears on recent Delaware State Highway Department maps. Such variations may depend, in part, at least, on how much of the Delaware Bay and river area is included in calculations.

mont tributaries, dumping boulders from the glaciated region in their path. For the last twelve thousand years, the ocean has been encroaching on the shoreline at a relentless but increasingly slow rate. Thus, geological formations continue a ceaseless process of change and adaptation.[2]

Remote as these geological periods may seem to modern man, they quite literally form the basis for all life in the present. The upstate-downstate split in life style, ethnicity, and politics that has been so prominent in the history of even so small a state as Delaware conforms with surprising regularity to the division between the piedmont and the coastal plain. In the northernmost part of the state, thin clay soil covers gently rolling hills incised by rapid-flowing, rock-filled streams—the Brandywine, the White Clay, the Red Clay—that flow from the hills of Pennsylvania southward to disgorge into the Christina. The Christina, the most northerly river of the coastal plain, meanders slowly eastward into the Delaware River. Southward from the Christina the land is flat and loamy, the rivers shallow and wide with well-developed flood plains that carry the Delaware's tidal waters far inland and feed extensive coastal marshlands. The names of the rivers—Appoquinimink, St. Jones, Murderkill, Mispillion, Broadkill—reflect the languages of the many peoples who have occupied the region at various times in its history. Only one river in the state, the Nanticoke, in the extreme southwest, flows westward into Maryland to the Chesapeake Bay; the other streams on the Chesapeake side of the watershed are sluggish and provide poor natural drainage. Below Cape Henlopen, where the Delaware Bay meets the Atlantic, are two smaller, shallow, saltwater bays fed by ocean tides and inland streams and separated from the ocean by a thin strip of sandy,

2. Nenad Spoljaric, *Pleistocene Channels of New Castle County, Delaware,* Delaware Geological Survey Report no. 10 (Newark: University of Delaware, 1967), pp. 2–4; K. D. Woodruff et al., *Geology and Ground Water,* Delaware Geological Survey Report no. 18 (Newark: University of Delaware, 1972), pp. 7–9; Nenad Spoljaric, *Geology of the Fall Zone in Delaware,* Delaware Geological Survey Report no. 19 (Newark: University of Delaware, 1972), pp. 6–7; the Governor's Task Force on Marine and Coastal Affairs, *The Coastal Zone of Delaware: A Plan for Action in Delaware* (Newark: College of Marine Studies of the University of Delaware, 1972), p. 96.

duned beach left by the ocean when it last receded from the land.

This well-watered territory, surprisingly varied for its size, contains both thick forests and treeless marshlands. In the sandy soil of Sussex County, in southern Delaware, where the sea's encroachments were most recent, tall pines intermix with colorful hollies and hardwoods, oaks, maples, sweet and black gums, and yellow poplar. A few miles inland from the ocean-beach dunes and coastal bays of Sussex is the most northerly cypress swamp in the United States, out of whose dark, tranquil waters grow bald cypress and cedar. Marshlands fringe Kent, Delaware's middle county, along the bay estuary that provides a rare ecological environment mingling fresh and salt water. In colonial times, oysters proliferated, each generation clinging to the shells of its ancestors. Crabs, snapping turtles, diamondback terrapins, shad, sturgeon, and numerous other species of fish and marine wildlife thrived on nourishment from the nearby wetlands, as did migratory waterfowl—ibis, herons, Canada geese, and ducks. Inland, the flat fastlands, or uplands, of Kent and of hilly New Castle counties were once covered with a dense hardwood forest of oak, walnut, beech, dogwood, and maple, the home of white-tailed deer, fox, panther, bear, as well as smaller creatures such as woodchucks, squirrels, and chipmunks.

The very name *Delaware,* derived from that of Sir Thomas West, Lord de La Warr, an early governor of Virginia, was applied to the bay and river before it became associated with the land. Until very recently in its history, development of the region was conditioned solely by natural forces: wind, sea, land, and animals. We do not know when man first appeared in Delaware; but since that time, the story of the land, river, and bay have been inexorably intertwined with human needs, desires, and the technological and cultural means to fulfill them.

Near the point where the Murderkill winds its way through salt marshes toward its confluence with the Delaware Bay is a tuft of pasture land called the Island Field that is the site of the earliest human settlement as yet uncovered in Delaware. The site, discovered by accident during road construction in 1928, was not fully explored until 1967, when archaeologists working there excavated a burial ground measuring thirty feet by forty feet that contained upwards of ninety graves. Examination of the artifacts of animal bone, shell, stone, and ceramics in the graves, together with evidence from radio-carbon dating of one cremated burial suggest that the ground was occupied between A.D. 500 and A.D. 1000. These early Delawareans chose their site close to the bay on the basis of the abundant food supplies available in the area. Their remains indicate that they ate fish, oysters, and clams from the bay and such land animals as deer, fox, beaver, and elk, as well as birds, for they were located along the Atlantic Flyway used annually by hundreds of thousands of migrating large game fowl. Although the cache of human remains has provided little information about the social customs, religion, or political organization of that stone-age society, the findings do reveal a lively commerce with other primitive peoples in places as far away as the Ohio and Mississippi valleys and New England. The people at the Island Field bartered shells, highly prized for ornamentation, in exchange for types of stoneware not available nearby.

While the fate of that intriguing primitive society is unknown, our knowledge of later Indian culture is much more complete. To comprehend the world of these woodland peoples, it is necessary to ignore modern political boundaries often based upon charters drawn up from inaccurate maps in remote European palaces. Instead, one must perceive the land in terms of its Indian settlements. Like their remote predecessors, the Indians whom European explorers first encountered along the Delaware in the early seventeenth century were closely tied to the river and its tributaries. The villages of the Delawares, as the Europeans named them, or Lenni-Lenape, as they called themselves, covered an extensive area surrounding the Delaware River, including New Jersey, most of Delaware, and eastern Pennsylvania. Located between the powerful Five Nations Confederacy of the Iroquois in New York State and the empire of Chief Powhatan in Virginia, the Delawares were a remarkably peaceable and politically undeveloped people. Their basic social units were the nuclear family and the village, not the tribe or nation.

Autonomous villages averaging fifty to two hundred Delawares were scattered throughout the river valley along the banks of tributary streams such as the Brandywine, Schuylkill, and Maurice. Their primitive social organization reflects the Delawares' lack of concern for defense, which must have been related to their contentment with the plenteous natural resources of their homeland.

The Delawares, like all American Indians, did not attempt to dominate nature as if they were outside it, but, rather, imagined themselves as part of the natural world around them. Their religious beliefs reinforced the concept that nature was essentially a benign helpmate for man. The Great Manito had created the world with the assistance of twelve lesser gods whose powers were immense compared with the weakness of mortal men. The Indians bowed before the power of these pantheistic deities and sought communion with them through spiritual exercises such as fasting and tobacco smoking. The demands of their subsistence economy imposed on them a life style that was busy but not burdensome. They lived outdoors except at night or in bad weather, when each family retreated into a crude one-room hut built of tree limbs, bark, and grass. Tasks were divided along sex lines. The women were charged with making clothing, weaving baskets, caring for the young, and, most importantly, with growing and cooking the corn that was the Indians' staple food. Men hunted for deer, beaver, and other animals useful both for food and clothing. They also fished by building stone or wooden walls or fences, called wiers, across streams, forcing the fish to swim through narrow openings where they were easily caught.

The construction of huts, dugout canoes, and animal traps were also male jobs. Semiannually, the Delawares journeyed from their agricultural villages along the river bank to interior hunting grounds; the men traveled light to provide protection, while their wives, used to the heavy labor of carrying water and firewood, bore the family possessions.[3]

3. C. A. Weslager, *The Delaware Indians, A History* (New Brunswick: Rutgers University Press, 1972), pp. 50–76.

Nothing in the Indians' culture prepared them for their "discovery" by European explorers. It is hard to imagine two societies more different than those whose values met in culture-shock along the Delaware River in the early years of the seventeenth century. The Indians were nonacquisitive; the Europeans, intent upon gaining riches. The Indians accepted a static Stone Age technology, while the Europeans, already possessing far more complex techniques for manufacture, transportation, and social organization, were in the early stages of yet more dramatic technological breakthroughs. The imprint of the whites on the lives of the Indians and on the river valleys was swift, decisive, and inexorable. One hundred years after European settlement, an old Indian from southern Delaware was regaling a settler with the recent history of his family's relations with the whites. He was poor as a raccoon, he said, because his father had been tricked into giving up his land for rum. "You white people make slaves of everything, the wind, the fire, and the earth." At that, the Indian laughed. The puzzled white man inquired why. "Because everything makes slaves of you white people," he answered.[4]

The Dutchmen who sailed with their English-born captain, Henry Hudson, into the Delaware Bay in August 1609 were the harbingers of an entirely new kind of interaction between man and the land. The Dutch had grown strong by defying the forces of nature. For centuries, through the most impressive demonstration of human organization and engineering, they had methodically pushed back the sea that threatened to engulf their small, flat country. Situated strategically along the English Channel, the Netherlanders turned to trade and manufacture to supplement their meager natural resources.

The two centuries that followed Columbus's discovery of America brought great changes in European life. As discoveries of sea routes, products, and peoples followed one upon another, the balance of trade shifted from the Mediterranean and Baltic states to the Atlantic coastal nations. Portugal, Spain, England,

4. "Description of the Cypress Swamps in Delaware and Maryland States (1797)," *Delaware History* 3 (March 1949):137.

and the Netherlands contested among themselves for control over the fabulous riches of America and the Orient. Their struggles were intensified by the Reformation and the Counter-Reformation that pitted Catholic against Protestant nations, justified the expanding powers of central governments, and gave religious sanction to intermittent trade wars. The Netherlanders not only played a major role in these developments, but emerged for a time in the mid-seventeenth century as the most successful commercial nation in the world.

The rise of the Dutch sea empire had its origins in a savage and seemingly interminable war in which the United Provinces successfully opposed the Spanish Hapsburg empire. The Protestant merchant oligarchy that ruled the United Provinces made trade their most effective weapon. Initially, trading expeditions were financed by individuals or small companies who bought shares in particular ships or voyages. Experience showed, however, the advantages of a more long-term and larger-scale business organization. Consequently, in 1602, the Estates-General chartered the East India Company, which was given a monopoly on Dutch trade from the Cape of Good Hope at the tip of Africa eastward to the Pacific. The company was empowered to establish diplomatic relations with the nations within this broad territory, to build and maintain fortifications for the protection of company property, and, if necessary, to make war. One of the most successful business operations in history, the East India Company was primarily interested in trade, not colonization. Its representatives seldom penetrated far into the interiors of the Oriental lands in which it did business, but preferred to remain in their compounds, called "factories," which were located in port cities. There, company employees bought spices, porcelain, silk, and other luxury items from native merchants in exchange for European goods.

It was the East India Company that sent Henry Hudson to America in 1609 to search for a western route to its East Indies ports. Although Hudson failed to find the "North-west Passage," his reports on the lands he had seen aroused interest among the enterprising Dutch, who reasoned that trade with the natives of North America might prove as lucrative as that with Orientals. In the following decade, numerous parties of Dutch explorers and traders visited the American coastline between what they termed the North and South rivers—to us, the Hudson and the Delaware. One of these explorers, Cornelius May, who suffered from no false modesty, named the capes at the mouth of the South River bay Cape Cornelius and Cape May. A small island that appeared to be another cape below Cape Cornelius he dubbed Cape Hindlopen, in honor of his home town.

Most of the Dutch visitors to the South River were more intent upon trade than on immortalizing themselves. We lack an account of the first encounter between the Lenni-Lenape and the Dutchmen at the South River, but if it followed the course of their initial meeting on Manhattan Island, the Indians, believing that their visitors were either the gods themselves or at least divine messengers, greeted the Dutch with fear and awe. The Dutchmen, in their turn, wished to gain the natives' trust to smooth the way for trade relations. As a sign of friendship, they offered the Indians liquor, which the latter drank at first with trepidation. It was soon evident that the natives, unaccustomed to alcoholic spirits and reared in a culture that discouraged emotional outbursts, were susceptible to drunkenness and to alcoholism. The Indians were equally fascinated by the seemingly miraculous manufactured goods that were offered them—woven cloth, iron utensils, and most especially, firearms. The Dutch, in their turn, were not accustomed to dealing with such primitive people whose economy was so little concerned with commerce. It was readily apparent that the most valuable local commodity was neither manufactures nor precious stones nor spices, but furs. Furs were used extensively in Europe for the manufacture of winter hats and coats, but since the furbearing animals had long since been depleted in the most populous sections of Europe, the price of fur was extremely high, more than offsetting the cost of importation from America. Furthermore, the Indians, heretofore used to an economy of self-sufficiency, could be converted into trappers for the price of cheap cloth, pots and pans, liquor, and muskets. And so in the second decade of the seventeenth century, the resources from the region that encompasses Delaware first entered intercontinental trade.

Contacts with the Europeans profoundly altered the lives of the Lenni-Lenape. For one thing, they fell prey to the attacks of war parties of Minquas Indians from the Susquehanna River Valley who sought to control their coastal neighbors and claim some of the trade for themselves. War parties of Minquas came by canoe down the Chesapeake and crossed over to the Delaware River at the two most convenient portage points, from the Elk River, the most northeasterly tributary of the Chesapeake, to the Christina, and a few miles farther south from the Bohemia River to the Appoquinimink. The Lenni-Lenape called these river highways "Minquas" rivers, because of their association with the interloping tribe. Poorly organized for defense, the Lenapes were ineffectual in stopping the raids. But the demand to seek furs was even more disturbing to their traditional way of life. C. A. Weslager, a modern student of the Delaware Indians, discovered that, although the native women continued their agrarian pursuits, the men gave up their former pattern of hunting and fishing and devoted most of their time to supplying pelts to the traders. Thus, Weslager says, the Lenapes' "simple gardening-hunting-fishing subsistence pattern became a predominantly hunting-for-barter economy in order to obtain furs for European merchandise." [5] But that was not all, for the fur trade, by its very nature, depleted resources with spectacular rapidity. Beaver, whose pelts were the most prized for warmth and beauty, were intially plentiful in Delaware, where their dams could be seen on every little creek. But beaver were also easy to trap and kill. Soon they and their dams disappeared, an event of some ecological significance not only because a species had been eliminated from the regional environment, but because the beaver dams had influenced watercourses. Within twenty years of their first contacts with the Dutch, the Lenni-Lenape had lost their importance in trade to the Minquas as the hunting ground for beaver moved steadily westward.

5. Weslager, *The Delaware Indians,* p. 116.

The Dutch, eager to expand their trade throughout the entirety of the Atlantic, created a new giant trading company in 1621, the West India Company. Modeled upon its sister company for the East Indies, the western company was expected to do two things: to frustrate and destroy the power and wealth of the Iberian Catholic kingdoms of Spain and Portugal, and to make money for its investors. The company's most notable successes on both fronts were in the South Atlantic, where the Dutch wrested much of the West African slave trade from the Portuguese and penetrated Brazil's lucrative sugar market. The West India Company's achievements in the North Atlantic were comparatively minor, particularly in light of the money and manpower invested, because the company could see little value in North America beyond the fur trade. West African blacks summed up Dutch motivation correctly when they remarked to Dutch traders that "Gold is your god." [6] The West India Company made only one effort at colonization on the west bank of the South River, a short-lived, all-male settlement called Zwaanendael—now Lewes, Delaware. Founded in 1631 as a whale-fishing camp, the settlement apparently stirred up considerable antagonism among the initially benign natives, for its inhabitants were massacred within a few months. In general, the company was content to direct its trade operations from New Amsterdam, its permanent settlement on Manhattan Island.

Among the principal investors in the West India Company was William Usselinx, a pamphleteer, promoter of joint-stock companies, and a devoted Calvinist. Usselinx grew disenchanted with his position in the Dutch monopoly and set out to create a new transoceanic trading company through the cooperation of a foreign Protestant power. In 1624, he journeyed to Stockholm, where he presented his plans to Gustavus Adolphus, the Swedish king, and his chancellor Oxenstierna. Usselinx persuaded the Swedes that, with the assistance of Dutch capital and experience, Sweden could join other western Euro-

6. C. R. Boxer, *The Dutch Seaborne Empire, 1600–1800* (London: Penguin Books, 1973), p. 128.

pean nations as a trading power in the Atlantic. Lutheran Sweden, on the fringes of Europe, was then just beginning to assert itself in the wider theater of European affairs outside of Scandinavia. Under Gustavus Adolphus, the most outstanding military commander of a martial age, Sweden won victories in wars with its neighbors Denmark, Poland, and Russia and became a principal contestant on the Protestant, anti-imperial side in the Thirty Years' War in Germany. Swelled by these successes, the Swedish officials were convinced that their kingdom was equipped to take on the responsibilities of a trading company and thus add yet more to her fame, power, and wealth.

After a series of false starts involving grandiose schemes for worldwide trading expositions, Peter Minuit, like Usselinx, a former associate in the Dutch West India Company, urged the Swedes to plant a colony in North America. Minuit pointed out that, although the Dutch traded on the South River and claimed the region by right of Henry Hudson's discovery, they lacked any permanent settlements there. Thus persuaded, the Swedes authorized the formation of the New Sweden Company, which, in 1638, sent Minuit with two tiny shiploads of Dutch sailors, together with Swedish and Finnish soldiers and colonists to the South River. They founded the first permanent European settlement in Delaware, a little colony called New Sweden, on the banks of a navigable tributary of the South River—which they named the Christina River in honor of their twelve-year-old queen, the only child of Gustavus Adolphus.

The seventeen-year history of New Sweden illustrates both the frustrations of colonization and the particular aptitude of the Swedes for pioneer living. As a profit-making venture, the colony was a dismal failure, largely because it was continuously undercapitalized. Nor did the existence of the colony automatically expand Swedish power within Europe, where it was instead a stumbling block to co-operation with the Netherlands and England. The colonists received very little attention or support from a government that was preoccupied with continual foreign wars or from the young queen who was devoted to culture and the maintenance of a lavish court. It proved impossible, for example, for the Swedes to compete with the Dutch and the English in the potentially lucrative fur trade, when the mother country failed to send goods for trade with the Indians on a regular basis. In a word, Sweden lacked the resources of money and personnel and the ardent desire necessary to support a colonial effort.

From the first, the Swedes had difficulty in making good their claim to American territory. Since the land was not theirs by right of discovery, they attempted to legitimize their presence by purchasing land from its Indian inhabitants. Minuit bought, or thought he bought, all the land along the South River from the capes northward 135 miles to the present site of Trenton. Even though the exact area of purchase was vague, the Swedes assumed that by giving gifts to its Indian "owners," they were acquiring sole ownership of the land in the name of the New Sweden Company. The European concept of land-holding was unknown to the Indians, however, and incompatible with their culture. It did not occur to the natives that the Europeans might demand that the Indians quit some or all of the lands along the river and move elsewhere; they understood that the "purchase" conferred on the Swedes the right to share the land with them— to hunt, fish, plant crops, and build houses, but not to *own* it in the sense that a man owned his bows and arrows. In the Indians' way of thinking, land was comparable to water and air—it was free for the use of all. That concept, an important part of the Indians' belief that man was a part of nature, led to numerous misunderstandings between natives and newcomers, especially when the wily Dutch, more used to dealing with the natives, made haste to "buy" the same land for themselves to undermine Sweden's tenuous claim. The Indians, of course, understood only that they had agreed, for the price of some foreign artifacts, to share their land with yet another European nation. To the Swedes, the Indians' action was proof of a despicable lack of integrity. Thus, Delaware came under the laws of land ownership as practiced in Europe.

The few Swedes and Finns sent out by the company to fulfill the grand designs of a New Sweden adapted to their new environment with remarkable ease, especially in light of the difficulties inherent in their situation. Most of the first settlers were soldiers chosen to secure the land. They built a log fortification facing the Christina, on ground surrounded on three sides by swampland, as defense against Indian attacks. It was soon evident, however, that these men lacked the skills necessary for survival in a wildernesss. Fortunately, other settlers were sent, including artisans competent to build ships, sawmills, and gristmills, plus an expert tobacco grower. These Swedish and Finnish peasants knew how to be nearly self-sufficient in the woods. They were used to making most of their own utensils and to building and living in crude but adequate log houses. We know something of their homes from Peter Kalm, an observant scientist who visited Delaware a century after the Swedish colony had been established. He wrote that

> the houses which the Swedes built when they first settled were very
> poor. The whole house consisted of one little room, the door of
> which was so low that one was obliged to stoop in order to get in.
> As they brought no glass with them they were obliged to be content
> with little holes before which a moveable board was fastened. . . .
> The chimneys were masoned in a corner, either of gray stone, or in
> places where there were no stones, of mere clay, which they laid
> very thick in one corner of the house.[7]

Ironically, these rude shelters proved to be the most significant contribution of Swedish culture to America, for they were the first horizontally laid, notched-log cabins built in the New World. Two examples of Delaware's earliest European domestic architecture have been preserved. A one-room dwelling found south of the Christina River near Wilmington, laid out very much in the manner described by Kalm, is in the state museum at Dover. Another, a two-story structure with brick fireplaces, probably dating from the early eighteenth century, was rescued from highway construction at Price's Corner, southwest of Wilming-

7. C. A. Weslager, *The Log Cabin in America: From Pioneer Days to the Present* (New Brunswick: Rutgers University Press, 1969), pp. 158–159.

ton, and moved fittingly to a spot near the location of Fort Christina.

In 1642, members of the Swedish government took control of the faltering, debt-ridden New Sweden Company and appointed Johan Printz, a corpulent and competent officer of cavalry, governor of New Sweden in the hope that he might accomplish wonders of economic productivity in a variety of enterprises without, of course, increasing the funding or personnel of the enterprise significantly. The new governor's instructions recognized the need to go beyond the mere gleaning of surface resources, such as furs and fish, into more difficult, long-range production that, by its very nature, demanded large-scale, permanent European settlement. Printz was expected to defend the colony against encroachments by the Dutch or the English; maintain friendly trade relations with the Indians; cultivate tobacco; increase the number of livestock, especially sheep; manufacture salt from ocean water; grow grapes; search for minerals; find commercial uses for forest products, such as walnut oil; establish commercial fishing, for whales if possible; keep silkworms; see to the planting of grain for the inhabitants; and do "whatever else could be done for the good care of the land, and cannot be introduced in detail [for] . . . the advantage, benefit and interest of the members of the Company in the conservation of this land, New Sweden, with all possible and feasible progress and commerce growing therefrom." [8] The image of America underlying that remarkable document is that of a giant cornucopia, a land of limitless potential, ripe for mercantile exploitation. That image is present also in an enthusiastic firsthand description of the colony written by Peter Lindestrom, an engineer who visited New Sweden in 1654. "The Christina River," he says,

> is a deep river, rich in fish; [it] extends far up into the country [and] can be navigated with sloops and other large vessels a considerable distance. On both sides of this river . . . the soil is by nature

8. Amandus Johnson, *Instructions For Johan Printz* (Philadelphia: The Swedish Colonial Society, 1930), pp. 62–92.

suitable for all kinds of agriculture and the cultivation of all kinds of rare fruit-bearing trees. Yes [it is] such a fertile country that the pen is too weak to describe, praise and extol it; on account of its fertility it may well be called a land flowing with milk and honey.[9]

In reality, the actual production of the colony fell far short of these exaggerated expectations. In the first place, the total population of New Sweden in the 1640s was something less than two hundred persons. In addition, Printz discovered that the nearby Lenni-Lenape Indians were useless for the fur trade and that he must trade with the more distant Minquas. Despite his instructions to treat "the wild nations . . . with all humanity and respect," [10] the governor was soon urging Stockholm

to send over here a couple of hundred soldiers . . . until we broke the necks of all of them [the Lenape] in this River, especially since we have no beaver trade whatsoever with them but only the maize trade. They are a lot of poor rogues. Then each one could be secure here at his work and feed and nourish himself unmolested without their maize, and also we could take possession of the places (which are the most fruitful) that the savages now possess.[11]

Had the Swedes been content to develop agriculture solely for the subsistence of the colony, the results of their labors might be judged highly successful, but as the instructions make plain, the prime purpose of the colony and, hence, the reason for its agricultural production was to be profit for the company. There were three Swedish farming areas, one next to Fort Christina, another at Uplands (now Chester, Pennsylvania), where some Dutch families had settled under the auspices of the Swedish Company, and a third at Tinicum Island, just south of modern-day Philadelphia, where Printz established his seat of government. At first, the Swedes concentrated on growing tobacco. To feed themselves, they bought maize from the Indians. Tobacco

9. Peter Lindestrom, *Geographia Americae,* translated by Amandus Johnson (Philadelphia: The Swedish Colonial Society, 1925), pp. 172–173.

10. Johnson, *Instructions,* p. 78.

11. Johnson, *Instructions,* p. 117.

culture proved unprofitable, however, and the colonists turned to growing rye from seed brought from home. They also planted Indian corn, a native product that they learned to use in a variety of ways. Lindestrom found that heating ripe ears of corn on hot embers rendered them "beyond measure, good and palatable to eat." [12] The colonists also made corn bread and a strong, thick corn beer. They planted vegetables, pumpkins, cucumbers, wild turnips, and watermelons, which Lindestrom praised as a hot-weather refreshment.

Sweden could not maintain her toe hold in the New World indefinitely. In the 1650s, the Dutch, still smarting because of Swedish interference in the fur trade, began deliberate acts of provocation designed to intimidate the smaller, weaker colony. Stuyvesant sailed warships up the South River and, in 1651, erected Fort Casimir on the west bank, a few miles south of the Fort Christina settlement. From that vantage point, the Dutchmen could control all commerce moving upriver to New Sweden. Governor Printz recognized the futility of mounting aggressive movements in retaliation, but his successor, Johan Rising, on first sailing up the river to begin his administration, demanded that the fort surrender to the Swedish crown. The nine-man Dutch garrison lacked muskets and gunpowder for their cannon and thus readily capitulated. Rising, believing that he had eliminated the Dutch menace from the colony, proceeded to Fort Christina, where he and a number of new colonists, including Peter Lindestrom, disembarked.

New Sweden now contained nearly four hundred people, and Rising optimistically set about expanding his scope of operations. Behind the original farms laid out on treeless lands along the riverbanks, new wooded farmlands were cleared, sometimes by means of a method called *svedjebruket* in Swedish, or "agriculture by burning." When the trees were chopped down, they were left to dry out where they lay. The following season, they were burned, thus fertilizing the soil as well as removing the trees. Under Rising, the Swedes began to venture farther

---

12. Lindestrom, *Geographia,* p. 180.

downriver. They occupied the land between the former Dutch fort and Fort Christina, made plans to develop a town behind the latter fort, and negotiated with the Minquas Indians for land facing the Chesapeake Bay along the Elk River. Rising expected to develop an overland trade route linking New Sweden with the English colonies Maryland and Virginia on the Chesapeake Bay, so that the Swedes could more easily engage in the tobacco trade.

The progress of the Swedish colony was rudely interrupted, however, about a year after Rising's arrival, when a flotilla of seven Dutch warships, under the command of Peter Stuyvesant, sailed up the river and demanded, first, the restoration of Fort Casimir and then the capitulation of all New Sweden to the Dutch West India Company. The Swedes, knowing that they could not withstand a siege in either fort, agreed to surrender terms that permitted the settlers to retain their farms.

The period of Dutch rule, from 1655 until 1664, was too brief to produce many long-lasting marks on the land along the west bank of the South River. Unlike the Swedes and the Finns, who were principally farmers, the Dutch were tradesmen and town dwellers. They discounted the Swedes' plan for a town on the Christina in favor of a site adjacent to Fort Casimir. The town, named New Amstel, was built on flat marsh ground that closely resembled urban sites in Holland. New Amstel planners laid out two streets of narrow house lots parallel to the river. Within a few years, the town could boast 110 houses built of wooden planks and clapboards, because bricks were scarce. Unfortunately, no examples of Dutch domestic architecture in New Amstel have survived. The Dutch also undertook to drain the marshes near the town by means of a series of dikes, used also as roadways, and a windmill that doubled for grinding grain.[13] The Dutch thus recreated a new Holland along the South River.

Like Johan Rising, the Dutch, too, recognized the importance of the portage point used by the Indians to connect the South

13. C. A. Weslager, *Dutch Explorers, Traders and Settlers in the Delaware Valley* (Philadelphia: University of Pennsylvania Press, 1961), pp. 195, 204–205, 209.

River with the Chesapeake Bay via the Elk and Appoquinimink rivers as a potential avenue for the tobacco trade. At the time when their colony was absorbed by the English Duke of York in 1664, the Dutch had already taken steps to plan a new settlement south of New Amstel along the Appoquinimink. Here, as in their other towns, the lots were long and narrow, providing the maximum number of owners with direct access to the stream. The Dutchmen were also concerned about the safety of navigation among the treacherous shoals of the bay and the river, and with their characteristic willingness to improve on nature, they placed buoys in the river and entertained the notion of dredging its most shallow sections.

The duke's government introduced new policies that encouraged the dispersement of farming throughout the colony. Unlike the Dutch and Swedish companies that had jealously guarded their ownership of the land, the English proved eager to grant land in fee simple to prospective farmers. To appreciate the significance of the English period of rule on the history of Delaware, it is necessary to understand something of the knotty legal argument over boundaries that was responsible for making the area's three counties into a state. When James, Duke of York, brother of Charles II, conquered New Netherland in the opening salvo of what the English call the Second Dutch War, he inherited a festering boundary dispute with another Englishman, Calvert, Lord Baltimore, proprietor of Maryland. Calvert's charter dated from 1632, in the reign of the duke's father, Charles I. Like many colonial charters drafted in European halls of state, the charter for Maryland described the area of that colony in imprecise language. Calvert's grant was purposely located in the no man's land between the overlapping claims of Virginia and Massachusetts. The boundaries of Maryland were described as the fortieth parallel line to the north, the Potomac River to the south, and the falls of the Potomac in the west. The eastern boundary extended to the Delaware Bay and Delaware River, except in those places that had been previously settled by Europeans. It was that seemingly innocent and exacting phrase *hactenus inculta* (''hitherto uncultivated'') that proved to be the

despair of numerous proprietors and a living for an army of lawyers.

In Lewes, Delaware, stands a monument to the short-lived
Dutch whaling settlement of 1631, Zwaanendael. The inscrip-
tion at its base reads "THAT DELAWARE EXISTS AS A SEPARATE
COMMONWEALTH IS DUE TO THIS COLONY." The complete explanation of that cryptic phrase is highly complicated, but it ultimately goes back to those two Latin words *hactenus inculta,*
for Calvert's warrant was written just one year after the tragi-
cally short-lived Zwaanendael settlement. Cecil Calvert made
overtures to gain control of lands along the Delaware during the
Dutch and Swedish period, but it was not until the duke took
possession that the case could be adjudicated in an English
court. In 1669, Calvert launched a campaign to settle lower Delaware, which he dubbed Durham County, Maryland. Between
1670 and 1682, Calvert made forty-seven separate grants of
land there to forty-five individuals.[14] The boundary was being
disputed by the Duke of York's representatives at New York in
1681 when Charles II made his famous grant of land to William
Penn. To mark off Penn's lands from the duke's territory on the
Delaware, it was decided that Pennsylvania should nowhere
come closer than twelve miles to New Castle, the English name
for New Amstel, the primary port town on the Delaware. In that
way, the northern boundary of the duke's colony became an arc
measured twelve miles from the New Castle Court House.

Penn was pleased with the princely size of his province, but
he was also apprehensive about its survival, because, unlike
other American colonies, Pennsylvania did not touch the ocean
at any point. Its only access route was via the Delaware River.
He therefore asked James for a deed to the lands that the duke
held on the river by virtue of his conquest of the Dutch. When
the duke obliged the Quaker proprietor, Penn inherited not only
the "three counties on Delaware," as the region was then
called, but also the boundary quarrel with Calvert. The Penn-

14. Percy G. Skirven, "Durham County: Lord Baltimore's Attempt at Settlement of
His Lands on the Delaware Bay," *Maryland Historical Magazine* 25 (1930):161.

Calvert dispute absorbed the time and drained the energies of the proprietors for many years, keeping them both in England when they could well have been useful in their colonies in America. In 1685, an English court proclaimed the basis for a settlement that in effect vindicated Penn. A line was to be drawn from Cape Henlopen westward to a point midway between the Chesapeake and the ocean and then due north to intersect with the arc. Calvert reluctantly accepted that decision, but his losses were not yet over, for the map used by the court to define the boundaries was based on Cornelius May's expedition of the early 1600s that incorrectly marked what the English had come to call "Cape Henlopen" not at the mouth of the bay, but at the false cape thirty miles below. Maryland therefore lost its Durham County, and Penn's three Lower Counties remained indeed three, as he had named them: New Castle, Kent, and Sussex. The final disposition of that decision did not come until the 1760s, a century after Cecil Calvert proclaimed his sovereignty over Delaware, when Charles Mason and Jeremiah Dixon, court-appointed surveyors, tramped through swampland and forest to determine the exact boundaries. Their markers, bearing the coat of arms of the Penns on the east side and that of the Calverts on the west may still be seen along the border between Delaware and Maryland, mementos of their remarkably accurate survey.

The Penn-Calvert controversy not only defined the borders of Delaware, it also exercised a strong influence on the rate and pattern of settlement, especially in Sussex County. Calvert, acting on the proposition that possession is nine-tenths of the law, awarded large land grants in the disputed territory as late as 1758, when, for example, Lord Baltimore awarded Captain John Dagworthy more than twenty thousand acres behind Rehoboth Bay for his services in the French and Indian Wars. That land, like other Maryland grants in Delaware, was later resurveyed by order of the Penns. Indeed, many of the early farmers in lower Delaware were Marylanders who thought that they had merely exchanged one part of their colony for another. Agents of the Duke of York, and, later those of Penn, also gave out sections of land throughout the state that attracted new settlers from England or from other English colonies, but since people preferred to settle on undisputed land, Sussex County filled up slowly.

The establishment of Pennsylvania proved to be the single most significant factor in Delaware's late colonial development. The Quaker colony brought to the Delaware Valley large numbers of people who settled in the new town of Philadelphia and its environs. Among these newcomers were experienced merchants who moved vigorously to make their town a leading Atlantic port. Philadelphia quickly surpassed New Castle as a commercial center and established trade not only with England but with the West Indies, Ireland, Spain, and Portugal. The Philadelphia traders' need for a large hinterland well stocked with marketable goods for trade encouraged not only the creation of new farms but a change from subsistence to market-oriented agriculture on old ones. Since the farmers with direct access to navigable rivers could most easily send their crops to market, lands along the banks of Delaware's many streams were taken up first.

Farming was the most significant economic activity in eighteenth-century Delaware. The land itself had long since replaced furs as the colony's most valuable resource and the focus of its regional economy. Delaware farmers, unable to duplicate the success of those along the Chesapeake in raising tobacco, gave up the sotweed for wheat, rye, barley, and the ubiquitous corn. Wheat and flour were taken to Philadelphia, where grain shipments were directed mainly to the semitropical Caribbean sugar islands.

There are no statistics on agriculture before the Revolution; however, several European travelers' accounts have survived. A Swedish clergyman, Israel Acrelius, described Delaware farms he visited in 1756 in some detail. He observed that most of the farms were "newly cleared," since tree stumps still covered much of the ground. The Swedish practice of burning trees had been outlawed under the Duke of York, because of the danger of uncontrolled forest fires that also destroyed existing crop lands. Instead, farmers were removing trees by girdling them, a practice that quickly killed the tree and made it wither and fall down. "One may often see fields filled with dry trees," he said, "and a heavy crop of grain growing under them." He noted that older farms were not nearly so productive as the newer ones, because the farmers had failed to fertilize them adequately. As settlement progressed, the grass that had grown among the forest trees was eaten by farm animals, destroyed by plowing, or dried out. Consequently, it was necessary for farmers to give attention to pasture, as well as arable land. Cattle and horses were pastured in orchards among the peach, cherry, and apple trees that grew so well in Delaware, or they were put out into swamp meadows along the Delaware River and other streams. These swamplands, strange to say, brought on Delaware's first agricultural land boom and bust. The cost of preparing swampland for pasture was considerable, since the land had to be enclosed with earthen dikes to keep out tidal water. Experimental use of such reclaimed land for both pasture and planting proved so successful that the price of swampland soared in the 1750s. The euphoria was short-lived; soon afterward, a series of high tides swept away embankments, and those left standing were so riddled with muskrat holes as to be useless. "Thus," Acrelius writes, "the grass and grain were destroyed, the land returned again to its wild nature, and there was no end of patching and mending. Then the price of the land fell to half its value, and he thought himself best off who had none of it." [15]

In addition to the major cash crops, farmers kept gardens for their own use, where they raised tobacco, potatoes, cabbages, beets, lettuce, beans, peas, and an assortment of herbs for flavoring and medicinal purposes. Planting and harvesting went on in every season. Flax and oats were sown in early March, corn in late April, buckwheat—used mostly as animal fodder—in July, wheat in September, and rye in November.

About five miles southeast of Dover, a stately brick mansion

15. Israel Acrelius, *A History of New Sweden,* translated by William M. Reynolds (Philadelphia: The Historical Society of Pennsylvania, 1874), p. 147, p. 155.

house faces a marshy tidal stream called, inexplicably, the St. Jones River. Here once lived John Dickinson, the man who in 1768 awoke Americans to a fuller understanding of their rights and liberties in his famous series of letters that began "I am a *Farmer,* settled . . . near the banks of the river *Delaware,* in the Province of Pennsylvania." [16] The Dickinson mansion is one of the many links that modern Delawareans have kept with their colonial past. It does not "typify" country life of the eighteenth century any more than any other single farm or house of that age before mass production can be called typical. But to know something of its history is to enter into a deeper understanding of the rural world of that period. John Dickinson's father, Samuel, built the house and in 1740 brought his Philadelphia-born Quaker wife and two young sons to live there. The family moved from Samuel's plantation in Talbot County, Maryland, where several generations of Dickinsons had been well-to-do tobacco farmers. Lord Baltimore granted to Samuel's grandfather lands along the Delaware Bay in the 1670s, when the Maryland proprietor was attempting to buttress his own land claims there by settling the country with men beholden to him for their land titles. Nearly seventy years and many confused land grants later, Samuel left his extensive tobacco fields to his older children and came to Delaware to raise wheat. He bought up small farms in the area until his Kent County estate exceeded three thousand acres. Some of his land was farmed by slaves, but most of it was let out to tenants who paid for its use in produce. These people lived in one- or two-room wooden houses that, together with the barns and sheds that once dotted the plantation and the wharfage on the St. Jones, have since disappeared. All that remains is the mansion house itself, a five-bay rectangular structure, its masonry laid in Flemish bond, with two appendages that were added to the west side in the 1750s. The main entrance leads into a large central hall; on the right is the front parlor, the most elegant room in the house. In

16. John Dickinson, *The Writings of John Dickinson,* 2 vols., edited by Paul L. Ford (Philadelphia: The Historical Society of Pennsylvania, 1895), 1:307.

that imposing, wood-paneled room, tradition says, Samuel Dickinson, a judge of the Kent County Court of Common Pleas, held court. To the left of the hall are two smaller parlors, one of which served as the library. The dining room and kitchen are contained in the two west wings. Over the kitchen is a small room reached by a tiny stairway and a crawl hole—a sleeping chamber, doubtless for the slave who was most responsible for the many activities of the kitchen. The house has suffered various tragedies, two in John Dickinson's time, when it was ransacked during the Revolution by a group of New York Tories and in 1804, when a fire destroyed the hip roof, the third floor, and some of the wood paneling on the lower floors. It has recently been restored and is now part of the state museum system.

Not many farms were such extensive enterprises as Dickinson's, but the Duke of York and later the Penn family gave out or sold large tracts to individuals, because it was desirable from the proprietors' point of view to distribute the land as quickly as possible so that they could begin to tax it for revenue. The size of farms tended to become smaller over time, however, as land speculators resold smaller parcels to farmers.

Land was expensive near urban markets in New Castle County, and farmers there were inclined to use crop rotation and fertilizer to maintain the land's fertility, whereas farther south, where land was both plentiful and cheap, less care was taken to preserve its value. As one writer put it, "So soon as one field was worn out, another was cleared, and the first left to grow up again in woods." [17]

In their free time, many farmers turned to hunting, fishing, and other pursuits, depending on the resources of the areas in which they lived. Along the coast, fishing, crabbing, and especially oystering provided additional food and products for sale in Philadelphia and nearby towns. In the forests of Sussex County, lumbermen cut cypress and cedar for shingles and

17. John A. Munroe, *Federalist Delaware* (New Brunswick: Rutgers University Press, 1954), p. 26.

house siding, both for local use and for trade. Delaware's abundant white oak, prized for shipbuilding, was soon overcut, but pine and other hardwoods continued to be important items in trade, building, and manufacture. Iron, discovered in Iron Hill near Newark in New Castle County and at the bottom of ponds and swamps in Sussex, provided the raw material for country forges, which also used large quantities of forest timber to make charcoal.

Among the most lucrative country industries was the Corbit tannery in Cantwell's Bridge, New Castle County. The Corbits had already been prosperous Delaware farmers for two generations when William Corbit went to Philadelphia to learn the art of tanning hides in 1765. Upon his return, he established a tanyard close to the banks of the Appoquinimink. The river not only served as transportation, but also supplied the extensive water needed for the tanning process. The Corbits bred cattle for both meat and hides in their extensive marsh pasture. The area also afforded the one other prime ingredient necessary in colonial tanyard technology: a ready supply of oak bark. The wealth gained from his farms, land speculations, and tannery paid for the very large and elegant Georgian home that William began constructing adjacent to the smelly tanning vats in 1772. Now a museum, the five-bay brick mansion standing on a bluff overlooking the meandering Appoquinimink is one of the finest Georgian residences to be found anywhere in America. Viewing its stately proportions and richly decorated woodwork both inside and out, the modern visitor is hard put to realize that the manion was once headquarters for an odoriferous and messy, but productive, industry.

The increase of population and commerce resulted in the growth of towns and the development of transportation and industry. By the 1750s, New Castle, reported as having 240 houses, had been supplanted as the chief Delaware River town, not only by Philadelphia, then nearly ten times larger, but also by Wilmington, an upstart town only twenty years old, with 260 homes. Located near the site of the old Swedish fort, Wilmington faced the Christina just before its confluence with the Brandywine. Unlike New Castle, which lacked a water route to the interior, Wilmington's situation was ideal for trade with the growing farm regions of New Castle County and southeastern Pennsylvania. Quaker merchants, millers, and artisans founded Wilmington in the 1730s as a port for the grain trade. Its prosperity depended upon its rivers—the Christina, which carried wheat from upstream hamlets, Christiana Bridge, and Newport; and the Brandywine, one of America's best sources of water power, which turned the mill wheels of its gristmills. Wilmington's merchant millers not only sold flour in the Philadelphia market, but they also carried their well-known ''Brandywine Superfine'' and coarser flour to foreign ports in Europe and the West Indies in their own home-built vessels. Among Delaware's other towns, New Castle, Dover, and Lewes were county seats and centers for local trade. Lewes, sheltered from the ocean by the sand dunes of Cape Henlopen, was, in the eighteenth century, as now, the home for pilots who brought ships up and down the often treacherously shallow waters of the Delaware Bay and Delaware River to Philadelphia and Wilmington. Farther north, little villages sprang up at the head of navigation of the various streams that empty into the Delaware. Fast Landing (Leipsic) was founded in 1723 at the most easterly edge of dry land, before the swamps of Leipsic Creek. It was a shipping point for farmers in the area, as was Johnnycake Landing (Frederica) on the Murderkill. Johnnycake Landing also specialized in building the shallops, brigs, and other craft that plied the river.

Thus, as the eighteenth century progressed, the face of Delaware was changing. The area was no longer a rude frontier of woodland simplicity; the best lands had been divided up and converted to planting or pasture. Likewise, architecture, at least for the wealthy, had become more sophisticated, stylish, and permanent. Georgian-period structures, mostly homes and churches, are still standing and are among Delaware's most attractive features, the objects of great pride among Delawareans.

In Sussex County, where lumbering was an important local industry, most buildings continued to be constructed of wood, often covered with unpainted cedar shingles that have weathered, over the centuries, to a grayish-brown color. A few gambrel roofs are still to be seen, but most of the surviving houses had low-pitched gabled rooflines. In Kent and New Castle counties, brick construction prevailed, usually laid in Flemish bond, a black-glazed header followed by a stretcher. That masonry technique, which used so many headers, was expensive, but it was strong and decorative in an age when vernacular architecture included intricate brick-work patterns that, for example, might work into a brick wall the initials of the homeowner and the year of construction. Not surprisingly, Philadelphia fashions prevailed, not only in high-style houses like William Corbit's mansion, but also in less costly homes. Early eighteenth-century houses have a sturdy look, with uncomplicated woodwork and small windows; they often featured a pent eave overhanging the first floor. As the century progressed, the houses became more refined-looking, their windows larger, and the woodwork more complex. In the country, five-bay, two-story-and-attic homes, one room deep, prevailed; in towns, where street-front lots were expensive, three-bay houses, two rooms deep, were more common. Each bay represented a discrete section of timber framing surrounding a door or window on the front of the house. As in Philadelphia, the Quaker influence can be seen in the restrained simplicity of houses built by members of the Society of Friends. Some of the best examples of Quaker architecture in Delaware are in a section of north Wilmington that was once the independent community of Brandywine Village. Here, a few steps from their mills along the post road that led to Philadelphia, the millers erected their homes in a row. Brandywine granite, so generously scattered in the river and on its banks just upstream from the mill seats, provided the major building material for homes and mills alike. Historically, the most interesting house in the village is the Joseph Tatnall house. Tatnall was the leading miller at Brandywine Bridge in the Revolutionary generation. He was a civic-minded man, but as a Quaker, could not in good conscience participate in the war. On several occasions when General George Washington passed through Wilmington, he stopped at the Tatnall home, no doubt not only for the hospitality, but because the miller, whose flour was important to the

American army, had reputedly pledged to him, "I can not fight for thee, but I can and will feed thee." [18]

The mills at Brandywine Bridge were representative of another aspect of Delaware's changing land use, as expressed in technological development. In the eighteenth century and early nineteenth century, water-powered techniques of manufacture reached their zenith. In those days, the only available sources of power for machines were either direct human or animal effort or the harnessing of two natural forces, wind and water. Water power was the best of these, because it was steadier than the wind and stronger than any team of oxen. But water suitable for power transmission could not be found everywhere, and even when available, it required considerable investment of capital and engineering skill to be made useful.

Several streams in New Castle County had the potential to be excellent power sources, because they fell rapidly from the hilly high ground of the piedmont to the nearly sea-level land of the coastal plain. As the largest of these streams, the Brandywine was not only the most desirable industrial site in Delaware, but one of the best in the entire mid-Atlantic region. It is not surprising then that a number of industrialists established various sorts of mills along its banks. The story of these mills is an important part of the whole pattern of resource use in Delaware's age of water power.

A visitor to the Brandywine in the first decade of the nineteenth century would have begun his inspection of the mills at Brandywine Village. Dr. James Tilton, surgeon-general of the United States in the War of 1812 and a native Wilmingtonian, claimed that these were "the largest and most perfect [for the] manufacture of flour within a like space of ground known in the world." [19] Here the main road from Philadelphia bridged the

18. Although it appears in several nineteenth-century writings, this traditional quotation cannot be traced to a contemporary source. Over the years, it has slipped into the realm of folklore and become more traditional than real.

19. Harold B. Hancock, "The Industrial Worker along the Brandywine, 1800–1840," 3 vols. (Wilmington: Eleutherian Mills-Hagley Foundation Research Report, 1956), 1:1.

river and entered Wilmington. The first Brandywine Bridge had been built in 1760, at the time when the mills were undergoing significant expansion. The keys to successful milling lay in securing sufficient supplies of grain and constructing the mills in the place most accessible to both ocean shipping and water power. Brandywine Village was ideally situated with regard to all three factors. The mills were constructed close together on both sides of the river, just below the bridge, since ships of considerable draft could sail that far up the Brandywine.

Above the bridge, the stream was rocky and fell rapidly, excellent for energy production, but impossible for navigation. To tap this power source, it was necessary to dam the river and carry some of its water off into races along each bank. Each race was designed to maintain the same height above sea level as that behind the dam. Thus, when the race water reached the mill wheels, it was much higher than that in the river parallel to it and could turn the wheel around as it fell back into the stream.

To that hydraulic technology were added significant home-grown improvements in mill design in the years following the Revolution. The ideas that constituted the new system did not originate along the Brandywine, however, but in the ingenious mind of a man named Oliver Evans, one of many children born to a Newport, Delaware, leatherworker turned farmer. Oliver's youthful preoccupation with mechanics led to his apprenticeship at age sixteen to a local wheelwright. It was at that time, he later recalled, that he began to study the problem of transferring steam power into an energy source for man. Years later, he was the first American to build a high-pressure steam engine. Evans's irrepressible inventiveness took him in many other directions, as well. At age twenty-two, he invented an improved method to make carding devices that could be used to prepare wool, cotton, and flax for spinning. A few years later, he turned his mind to the operation of flour mills. It occurred to him that much of the tedious, back-breaking labor of carrying the grain from one operation to the next could be eliminated by the application of a horizontal endless screw and a vertical continuous canvas belt equipped with pockets. He also invented a circular raking device that replaced the work of the hopper boys employed by millers to cool the flour between the grinding and bolting operations. All of his improvements could be powered by the same water wheel that turned the grinding wheel and shook the bolting screen to sift the flour into various categories of fineness.

In his enthusiasm for his new system of milling, Evans persuaded his brothers, in the early 1780s, to join him in a milling venture on Red Clay Creek, near Newport, where he planned to demonstrate his ideas and to sell them to millers. Like inventors before and since, he soon learned, however, that it was easier to conceive a new idea than to make it pay. At first, millers were reluctant to give up methods that they had learned as apprentices. The Brandywine millers, who ran the most extensive operations in the area, were particularly backward, in spite of Evans's entreaties. He even went so far as to construct a working model of his entire scheme that he displayed in Wilmington for their benefit. Only after the new methods had been successfully proved in Baltimore and at Evans's own mill and after President George Washington had decided to use them at his Mount Vernon mill did Joseph Tatnall and his fellow Brandywine millers agree to install the new equipment. Not only was acceptance slow, but equally discouraging was Evans's discovery that his supposed U.S. patent protection was not preventing millers from copying his ideas without paying him the required fees. In the face of these disappointments, Evans wisely published a handbook for millers, the first and best of its kind, entitled *The Young Mill-Wright and Miller's Guide,* which realized some profit.

In later years, Oliver Evans left his mill and moved to Philadelphia, where he at first ran a millers' supply shop and then engaged in the manufacture of steam engines. In that work, also, he was sorely disappointed by the refusal of many people to recognize him as the inventor of the high-pressure engine. In 1809, in a fit of despair, he gathered his family together as witnesses as he bitterly burned all his many inventive drawings.

His life was constantly filled with lawsuits and arguments with other engineers concerning the practicality of using steam to power vehicles on land and sea—an idea in which Evans's passionate belief was ultimately vindicated. When he died in 1819, he left behind his own epitaph, written some four years earlier: "While Oliver Evans lived, he laboured incessantly for the benefit of generations yet unborn by making new and useful inventions." [20] Although the struggles of his life excited little appreciation from his contemporaries, Oliver Evans's incessant labors have placed him among the most important American inventors, a living embodiment of the faith of his era and of society in technological progress as a way to personal wealth and social benefit.

A short distance upstream from Brandywine Village was the Gilpin Paper Mill, another local center of manufacturing innovation. Joshua and Thomas Gilpin, descendants of a prominent Philadelphia Quaker mercantile family, began Delaware's first paper mill there in 1787. In the mill, rags collected from surrounding towns were reduced to a pulp by water-powered pummels, then mixed with a water solution and poured into molds to dry. The process—old, slow, and requiring the services of skilled papermakers—was ripe for improvement. In 1798, a Frenchman invented a machine that could make rag paper on an endless roll. A few years later, an Englishman, working independently, designed a similar machine that used cylinders to move the solution along and squeeze out excess water. The Gilpins eagerly sought information about these improvements so that they could introduce the new processes to America. They hoped thereby to cut the size and costliness of their staff, since the most skilled job in the old process, that of putting the proper amount of solution into the molds, would be eliminated. It is typical of such undertakings that, although the Gilpins did initially reduce their staff, the rise in the production and cheapness of paper made it more popular and, hence, in-

---

20. Greville Bathe and Dorothy Bathe, *Oliver Evans: A Chronicle of Early American Engineering* (Philadelphia: The Historical Society of Pennsylvania, 1935), p. 211.

creased demand so that ultimately their employment rolls went up from twenty-seven workers in the days before the new process to sixty by 1820. But the nature of employment in the mill was shifted from the earlier, skilled jobs to low-paying, unskilled work, such as preparing the rags for processing, which was done by women and children. Females and youths received pitifully small wages, from one-third to one-seventh the amount paid to men. Innovation and a good product, normally the keys to success in industry, were not sufficient to make the Gilpins' mill prosper for long, however. They lost money in other ventures, while nature conspired to wreak damages on the mill through fire and by a memorable flood in 1822 that destroyed property all along the Brandywine.

While the Gilpin mill lasted only three decades, the Bancroft Textile Mills, built farther upstream in the 1830s, survived well into the twentieth century. Changes in English textile manufacture in the late eighteenth century introduced the industrial revolution to the world. Although the new processes for carding, spinning, and weaving cloth were jealously guarded, construction plans for the machines could not long be kept secret, and the Brandywine, like New England's Merrimac, Connecticut, and Housatonic rivers, became a center for textile factories. The Bancrofts were the most famous and successful Delaware textile manufacturers, but they were hardly the first. As early as 1795, Jacob Broom, a Wilmington merchant and member of Delaware's delegation to the Constitutional Convention, began spinning cotton by horsepower in Wilmington. He soon abandoned that crude factory for a water-powered site a few miles up the Brandywine, but the mill burned, and he lacked the capital to replace it. Along the Brandywine, as elsewhere in America, the Napoleonic wars furnished the big impetus to sustain the homemade-textile industry. During the war, British textiles were hard to get, and, with the outbreak of the War of 1812, it became impossible to import anything from England. American merchants saw the advantages of investing the profits of wartime trade into manufactories that promised to make the United States economically self-sufficient. There was a flurry of mill construction along the Brandywine in 1813, when three large stone mills—Brecks, Henry Clay, and Walkers, all still standing—were built, just below Broom's original textile factory.

Like many another ambitious industrial scheme undertaken on the crest of a wave of economic good fortune, not all of these mills survived through the slough of despond that followed the war, when the government ceased contracting for American-made uniforms and the British began dumping cheap textiles in the United States to win back their market here. Those companies that produced inferior goods or suffered from poor management failed. With the euphoria behind them, capable textile millers recovered, however, and prospered. One such was Joseph Bancroft, a young English Quaker who came to Wilmington in 1824 after having served seven years as apprentice in his uncle's cotton mill. Joseph joined his father and brothers in manufacturing flannels at Brandywine Bridge, but that enterprise, like so many at that time, lasted for only a few years before his partners drifted away to more enticing opportunities. He then served as a plant superintendent until 1831, when a local entrepreneur set Bancroft up in business to manufacture cambric muslin at Rockford, just above Wilmington. Recognizing that American textile makers were behind the English in finishing fabrics, Bancroft returned to England in 1854 to study the process for producing "Hollands," a heavy, durable finish used in such items as window shades. On his return, Bancroft installed finishing machinery to bleach, starch, and dye textiles; thereafter, although he continued to manufacture some cloth, he specialized in finishing textiles bought from New England mills. The firm's prosperity, particularly during the Civil War years, led Bancroft to form a partnership with his sons, who, in their turn, continued to expand the business so that, when they incorporated in 1889, it had become the largest textile-finishing company in the United States.

The Bancrofts were admirable citizens, noted for their paternal care for employees. Joseph's son, William Poole Bancroft, was nineteenth-century Wilmington's most outstanding philanthropist, the father of the city's park system and of its public

library. Through a trusteeship, his estate has continued to preserve the beauty of hundreds of acres of Brandywine Valley
land. But, ironically, the factory that created the means to
achieve these good works was cited by the Wilmington Board of
Health as among the most dangerous polluters of the city of
Wilmington's water source in the late nineteenth century. The
snake of industrial pollution had entered the Eden of the Brandywine.

Upstream from Bancroft's mills was the land on which Jacob
Broom had built his short-lived cotton mill. When it burned,
Broom decided to sell his ninety-five acres of densely wooded
land and the water rights involved. Simultaneously, a French
émigré with the lofty philosophical name of Eleuthère Irénée du
Pont was searching for a site on which to construct mills to
make black powder. Du Pont's father, Pierre Samuel du Pont de
Nemours, had risen from the obscurity of the minor nobility to
prominence in the ancien régime as an intellectual, an economic theorist, and an advisor to Louis XVI. When the Revolution shook the foundations of French society, the moderately
liberal du Pont looked to the United States for some new opportunity to combine his concerns for economics, social theory,
and the prosperity of his family. He dreamed on a large scale,
planning, first, a vast province in the West called Pontania.
When that and other ideas proved unworkable, his son E. I.
decided to put to use his own superb training as former assistant
to the chemist Antoine Lavoisier in the French government's
powder works. Supported by funds from his father and other
French investors, E. I. began the search for a suitable location
that brought him to Jacob Broom's land. Here, in 1801, he
found all that his enterprise would require: adequate water
power, a location between the major cities of Philadelphia and
New York and the new national capital at Washington, and sufficient timber to begin construction of his mills. The Du Pont
Company's initial successes were due to its capitalization—
quite large for that day—the knowledge, skill, and perseverance
of its leader, and the willingness of the Jefferson administration
to buy military powder from the president's old friends from his
days as ambassador to France.

E. I. du Pont quickly became the most important factory owner in a district that was already among the leading manufacturing areas of the United States. His carefully planned and well-maintained property, combined with its aura of constant danger, inspired the awe of visitors. Du Pont turned his land into a total industrial community. Overlooking the many buildings, separated in the interests of safety, where the powder was made, he constructed a large home for his own family, row-houses for the families of workmen, and dormitory-style housing for those who were single. When his daughters became interested in teaching workers' children, du Pont built a special building to house the Brandywine Manufacturers' Sunday School. A large part of his property was used to pasture the mules and horses that pulled wagonloads of ingredients around the mills and took the finished product to docks on the Delaware River.

In their style of paternalism, these early factory owners resembled the old master craftsmen who had boarded their workers more than they resembled modern industrial employers. Yet, the most noteworthy changes wrought by industrialization lay in the area of the new relationship of people to their work and to their employer. Instead of employees working singly, or in small groups where apprentices and journeymen labored and lived side by side with a master craftsman and his family, labor was transferred to the factory, where the workers were subject to strenuous but impersonal discipline. The work day was generally twelve hours long, beginning at 6:00 A.M., and, depending on the operation involved and the state of technology, the machines set the pace. The more sophisticated the machinery became, the less training was required to perform those tasks that remained, and the man who could build and repair machinery replaced the skilled craftsman as the most important human link in carrying out the manufacturing operation. Since the factories were strung out along the heretofore sparsely inhabited banks of the Brandywine, E. I. du Pont was not alone in constructing housing that would keep workers close to the factory and its discipline. Groups of workers' houses, distinguished by names such as Duck Street, Chicken Alley, Fountain Row, Pigeon Row, and Wagoners Row, were built in the river valley. Wage rates for unskilled males were closely tied to the prevailing pay for agricultural labor, while those for women and children were so low as to be mere supplementary income to a family, not a living wage for an individual who might need to support herself. Since most workers lived in housing provided by the company that employed them and either boarded there or bought the food they did not raise in their own gardens from a company store, payday was an exercise in accounting rather than a time of actual transfer of money.

Economic growth inspired a need for cheap, efficient transportation such as colonial Delaware had never known. Natural waterways were no longer sufficient to meet the demands of the Brandywine millers for flour or to provide other manufacturers with the raw materials they required or with the means to sell their products. The prosperity of New Castle County's industrialists made it possible for them to join in the rush of the large northeastern cities to construct "internal improvements," roadways, canals, and—finally—railroads. The revolution in transportation in the first half of the nineteenth century had completely unforeseen ramifications that remade Delaware, as improved transportation remade other parts of America, casting into insignificance places that had once been important and creating new urban centers in former cornfields.

The transportation revolution started with the turnpikes, relatively cheap, technically simple roadways that were improved by crown grading, the scattering of crushed stones on the road surface, and the construction of bridges over small rivers and ravines. Beginning in 1792, when Philadelphia merchants chartered the Lancaster Pike, businessmen in every city sought state charters to construct and administer toll roads. In Delaware, Wilmington was the only city with sufficient commercial interests to join the trend. Her flour millers in particular had to emulate Philadelphia's initiative or lose their trade with Lancaster and Delaware counties. Soon four turnpikes radiated northward from Wilmington into the Pennsylvania countryside, while another went southwest toward the Cheasapeake. About the same time, in 1807, a company bridged the Christina between Wilmington and New Castle, thus replacing a ferry that a local historian of the time claimed had been "tedious" and "vexatious," especially in winter when travelers to and from the county seat "were subjected to much suffering, delay, and anger, by reason of the floating ice." The bridge brought new trade and doubled the value of marshlands on the shore of the river opposite the city, thus "inducing the owners to drain and cultivate them, by which the healthfulness both of the town and country have been improved." [21]

Although turnpikes partially succeeded in improving overland transportation, all-water routes were still preferable both for ease and cheapness, and in the three decades following the War of 1812, the country developed a mania for canal building. A canal to link the Cheasapeake and Delaware bays was one of the earliest such projects ever suggested in America and one of the few that continues in operation today. The last governor of New Sweden, Johan Rising, pointed out the potential value of a cross-peninsular canal in 1654, and subsequent colonial leaders continued to contemplate such an undertaking. Following the Revolutionary War, Philadelphia merchants revived the idea as they gnashed their teeth watching the extensive trade of central Pennsylvania follow the Susquehanna River into the Chesapeake Bay and hence to their upstart rival, Baltimore. Not surprisingly, there was less enthusiasm for the improvement in Maryland, while in Delaware, where nearly all of the canal would be located, there was considerable fear that the project would destroy the state's overland carrying trade. In spite of these suspicions, a canal company was formed in 1802 by Philadelphians who placated Delaware with arguments such as that improved transportation would bring more Maryland wheat to the Brandywine mills and that the most likely route for the canal to follow would place the eastern terminus on the Christina River alongside Wilmington. The Philadelphians who dominated the company, eager to maintain good relations with the leading

21. Benjamin Ferris, *A History of the Original Settlements on the Delaware* (Wilmington: Wilson & Heald, Printers, 1846), pp. 240–241.

businessmen in the little state through which the canal would flow, wisely chose Joseph Tatnall, miller, as president of the Cheasapeake and Delaware Canal Company. They then hired Benjamin Latrobe, the noted engineer and architect, to perform the difficult task of laying out the best route. After much study, Latrobe decided on a route linking the Chesapeake to the Christina River and began construction, but the costs were greater than the company could afford, and, after failing to get financial assistance from the United States government, the company suspended construction, which was not resumed for two decades.

When the enterprise was revived, William Strickland, a student of Latrobe's who was hired to restudy all possible routes, concluded that the canal should terminate well below New Castle, opposite Pea Patch Island, at a point called Newbold's Landing. Not surprisingly, the Wilmington investors were incensed and could not be persuaded that any considerations other than the jealousy of Philadelphia toward a potential rival was the cause. Strickland countered that the Christina was too narrow and shallow to sustain the canal's traffic, especially since the construction of the bridge at Wilmington and subsequent draining of nearby swampland had reduced the tidal flow. The objections from Delaware were thus brushed aside and construction on the canal got under way in 1824. When it was completed, five years later, at the huge sum of $2,250,000, the canal shaved more than three hundred miles off the travel distance by sea from Philadelphia to Baltimore.[22] The waterway also created a new town at Newbold's Landing, optimistically renamed Delaware City. The town's promoters anticipated that the canal would do for them what the Erie Canal was doing to promote Buffalo, Syracuse, and Troy. They even named their main street after New York's canal-booster governor, De Witt Clinton. But the Chesapeake and Delaware Canal failed to make either Delaware City or any other place along its 13.6-mile path

22. Ralph Gray, *The National Waterway: A History of the Chesapeake and Delaware Canal, 1769–1965* (Urbana: University of Illinois Press, 1967), pp. 11–14, 43, 49, 50, 66.

into a commercial entrepôt. The best that could be said for it from Delaware's point of view was that it provided better transportation to market for farmers in its immediate vicinity.

Shipping and shipbuilding continued to be the lifeblood of Delaware's commerce well into the nineteenth century. Shipyards were located in all the port towns at the head of navigation along the rivers that flow into the Delaware. In 1859, there were three yards in Milton on the Broadkill, three in Milford on the Mispillion, two in Frederica on the Murderkill, and three at Lebanon on the St. Jones. In addition, Bethel and Seaford built ships for the Chesapeake. The ships were mostly wooden sloops, schooners, and fishing boats that made use of local forest products, especially white oak and pine. A six-hundred-ton schooner consumed upwards of 190,000 feet of white oak alone. Frederica, in Kent County, was typical of these little port towns. Nathaniel Lank, Sr., and his son Nathaniel Lank, Jr., maintained a shipyard there that employed about thirty-five people at the height of the industry in the mid-nineteenth century. They built three-masted schooners, one at a time, each ship needing about one and a half years for completion. But because the Murderkill was too shallow to support a fully rigged schooner, the ships were launched without masts and taken to Philadelphia for their final fittings, unable ever again to sail the six miles upstream to the town where they had been built. The inevitable decline in shipbuilding set in during the 1880s, when wooden sailing ships were being phased out of coastal freighting and as the once-plentiful virgin white oak and other trees used in their construction had been depleted.

Steam navigation ushered in important changes in transportation on the Delaware, where, in 1787, John Fitch demonstrated the first successful steam-powered vessel, a noisy, inefficient machine that failed to catch the public's imagination. Oliver Evans also built a remarkable steam-powered amphibious contraption designed to dredge the harbor at Philadelphia, but it was not until after Robert Fulton's *Clermont* had chugged up the Hudson in 1807 that commercially successful steamboating began on the Delaware.

Two Wilmington-based packet lines, the Bush Line and the Charles Warner Company, were already operating when the new-style riverboats were introduced in 1814. Their boats were familiar sights on the river, carrying passengers and heavy freight, coal, lumber, and gravel, from Philadelphia to Wilmington and beyond. The opening of the Chesapeake and Delaware Canal spurred another packet line, the Ericsson Line, that used narrow boats driven by a screw propeller to navigate the canal between Baltimore and Philadelphia. The true queens of steamboating on the Delaware, however, were the big side-wheelers, sometimes weighing in excess of six hundred tons, that dominated the river during the second half of the nineteenth century. Built on the Christina by Wilmington firms, these boats carried people and farm produce up and down the river to bay-side resorts, port towns, and cities. One such was the hundred-foot-long *Frederica,* owned by Frederica merchants, that as late as the beginning of the twentieth century was in successful competition with the railroad as a passenger carrier. The steel steamer made two trips a week from the little town to Philadelphia via Bowers Beach for a round-trip fare of $1.50 per person.[23]

The railroads began to challenge water carriers in America during the 1830s. Initially, when the technology of railroading was primitive, builders constructed their lines through territory not already served by a river or canal, usually as a connector to existing water routes. That practice is exemplified in Delaware by the New Castle and Frenchtown Railroad built across the peninsula in 1832. The short history of Delaware's first railroad also illustrates some of the difficulties inherent in free-market capitalist enterprise in an age of rapid expansion in transportation. New Castle's leaders organized a company in 1809 to build a gravel turnpike of 16½ miles to the Chesapeake in hope of restoring some of their town's long-lost commercial importance. Their initial joy at the successful completion of the road was dimmed, however, by the construction of the Chesapeake

23. Mary Emily Miller, "Port Town on the Starboard, A History of Frederica, Delaware," *Delaware History* 14 (1970):130–131.

and Delaware Canal, which threatened to undo New Castle's trade completely. But the New Castle men were not beaten yet—latching onto the latest advance in tranportation technology, they decided to build a railway parallel to their turnpike right-of-way. The project was costly and difficult, but at first the results were gratifying. The railroad company secured an agreement with the Union Steamboat Line on the Delaware that made them competitive with the canal, and since theirs was the shorter and faster route between Philadelphia and Baltimore, the railroad anticipated continued success. Horses pulled the stagecoach-shaped cars for the first few months until English-built locomotives could be introduced.

During the 1830s, a great many travelers, including some people of national and international fame, stopped in New Castle in transit between the large east-coast cities. But New Castle could not long maintain its premier position as a transportation center on the Delaware, because Wilmington had too many advantages of wealth, entrepreneurial zeal, and location to be beaten. Even as the portage railroad was under construction, Wilmington's business leaders, together with others in Philadelphia and Baltimore, were planning a much more ambitious railroad undertaking that would link their three cities without recourse to boats except to cross the Susquehanna River. The new line, called the Philadelphia, Wilmington and Baltimore Railroad, made the New Castle and Frenchtown route obsolete only six years after it had been built. The new road is still owned by the Penn-Central, while the New Castle route has long since all but disappeared.

While the PW & B Railroad influenced the economy of New Castle County generally, especially Wilmington, the railroad hardly touched most of Delaware. The farms and little towns that characterized the state below the canal remained solely dependent on river transportation nearly two decades longer. Indeed, in these same years, when industrialization and the transportation revolution were quickening and reshaping the economy of northern New Castle County, the rest of Delaware was suffering from economic blight. Lands too long cultivated without proper restoration of nutrients were producing pitiful yields, the price of farmland fell sometimes below the cost of the buildings on it, and the population stagnated as young people sought new opportunities in the West. A writer in *The Delaware Register and Farmers' Magazine* pleaded in 1838 that "There is territory enough, if properly managed in this State, to support comfortably five hundred thousand inhabitants; and yet we see thousands leaving it every year on account of the poverty of the soil, which might be made rich and highly productive with less expense of money and labor than it costs to clear and put in cultivation the wild lands of the West." [24] In Sussex, many farmers concentrated on cutting timber and neglected to improve their farms or to replace the cuttings. In Kent, the yield per acre of wheat slipped disastrously from fifteen to five bushels. "When I was a boy," a native son wrote in 1852, "I have frequently heard farmers in my neighborhood say they had not raised as much as they sowed." [25] A speaker before an Agricultural Society gathering in 1818 exaggerated little when he said that "our land for the last fifty years has done little more than starve its proprietors." [26]

The story of agriculture in New Castle County was very different. According to the editor of the *Delaware Register,* writing in 1839, "The land above Cantwell's Bridge (Odessa), which contains not more than a tenth part of the territory of the State, is worth more at present . . . than that of all the rest of the state—and four times as many people to the square mile reside there as do below." The northern county, described by the *Baltimore Sun* in 1846 as "the paradise, the garden spot of the State," [27] produced twice as much wheat as Kent and Sussex combined, according to the U.S. census for 1850. [28] The

24. *The Delaware Register and Farmers Magazine,* March 1838, p. 112.

25. "Readings in Delaware History: Economic Development," edited by H. Clay Reed, mimeographed (Newark: University of Delaware, Department of History and Political Science, 1939), pp. 80–83.

26. Harold B. Hancock, "Agriculture in Delaware, 1789–1900," in *Delaware: A History of the First State,* 3 vols. edited by H. Clay Reed (New York: Lewis Historical Publishing Co., 1947), 1:375.

27. Hancock, "Agriculture in Delaware," 1:376.

28. U.S., Department of Interior, Bureau of the Census, *Compendium of the Seventh Census,* 1850 (Washington: A. O. P. Nicholson, 1854), pp. 208–209.

twin keys to its success were transportation and fertilizers. The county's more progressive farmers founded agricultural societies, subscribed to journals that advocated improvements in farming, experimented with new crops, and used marl, lime, and guano to restore life to the soil. The most spectacular advances in agricultural production were made by those whose experiments with new crops took advantage of growing urban markets. E. I. du Pont introduced merino sheep herds to his farmlands to provide wool for the textile mills, and many other New Castle County farmers followed his example. Dairy farms along the canal route in southern New Castle County supplied butter to Baltimore.

By far the most profitable new crop was the peach. Peach trees flourished in Delaware during colonial times, but farmers saw no advantage in planting orchards on a large scale until the steamboat and the railroad made it possible to transport the fruit quickly to urban markets. Isaac Reeves, a New Jersey native, planted Delaware's first commercial peach orchard near Delaware City in 1832. The high prices paid for his crop in Philadelphia and New York prompted others whose farms were accessible to transportation to join in the bonanza. Along the roads of southern New Castle County, one can still see standing in fertile fields the "peach mansions," built during the agricultural boom of the 1840s and 1850s—big, square, flat-roofed, three-story houses decorated with ornate woodwork and peaked by widows' walks of the early Victorian Greek-Revival and Italianate styles. Major Philip Reybold soon emerged as the region's most successful peach grower. The Peach King, the son of a Philadelphia sheep-dresser, was already well established as an innovative agriculturalist in Delaware City when orchard crops became popular. He grew wealthy grazing sheep, planting castor beans, making bricks, and building a portion of the Chesapeake and Delaware Canal. By 1845, Reybold was filling up every available riverboat with thousands of baskets brimming with peaches from more than a hundred thousand trees.

Southern Delawareans found the agricultural successes of their northern neighbors easier to understand than to emulate. Farmers to the west of river navigation could not afford to import fertilizers. Much of western Kent and southern Sussex counties remained uncultivated swamps, because there was no incentive to development, and even the timber was not worth cutting where there was no transportation. On the urging of John M. Clayton, senator from Delaware, a company was formed in 1836 to build a railroad down the spine of the state, but its efforts died in the wake of worldwide depression the following year. By the mid-1840s, when the demand for a railroad had become critical, Samuel Maxwell Harrington, a Kent County jurist, revived the decade-old plan with his grand vision of a peninsular railroad linking New York City with Norfolk, Virginia. Many difficulties plagued the project. Because the depressed farmers who stood to profit most could not fund a railroad, the company eventually turned to the Philadelphia, Wilmington, and Baltimore line for support. The PW & B became the northern terminus for the Delaware Road, but the choice of route southward posed a major problem. Harrington's plan for the railroad to terminate at a wharfage on the Nanticoke in Seaford went unchallenged, but every little town and hamlet between there and Wilmington eagerly hoped for rail connections. Of the two possible routes—one in the east that would touch many of the river-port towns, the other west of the Delaware watershed—the engineers ultimately chose the flatter, western route—a fortuitous decision, since it brought transportation to the most neglected area of the state.

Many farmers in southern Delaware planted orchards in anticipation of a more market-oriented economy, and landowners who drained the swamps near Seaford discovered, as one wrote enthusiastically, that the "old causeway gutters, ditch banks, fence rows, and muckholes, instead of being left to breed disease, are cleaned out, and their contents turned into compost to improve the soil." [29] Finally, in late 1856, the first train from Wilmington pulled into Seaford, to be greeted by country people from miles around who descended on the station in spite of a downpour of rain to consume 120 turkeys and other foods provided by the railroad for the occasion.

29. Reed, editor, "Readings in Delaware History," p. 80.

As its promoters had foreseen, the railroad did have a quickening effect on the downstate economy. Between 1850 and 1870, improved acreage in Kent County expanded by about 25 percent; new towns began to grow up around railroad stations; and older towns such as Seaford, Dover, and Middletown enjoyed more rapid growth than the old port towns on the Delaware. But the spectacular changes in those years were in agricultural profits. Kent County's income from orchard products jumped in two decades from less than $10,000 to nearly $500,000.[30] By 1869, there were more than one million peach trees bearing fruit within shipping distance of the railroad, and it was claimed that Kent County produced "more peaches and of better quality than any other territory of the same size in the world." [31] During peach-harvest season, the PW & B diverted as many freight cars as possible to carry immense shipments. In 1869, a bumper-crop year, 41,000 carloads, each carrying five hundred baskets, went to New York alone, while steamboats continued to ship considerable quantities from the Appoquinimink and other rivers in central Delaware. Farmers soon realized that the railroad brought problems as well as profits. Convinced that the Delaware Railroad was overcharging them, they, like farmers in other parts of the country, formed a state chapter of the Patrons of Husbandry, or Grange, which, in 1887, petitioned the Interstate Commerce Commission for lower freight rates. In spite of a vigorous defense by the railroad company, the commission agreed with the farmers, but the rates were not reduced by much.

Delaware's reign as the "Peach State" was shortlived. Already, as the rails were being laid for the Delaware Road, farmers around Delaware City began noticing the ominous signs of a disease known as "the Yellows." "Slender wiry shoots" that produced "mean, starved-looking leaves" appeared on the trees, the fruit matured too rapidly, was spotted and tasteless,

30. U.S., Department of Interior, Bureau of the Census, *Compendium of the Seventh Census,* p. 211; U.S. Census, 1870, *Industry and Wealth* (Washington, D.C.: Government Printing Office, 1872), 3:114.

31. Hancock, "Agriculture in Delaware," 1:385.

then finally the foliage turned yellow, and, after two seasons, the affected tree died. There was no cure.[32] Slowly the disease spread southward, devastating orchards in its wake. The railroad had changed southern Delaware, however, and her farmers did not revert to subsistence agriculture, but sought out new crops on the basis of potential profits in urban markets.

The effects of railroad transportation on manufacturing and urban life were in every way as impressive as on the rural economy, and indeed a reciprocal relationship between the two made possible a more market-oriented agrarian economy. In the wake of the transportation revolution, America's industries were reshaped by coal, iron, and steel. Steam, not water, powered the machines of the new technology, thus encouraging businessmen to build their factories in cities where transportation, capital, and workers were at hand.

Delaware's sole industrial city was Wilmington. As an urban place, Wilmington could not compete in size with Philadelphia, but it was capable of holding its own as a manufacturing center. Its rail and water commerce brought in coal and iron from nearby Pennsylvania, lumber from southern Delaware and North Carolina, and other raw materials from around the world. Wilmington was equally fortunate to have workmen trained in various industrial skills from their association with the Brandywine mills and shipbuilding, as well as entrepreneurs who had grown wealthy as millers or shippers and were eager to invest in new industrial enterprises. About 1840, heavy industry began concentrating on the narrow strip between the Christina and the newly laid tracks of the PW & B. Railroad spurs, machine shops, and dry docks soon filled the area where the Swedes had built their fort and planted tobacco two centuries before. The new economic giants of the Christina were firms such as Harlan and Hollingsworth, builders of custom railroad cars, steam yachts, and boilers; they were also the first American company to build a cast-iron ship. Other firms included the

32. John J. Black, *The Cultivation of the Peach and the Pear on the Delaware and Chesapeake Peninsula* (Wilmington: Jones and Webb Printing Co., 1886), pp. 80–82.

Lobdell Car Wheel Company, largest manufacturer of iron railroad-car wheels in the United States through most of the nineteenth century; and Pusey and Jones, manufacturers of river boats and calendar rolls for paper mills. These companies, begun as partnerships and later incorporated, employed as many as a thousand workers and were among the largest of the foundries, car shops, and shipbuilding enterprises that gained the Christina the appellation, "the American Clyde." Most of the steamboats on the Delaware were built at Wilmington, as were numerous ferries, yachts, and other craft destined for service in rivers and bays along the East Coast and as far away as the Amazon in Brazil. Wilmington's railroad cars were equally famous. The Jackson and Sharp Company led the industry in the United States during the 1870s; they built cars for the nation's first transcontinental railroad and later successfully manufactured electric trolley cars for the national and international market. Many Paris trolleys and London underground cars were built on the banks of the Christina at Jackson and Sharp's shops, as were cars for the Manchurian Railroad.

Not far away from the river bank were other industries competing for space with working-class housing. Carriage-making was a major local industry until the Civil War cut off the builders' most lucrative markets in industrially backward Southern cities. Another local specialty was tanning, an industry that depended on imported hides and used huge quantities of the city's abundant water supplies. In the heyday of the city's tanneries, during the late nineteenth century, Wilmington ranked second only to Philadelphia in the tanning of goat hides into morocco, a soft leather very much in demand for book bindings, gloves, and uppers for ladies' shoes.

Wilmington's successes in manufacturing were not matched in the development of the city's commerce. In spite of the continuous efforts of her boosters, Wilmington could not compete with Philadelphia as the entrepôt of the Delaware Valley. During the post-Civil War boom years, Wilmingtonians built two new railroads, the Wilmington and Western and the Wilmington and Northern, that their promoters claimed would make the city

a major east-coast port competitive with her larger neighbor upstream on the Delaware. But it was not to be—both railroads
ran into financial difficulties and became small locally-oriented
feeder lines. Wilmington's merchants were equally disappointed
by their failure to attract the buying power of rural downstate
Delawareans who had the infuriating habit of steaming past the
city on train or boat enroute to shop in Philadelphia. When
downstate farmers formed the Delaware Fruit Exchange in
1883, which concentrated the big-city fruit buyers at one point
for peach auctions, the place selected was not Wilmington, but
Wyoming, Delaware—a tiny hamlet with a railroad siding,
south of Dover. Thus, although Wilmington was the largest,
most dynamic economic center in the state, its businessmen
were unable to establish reciprocal relations with other Delawareans.

The city's growth had a powerful impact on land use in its
immediate environs in New Castle County. Before the advent of
urban mass transit, working people walked from home to the
factory, and so builders clustered lower-class, brick row-houses
in the poorly drained, unhealthy lowlands of the Christina River
valley near the factories. By 1864, when the city's population
exceeded 22,000, land promoters built a horse-car line from the
PW & B station up Market Street and westward on Delaware
Avenue, along the crest of the hill that separates the watersheds
of the Brandywine and the Christina. Well-to-do people subsequently built homes and churches in this more fashionably attractive and healthful region. Two decades later, when the population had grown to more than 42,000, the city's transit
company was among the first in the nation to install electrically
powered trolleys that fanned out to the westward and northward
beyond Brandywine Village. The majority of nineteenth-century
Wilmingtonians paid rent for the two- or three-story brick row-
houses with narrow back yards that, as in Baltimore and Philadelphia, characterized most of the city's domestic architecture.
Only the more wealthy factory owners, bankers and shippers,
and lawyers could afford to build detached homes surrounded
by grounds and gardens. The maturing manufacturing sector

required more administrative direction than the factory owners could personally supply, and the number of office workers grew, thus expanding the middle class. As the trolley lines were extended, clerks, foremen, and small retailers flocked to the edges of the expanding city to buy larger row-houses featuring such amenities as slate roofs, oriel windows, and indoor plumbing, platted in checkerboard rows fronting on small yards. The physical form of the city thus reflected its economy, the size and relationship of its various social classes to the work available and to the prevailing transportation technologies of each period.

In all this expansion, some people gave thought to preserving places of natural beauty. While the Christina River presented a spectacle of nearly total industrial development, the Brandywine, because of the smaller, less obtrusive mills of an earlier day, retained much of its original appearance. William P. Bancroft, who had grown up along its picturesque banks, got strong support from other business leaders when, in 1883, he offered the public a large tract along the river on condition that the city purchase additional land downstream as the nucleus for a system of public parks. The city's prompt, positive response saved the Brandywine from industrial development and made available to all a scenic, wild retreat from the monotony of the prevailing grid-street pattern.

The pressure of population expansion required new means of supplying water and carrying off wastes. In the early days, Wilmingtonians took their water from back-yard wells or from springs, but growth rendered these sources both inadequate and unhealthful. In the 1820s, the city government assumed responsibility for water supply when it bought a steam-powered mill to pump water to a reservoir on a hilltop from which gravitational flow took the water to the population below. In time, the city found it necessary to expand its water system by creating new reservoirs, but it continued to rely upon the Brandywine as its sole source. Not surprisingly, industrial pollution and sewage plagued the water supply, producing typhoid fever and cholera. The first steps to solve these health problems did not come until the 1890s, when, after years of pleading from its Board of

Health, the city government undertook the expensive but necessary task of building a complete sewer system. Following a practice that was commonly employed by sanitary engineers at that time, the new system dumped raw sewage into the Delaware River at high tide to be carried past bayside beach resorts, oyster beds, and fishing grounds, out to sea. The sewers improved the healthfulness of the crowded, low-lying neighborhoods, where, heretofore, sewage from privy vaults had collected near ground level, fouling basements and causing illness. And although sewering also prevented some pollutants from entering the city's drinking water, it was only in 1909 that Wilmington built a water-purification plant. Lastly, the sewers helped to prevent the clogging of the Christina River. The Christina, like all the tributary tidal streams along the Delaware, was becoming ever more shallow as swamps were drained and the cleansing action of the tidal flow was reduced. The dumping of garbage and sewage into the river had only exacerbated the situation, and the sewers, together with expensive dredging, kept the river's depth adequate for its shipbuilding and shipping industries.

At the turn of the century, America's industrial economy had become truly national in scope, but little Delaware was once more falling behind, just as in earlier days, when her lands had lost their productivity. Downstate farmers sought profitable crops to replace their faltering peach orchards, while in Wilmington leading industries were encountering hard times from outside competition. The carriage-making trade never recovered fully after the Civil War, as manufacturers in the midwest undersold the local companies in the south by making cheaper products. More significant still was the steady decline of the railroad-car manufacturing and ship-building industries that formed the backbone of the city's economy. They, too, suffered from competitive disadvantages relative to bigger midwestern firms like the Pullman Company and American Car and Foundry Company. In addition, the Wilmington firms were subject to the voracious appetites of such giant trusts as U.S. Steel and Bethlehem Steel, which sought to dominate whole industrial sectors through vertical integration. Absorption by these huge compa-

nies brought both the blessings and the disadvantages of impersonal administrative efficiency. When any particular plant
proved more costly to operate than another somewhere else, the
managers in New York or Pittsburgh did not hesitate to shut it
down, and the Wilmington factories, with their aging machinery
and shallow river, were often at a disadvantage.

Delaware entered the twentieth century with a split personality. Down the peninsula, the depressed state of agriculture drove
rural people into a provincial state of mind in spite of their
railroad and their proximity to major cities. Wilmington had
never developed reciprocal relations with the state's farmers,
even during the halycon days of the peach harvests, and now it,
too, was in danger of economic decline.

At this critical time, when Delaware needed new direction
and enterprise, the Du Pont Company emerged as a dynamic
force in the state. Du Pont was, of course, by no means a new
element in Delaware's economy; the powder company had been
rooted in the same place on the Brandywine for a century,
growing to be the largest explosives manufacturer in the United
States. But no one looking at the state's economy in 1900 could
have guessed that this company employing about four hundred
people was destined to become so significant an economic factor
in the state that today, when people think of Delaware, they automatically think of Du Pont. In 1900, the company was owned
by a few members of the du Pont family and administered in a
highly conservative fashion by Eugene du Pont, a grandson of
the founder, E. I. In addition to the mills, which covered three
miles along the Brandywine, the company built, owned, and
maintained workers' housing and the nearby homes of the du
Ponts. The family had grown considerably in the course of a
century. E. I.'s three sons each produced several offspring,
most of whom lived on the Brandywine and participated in the
company's affairs. It was really impossible to separate family
and company business, and, as in most Victorian families, the
elders ruled. Although a few du Ponts were involved in state
politics, the family as a whole preferred to remain in the semi-
isolation of their Brandywine enclave.

In 1902, the company's centennial year, the du Ponts faced the greatest crisis in the entire history of the firm, when Eugene du Pont died, leaving no one among the senior partners willing to assume the responsibilities of leadership. The older du Ponts had decided to sell out to Laflin and Rand, the second-largest American powder-maker and a friendly rival, when the youngest partner, thirty-eight-year-old Alfred I. du Pont, a temperamental but skilled powder-maker, suddenly insisted that he would buy the company. The older men agreed, but only on the condition that he bring his cousins, T. Coleman and Pierre S., into the firm, since these men, unlike Alfred, had experience in executive management.

No one, certainly not Alfred himself, realized the implications of that decision—for T. Coleman and Pierre were not in the least interested in running the company in the old-fashioned ways of Eugene. Since the Civil War, the Du Pont Company had successfully controlled the pricing policy in the American explosives industry by means of agreements with the other major producers, such as Laflin and Rand, and by buying stock in smaller powder companies. The new leaders, admirers of the aggressive new-style business techniques of Andrew Carnegie and J. P. Morgan, were determined to make full use of this hodgepodge of company assets for the purpose of consolidating and rationalizing the entire domestic explosives market under their own direction. Thanks to T. Coleman's drive and Pierre's skills as a financier, they soon carried out that ambitious plan for buying control of a whole industry. Their swift and decisive success in the consolidation enterprise led logically to the adoption of the techniques of modern management to run the industrial empire they had so quickly acquired. Instead of permitting each subsidiary manufacturing plant to run its own affairs, so long as it kept its prices in line with those of Du Pont, the new managers reorganized the total administration of the company in such a way that they could maximize production and sales.

Because the newly created administrative structure required far more people and space than was available at the old company office on the Brandywine, the question of the best location for a large office building soon arose. The du Ponts could have followed the lead of other big corporations of the day and moved to New York City, but for Pierre and Alfred especially, Wilmington was home; they had grown up on the Brandywine, and it was the environment that they knew and loved. And, so, in 1906, they built a block-long, twelve-story modern office building, complete with a hotel and a theater, at the top of a hill in downtown Wilmington, where it dwarfed every other structure, and has been, ever since, the visible symbol of the Du Pont Company's relationship to the city. From the perspective of Delaware and Wilmington history, it is notable that the du Ponts did not stay because the state contained any valuable natural resources necessary to the production of powder. In fact, the mills on the Brandywine were quite out-of-date and were abandoned soon after World War I, their water power no longer an industrial necessity. Du Pont Company plants then, as now, were widely scattered throughout the United States. In deciding to keep the home office in Wilmington, the company managers were making their one significant bow to family tradition, and in so doing they changed Delaware more than anybody had since the Dutch first encountered the Indians.

When World War I erupted in 1914, the du Ponts were well organized to meet the challenge of the greater demand for explosives that followed. The company expanded rapidly, building several new plants and employing thousands of additional workers to fill the unprecedented orders from the allied governments in Europe and later from the U.S. War Department as well. In the course of the war, Du Pont manufactured nearly 1½ billion pounds of explosives for the allies, with an inflated payroll that rose to include more than a hundred thousand workers.[33] Enormous wartime profits, which reached $82 million in 1916, not only multiplied the personal fortunes of du Ponts and their close business and family associates, but were in large measure plowed back into the company's postwar expansion into the chemical industry. By using confiscated German dye patents and purchasing other European patents such as the one

---

33. William S. Dutton, *Du Pont, One Hundred and Forty Years* (New York: Charles Scribner's Sons, 1942), pp. 227–228.

for French-developed rayon, in addition to the growing expertise of their own chemists, the dynamic company maintained steady progress and profits through the "New Era" of the 1920s and even during the Great Depression. *Fortune* magazine reported, at the depths of the economic collapse, that "one share of Du Pont bought in 1914 for $125 would have been worth $2,844 by September 1934." [34] *The* Company, as Delawareans call it, had become the major force in the state's economy. Today, it employs 11 percent of Delaware's work force.

In the nineteenth century, railroads, peaches, and heavy industries using coal, iron, lumber, and hides dominated Delaware's land and resource use. In the twentieth century, these have been superseded by automobiles, chickens, diversified manufacturing, and the offices and laboratories of major chemical companies. Along the Delaware River, the old wood- and coal-powered steamboats and sailing vessels have given way to huge oil-powered, ocean-going tankers and cargo ships. Oil has become the center of a continuing and complex controversy along these coastal waters, pitting environmentalists against industrialists, and for the first time forcing the people of Delaware to think seriously about long-range resource management.

Transportation has always been the most significant factor in the patterns of land use in Delaware. First, rivers; then rails; and more recently, roads have determined where people live and how they make their living. It is especially difficult for late-twentieth-century Americans to imagine life one hundred years ago, when rural people were almost totally dependent on public transport in trains or steamboats, and city folk had only the additional option of trolley cars for local travel. In these circumstances, Delaware's farmers, like those elsewhere, felt trapped by the railroad companies and banded together to form the Grange. Meanwhile, the state's roads were of the teeth-rattling, dirt variety, until around 1900, when a few wealthy, adventurous people with a yen for speed and an enjoyment of machinery began America's love affair with the automobile.

In Delaware, not surprisingly, a du Pont, T. Coleman in this

34. *Fortune*, 10 (November 1934), p. 206.

case, was among the first motoring enthusiasts. A hearty, dynamic man, Coleman du Pont possessed a rapidly appreciating fortune due to the increased size, production, and efficiency of the powder company he headed, and he gave the state an ultramodern motor highway that runs from the southern border to Wilmington. Coleman du Pont conceptualized on a grand scale. "I will build a monument a hundred miles high and lay it on the ground," he is supposed to have boasted.[35] He planned to construct the highway along a two-hundred-foot right-of-way that would include separate lanes for trolley tracks, pedestrians, horse-drawn traffic, and both high-speed and slower, heavier, motorized vehicles. The trolleys and other utilities that shared this wide strip would pay for the privilege, and with these funds he thought the state could maintain the roadway and even make a profit. In 1911, the state legislature authorized T. Coleman's Boulevard Commission and granted to it the power of eminent domain. Not everyone in Delaware was initially persuaded that this seeming act of philanthropy was for the best, however. When du Pont began construction in Sussex County, some farmers suspecting his motives refused to accept his condemnation authority. The resulting legal struggle finally was resolved by the state supreme court in du Pont's favor, but he agreed to some concessions, such as narrowing the right-of-way, so that in many places the completed highway was only a two-lane concrete strip instead of the proposed dual-lane, multipurpose boulevard. The well-engineered road quickly won converts in Sussex, where Governor John G. Townsend proclaimed at the opening of its first section that "no one thing since the building of the railroad has done so much for the development of this section of our commonwealth as the construction of this road." The governor proudly noted the ironic fact that "It is no idle boast that Sussex County has the greatest road in the United States." [36]

35. John Rae, "Coleman du Pont and His Road," *Delaware History* 16 (1975):174.

36. Warren W. Mack, "A History of Motor Highways in Delaware," in *Delaware: A History of the First State,* 3 vols., edited by H. Clay Reed (New York: Lewis Historical Publishing Co., 1947), 2:543.

Once the highway project was under way, the rapidly increasing number of automobiles and trucks insured that it would be but the first step toward fulfilling the hopes of the advocates of the Good Roads movement for a complete system of improved roads. In 1916, Congress passed the Federal Aid Highway Act, which provided matching funds for road-building for those states that maintained professional highway departments. In the following year, Delaware's legislature created such a department, with T. Coleman du Pont and his chief engineer as prominent members. Coleman then turned over the job of completing his state road to the department, with a gift of $44,000 per mile to see the job through. His total expenditures on the highway that bears his name came to $3,917,004. Although the road as completed in 1924 fell short of Coleman's original intentions, it was still literally a path-breaking adventure, not only for Delaware but for the whole country. Its careful engineering included such advanced concepts as that of passing *near* towns, rather than *through* them, to make the roadway convenient but not congested. The road's success as a stimulus to traffic can be gauged by the fact that within three years the Highway Department had begun to widen some of its sections.

The Du Pont Highway became the spine of a statewide system of roads that changed Delaware life. Not only did the number of cars proliferate in the 1920s and '30s, but the trucking industry played an increasingly important role in the state's economy. In 1924, the state registered 6,061 trucks; by 1940, the number had risen to 15,000. By that latter date, trucks were hauling along the Du Pont Highway a million crates of poultry, plus thousands of bushels of peaches, cantaloupes, strawberries, potatoes, and other crops annually.

These figures on agricultural-commodity transportation demonstrate the rise of an important new crop. Just as orchard crops had been associated with the introduction of the steamboat and the railroad, so Delaware's modern broiler industry has grown up with the motor age. Broilers are young chickens weighing under three pounds. The rise of this multimillion-dollar industry in Delaware is closely tied to the state's proximity to population centers and to the local production of grain feeds. Mrs. Wilmer Steele of Ocean View, a small town near Bethany Beach in southeastern Sussex County, is credited with having started broiler production, when she raised a brood of five hundred chicks for quick and profitable sale in 1923. Within five years, Delaware farmers, mostly in Sussex, were producing two million birds, and the number kept on increasing at an astonishing rate. By the beginning of World War II, the number had climbed to thirty-five million; yet, during the war, it more than doubled, and in 1963 broiler production topped a hundred million and is still increasing. Between 1940 and 1970, the value of this single crop in Delaware has grown from about $17 million to over $77 million.[37] Hatcheries, long, low, pine-board chicken houses, and poultry-feed retailers sprang up throughout Sussex County. At first the chickens were trucked live to New York and other points, but since about 1940, automated dressing plants have been built that can kill, cut up, and pack thousands of broilers a day. In recent years, Delaware's independent poultry producers have signed contracts with the big feed and marketing companies that have come to dominate this highly organized and competitive business.

The demand of the poultry industry for grain feeds has sparked other changes in Delaware agriculture, particularly the successful introduction of soybeans as a major crop, second only to corn in acreage. Soybean meal accounts for about 20 percent of the broiler-feed ration, and the birds consume about ten million bushels of Delaware soybeans annually. Corn, which farmers rotate with soybeans, is also used primarily as chicken feed. Neither of these grain crops could be profitably grown in Delaware were it not for the broiler industry. Among Delaware's other major crops are dairy farming and truck farming. In the early 1950s, many potato growers, displaced by suburbanization in Long Island and the Philadelphia area, moved

37. W. T. McAllister, "Trends and Adjustments in Delaware's Agriculture, 1940–1970," mimeographed (Newark: University of Delaware, College of Agriculture, 1971), p. 1.

their operations to Kent County. With Delaware's good soils and ready access to major population centers, the state's agriculture has adjusted well to twentieth-century economic patterns. As of 1970, the state had the third-highest gross income per farm in the United States and was first among all the states east of the Mississippi. As farming has moved toward agri-business, farmers are making more intensive use of their land to increase yields. The trend is toward larger individual farms, while the total amount of land given over to agriculture has declined from 70 percent of the state in 1940 to 56 percent thirty years later.

The advent of the automobile simultaneously with the Du Pont Company's expansion brought dramatic changes to northern Delaware, typical of development throughout the Boston-Washington corridor that urbanologist Jean Gottman has called "megalopolis." [38] In the first part of the twentieth century, Wilmington continued to grow, reaching a peak population of more than 112,000 in 1940; but after the war, the predominantly white-collar work force of the chemical industry abandoned the city for new homes in the suburbs. Comparing the census years 1920 and 1960, the population of Wilmington dropped 13 percent, while the population of surrounding New Castle County soared by 455.9 percent. The impetus to suburbanization touched blue-collar workers, as well, when General Motors built an assembly plant in a suburban area southwest of Wilmington, and Chrysler opened a plant in nearby Newark. Du Pont, too, responded to the trend by locating many new facilities on the cheaper, more plentiful land outside the city. After the war, the company constructed a mammoth, campus-style experimental station near the location of the original powder mills, followed by other large-scale complexes between Wilmington and Newark.

Since Delawareans had never faced such rapid growth before, it is not surprising that the state and county initially lacked the means to plan for or control that expansion. New Castle County's weak Regional Planning Commission could only hope

38. Jean Gottman, *Megalopolis: The Urbanized Northeastern Seaboard of the United States* (New York: The Twentieth-Century Fund, 1961), pp. 3, 4.

to keep up with building the sewers and road systems to support the suburbanites. In the late 1950s, the state built a dual-lane highway to connect Wilmington with Newark. The farmland on either side was carved into sprawling suburban developments with astonishing rapidity, and the highway itself became an ugly commercial strip seemingly overnight. The most northeastern part of the county, Brandywine Hundred, was another concentrated suburb. Once the most beautiful farmland in Delaware, it now houses two thousand people per square mile. Meanwhile, enormously wealthy members of the du Pont and related families, together with top executives, continued to live in "chateau country" on their sylvan estates in the rolling country west of the Brandywine, thus maintaining an enclave relatively untouched by the great changes in land use that were going on around them.

As late as the mid-1960s, the prevailing attitude toward expansion into the county was positive. The fact that Wilmington's declining population was becoming progressively poorer, that much of the city was physically deteriorating, that it was well on its way to becoming a black ghetto, and that new industries were choosing to locate in the county rather than in the city aroused little concern. In 1963, the University of Delaware, in co-operation with the State Highway Department, published the first of three studies on the impact of newly built Interstate 95, a turnpike that crosses Delaware from Newark to New Castle and forks off through Wilmington toward Philadelphia. The tone of the first report was very optimistic. The researchers pointed out that new types of transportation had always led to economic growth in the past, and they predicted that I-95 would bring even higher levels of prosperity to an already dynamic area. Land values would rise, new homes would be built, new jobs created, the tax base strengthened, and land use would be intensified. They prophesied that I-95 would bring new industry to the city of Wilmington and would raise sagging urban land values.[39] In their second report, written shortly after the highway

39. Blaine G. Schmidt, *Delaware Highway Impact Study: Phase I, 1954–1958* (Newark: University of Delaware and Delaware State Highway Department, 1963), pp. 3–14.

was completed, they conceded that it had not produced quite the results they had foreseen. The highway had little impact on the already highly suburbanized corridor northeast of the city; it was badly hurting businesses along older routes such as the Du Pont Highway and Route 40 south of the city; and—most obviously—it had not prevented the continuing deterioration of Wilmington. They projected, however, that that last problem was only temporary, a result of the demolition of blocks of housing in the city, and that, as the urban scar healed, I-95 would still become the key to renewed urban vigor.[40] By the time of their third report, issued when the highway had been in operation for five years, they were forced to conclude that Wilmington was not recovering from its civic wound. The price per square foot of city land adjacent to the highway had dropped more precipitously than in a similar nearby area, from $1.71, just before the interstate road was built, to $0.35 a decade later.[41]

The study's over-all appraisal of the impact of I-95 on New Castle County remained favorable, however. They pointed out that the new road had brought a land boom to a formerly agricultural region near the already highly suburbanized town of Newark. There developers were building homes, apartments, and townhouses; new industries were coming in; and land values were increasing dramatically. The assumption that increased intensity of land use was always a social good that governed the first study ten years before was less tenable, however. The writer of the final report recognized that growth should be the cause for concern as well as pride and called for better planning to prevent the growth region from becoming another misadventure in suburban sprawl.[42]

The New Castle County government has responded to the ob-

40. Blaine G. Schmidt, *Delaware Highway Impact Study: Phase II, 1959–1963* (Newark: University of Delaware and Delaware State Highway Department, 1967), pp. 64–76.

41. Blaine G. Schmidt, *Delaware Highway Impact Study: Phase III, 1964–1968* (Newark: University of Delaware and Delaware State Highway Department, 1972), p. 57.

42. Schmidt, *Delaware Highway Study, Phase III*, p. 105.

vious need for planning. It has been reorganized in order to meet greater demands for community services and has created a professional planning department that is attempting to steer population growth into areas that are adequately supplied with water, highways, and other supports to residential and industrial development. Beneficial as that is, it is only the first step toward the control of land use that will be required to meet the future challenges of population expansion in an era of decreasing natural resources.

While academics, politicians, and the public were recognizing that uncontrolled suburban growth was a mixed blessing, the state was facing other serious land-use problems along the coast of Delaware Bay and Delaware River. One of the concomitants of the automobile age has been the growing importance of the oil industry. Since the turn of the century, several refineries have been built on the Delaware River near Philadelphia, and in 1957 the Getty Company opened the first refinery in Delaware, a huge facility at Delaware City. By the early 1970s, there were seven refineries on the Delaware River, with a joint capacity to refine 913.1 thousand barrels daily. About 70 percent of all the oil brought to the east coast of the United States came up the Delaware River. Furthermore, the state was under intense pressure to permit the construction of additional refineries on the land along the river banks. Ecologists argued strongly against further industrialization in these coastal wetlands because of the area's importance as a spawning ground for sea life and as a stop-over point for migratory birds. One study called the land "the most biologically productive area known." [43] Delaware's resort towns, Rehoboth, Lewes, and Bethany Beach, were also concerned about the possibility of oil pollution that might destroy the state's extensive summer-tourist business. In 1970, Governor Russell W. Peterson, a former chemist, approached that perplexing issue with its economic and ecological implications for Delaware's future with the self-confidence gained from

43. Governor's Task Force on Marine and Coastal Affairs, *The Coastal Zone of Delaware* (Newark: University of Delaware College of Marine Studies, 1971), p. 202.

. . .

his scientific training and the dedication of a citizen-reformer in politics. Peterson, a midwesterner brought to Delaware by Du Pont, was acutely aware of the unique beauty of the Delaware shoreline and the importance of recreation, tourism, and fisheries to the state's economic and social life. In 1971, following a lengthy public debate, the state legislature adopted the governor's proposed Coastal Zone Act that outlawed all new heavy industry "incompatible with the protection of the natural environment" along the shoreline.[44] The act was hailed nationally as a major step toward protecting the ecological balance of one of the most important wetland areas on the east coast. In the 1970s, the University of Delaware's recently established College of Marine Studies has been working to restore fish and commercially viable oyster beds to the bay, while monitoring the pollution problem and advising the state government and the public on the long-run economic advantages to be gained by fostering sea life in the coastal area. In spite of all this effort, the Coastal Zone Act cannot by itself solve the state's ecological problems, and it has continued to come under fire by those who claim that it is costing Delaware new industry.

One oil-related problem that has not gone away is that of lightering in the Delaware Bay. The size of tankers has increased so much since the 1950s that they require ever deeper water in which to operate. New tankers with drafts of fifty feet and more when fully loaded cannot navigate the Delaware, which is as shallow as thirty to thirty-eight feet in some places. The oil companies have met the problem by a procedure known as "lightering," whereby the ships unload part of their cargo onto barges just inside the bay's protected waters. Although there have been no major spills, so far, the practice is sufficiently dangerous to cause concern. One proposed solution is to construct a large, permanent marine terminal in the bay, where tankers can discharge their cargoes into a pipeline that

44. Joel M. Goodman, "Economic and Social Aspects of Delaware's Coastal Zone," Delaware Bay Report Series, 10 vols., edited by Dennis F. Polis, mimeographed (Newark: University of Delaware, College of Marine Studies, 1973), 8:20.

will go to the refineries upstream.[45] While the problem as yet
awaits resolution, another that has recently displaced it from the
public consciousness is the proposed exploration for oil off the
Delaware coast.

Today Delawareans, like other Americans, are sceptical of
the traditional view in our society that endless growth in population, land-use intensity, and the economy are for the best. The
constant push to improve the economic status of oneself and
one's community is, of course, still strong, but most people
have come to accept the need for land-use planning. The success of the Coastal Zone Act gives some hope that we can resist
the seemingly relentless demands for economic growth, but
there is no sure way to predict future needs. One is struck rather
by a disturbing lack of continuity as our concerns are shifted
with dizzying speed from one problem to another. A few years
ago, when the newspapers were filled with stories about the
lightering problem, it was assumed that oil flows from abroad
would continue to grow. More recently, since the Arab boycott,
concern has shifted to increasing domestic production, even at
the potential cost of ruining the state's ocean beaches. This
whirligig of change makes it especially hard for the public and
for planners alike to reach accord on how we wish to shape our
future. The one thing that can be said with assurance is that we
can no longer afford the solutions of the past.

From the time of the land's discovery by Europeans, Delaware's natural resources have been treated as things to be ex-
ploited for profit. The beaver, oak trees, oysters, terrapins,
marshlands—all were subject to ruthlessness that countenanced
wanton waste with little thought for future generations. Farmers
wore out the soil and moved on to newer frontiers in the West.
Those who stayed behind tried to keep pace with the times by
investing in railroads, constructing manufactories, planting
peach orchards, or raising poultry as conditions changed. It has
only been since the massive impact of the sophisticated, highly

45. W. S. Gaither et al., *Energy, Oil and the State of Delaware* (Dover: Delaware
Bay Oil Transport Committee of the State of Delaware, 1973), pp. 6, 11, 34.

dynamic economy of big business, urbanization, and the automobile age that the people of Delaware have recognized what the Indians knew instinctively: that man must live with his environment—or destroy himself.

Part II

A Diverse People

$\mathcal{M}$ODERN Delawareans often assume that, back in the old days, say before World War II, the people of their state were homogeneous and sedentary. Recently, with the rise of the big chemical companies that dominate the state's economy, Delawareans have joined the rest of the nation in moving from place to place with unprecedented frequency. Whenever I tell someone that not only was I born in Delaware but so were my parents, grandparents, and even earlier ancestors, the revelation precipitates gasps of wonder. Delaware today, in spite of its small size, is a diverse state with marked contrasts between the urban, industrial upstate and rural downstate, between natives and newcomers, between blacks and whites. But the notion that the state was once a homogeneous whole is largely a myth. Compared with some states among the original thirteen in New England and the South, Delaware, like the other states of the Middle Atlantic region, had a colonial heritage of ethnic, religious, and cultural pluralism. These contrasts have always been most marked in New Castle County, the crossroads between Maryland and Pennsylvania. As Wilmington became an industrial center in the nineteenth century, it attracted from a variety of European countries immigrants who further enriched the northernmost county's ethnic mix. More recently, with the spread of industry downstate and the introduction of new agricultural products and techniques, that heterogeneity is spreading southward. Social life in Delaware has thrust diverse people into one another's company, usually with the result of accommodation except in the crucial area of race relations.

69

Delaware's earliest recorded instance of the meeting of contrasting cultures occurred in the first decade of the seventeenth
century, when Dutch explorers met the Lenni-Lenape. The
meeting boded ill for the Indians, for, as we have seen, the impact of European economics had profoundly affected the natives' way of life even before the Swedes created the first permanent white settlement in Delaware—New Sweden, on the
Christina River, in 1638. As the white population increased during the second half of the seventeenth century, the Indians
ceded to whites more and more of their traditional living space
and became victims of a culture that they could neither assimi-
late into nor ignore. Many died from contracting the white
men's diseases, particularly smallpox; those who survived and
remained in the area were equally unable to escape maladjust-
ments from the new order of things. The goods that the Indians
received for their lands—pots, cheap woven garments, guns,
and liquor—were dazzling attractions, but they could not really
compensate the red men for the loss of their way of life.

The drunken Indian, a sadly recurring figure in American
frontier history, made his first appearance in colonial times. The
various efforts of the Europeans to cope with that social evil
proved futile. Dutch and Swedish leaders despaired of ridding
their communities of the embarrassment of Indian imbibers who
menaced the peace and provided poor examples for the colonists. Under the Duke of York's administration, a law designed
to protect white society from inebriated savages was adopted
without, however, denying liquor dealers the right to make a
profit on the Indian trade. The law permitted tavern keepers to
sell alcohol to an Indian, but only in large quantities and only if
the red man took his purchase out of the white man's town and
into the forest before consuming it. William Penn, motivated by
a much more humanitarian impulse, forbade any sale of liquor
to Indians. Like a more recent American experience in prohibition, his well-intended law proved to be unenforceable, especially after the proprietor returned to England and left the government in the hands of people who secretly profited from the
illicit trade.

The Lenni-Lenapes who survived for more than a generation or two after European settlement were those who left the region and joined other Indian communities. The last remnant of the Delawares, subsequently pushed westward by advancing whites, lives on today in a few communities, principally in Oklahoma. Their language now nearly lost, the remaining Delawares have attempted to hold together some bits and pieces of their ancestral heritage.

The only Indians still living in Delaware are descendants of the Nanticokes, Accomacks, Assateagues, and other Chesapeake Bay tribes related to the Powhatans of Virginia who once occupied the southern portion of the Delmarva Peninsula. Driven northward by English settlements in Virginia and Maryland, some of these natives established control over the area around the Indian River and its estuary in Sussex County during the early years of the eighteenth century. There, too, they were eventually harassed by settlers, and in 1742, they joined forces with tribes farther up the Chesapeake in plans for a revolt against the whites. The plot was revealed, however, and although the Maryland leaders who then governed the region dealt lightly with the conspirators, the aroused white population made life so difficult for the Indians that most of them migrated farther north and eventually settled in Ontario, Canada. The few remaining Nanticoke families retreated to their isolated cabins among the pine forests and small farms beside the Indian River Bay. Over the years, miscegenation with both whites and blacks diluted their Indian blood. In the nineteenth century, some of these people moved to a small crossroads community called Cheswold, northwest of Dover, in search of work. In both communities, the exotic, yellow-skinned mixed bloods were the source of many romantic stories that ignored the more pedestrian explanation of their unique racial characteristics. The Cheswold group called themselves Moors and claimed descent from a gang of Spanish-African privateers who were shipwrecked along the Delaware coast in colonial times and found refuge among the Indians. Another popular legend claimed that their common ancestors were a beautiful wealthy

Spanish (or in some version, Irish) lady plantation-owner in Sussex County and a Moorish chief.[1] Until the recent demise of legally enforced racial barriers in Delaware, their status as mixed bloods was a source of many problems and much bitterness, since state law generally recognized only two racial groups, Negro and white. Through resentment and pride, the Moors maintained fanciful legends of their supposed ancestry.

While most of the state's Indians were in the process of losing their lands, the Swedes were experiencing another common phenomenon among American immigrants, that of losing their cultural heritage to the more numerous English. These pioneering colonists from Sweden were a mixed lot. Many were Finns whose country had been under Swedish rule since the Middle Ages. The Swedish government had once encouraged Finnish peasants to enter Sweden and clear the vast forests of the northern part of the country, but in the seventeenth century, the Swedes discovered valuable copper reserves in the region and drove the Finnish farmers away. Many Finns were thus attracted by the chance to farm in a new territory. Some others among the first Swedish settlers were petty criminals, poachers, and army deserters, expendable people sent to America in an attempt to swell the size of the tiny colony. There were even some Dutchmen among the soldiers and seamen hired by the company. The colonists were divided into two types: "servants," who were employees of the company brought to America to produce a profit by farming the company's land, hunting, and building for the company; and "freemen," who came at their own expense, farmed private plots, and were free to come and go as they pleased. The malefactors, all of whom were in the first category, were chained and kept separate from the others. They were employed in the most onerous tasks, such as digging trenches and building fortifications, until Governor Printz discontinued the practice of bringing such undesirables into the colony.

1. C. A. Weslager, *Delaware's Forgotten Folk* (Philadelphia: University of Pennsylvania Press, 1943), pp. 25–39.

The scarcity of women was a major problem. Without them, not only was natural increase impeded, but the men were required to perform traditional female tasks, such as caring for animals, cooking, and making clothes. The paucity of females suggests the colony's most basic difficulty, its impermanence and inability to become a self-supporting enterprise. Ironically, it was shortly after the Dutch conquest that a ship carrying 105 passengers arrived in the Delaware River, bringing four Swedish and twenty-seven Finnish women and thirty-two children, whose presence did much to sustain the little Scandinavian ethnic community.

With such a small number of people, most of them peasants or soldiers, all struggling to make a living in the wilderness, it is not surprising that social organizations did not flourish in New Sweden. The only important institution outside the company itself was the Lutheran Church. A minister, Johan Campanius, was sent to New Sweden in 1642. A dedicated man, he wore himself out attempting to farm and to minister to a congregation strung out for twenty miles along the river. The Indians were amazed to see the Swedes' religious ceremonies, especially the way in which the newcomers patiently listened to the minister talk for such extended periods. They held Campanius in awe on that account and visited him often to be instructed in the mysteries of the Christian faith. For their benefit, he compiled a vocabulary of the Lenape language and translated Luther's Little Catechism into their native tongue in 1646, some years before the Puritan John Eliot made his translation of the Bible for the Massachusetts Indians. Campanius has not been forgotten by the remnant of Delaware Indians, as a touching scene enacted more than three centuries after his death reveals. In 1963, several members of the tribe journeyed to Sweden to participate in the three-hundred-and-twenty-fifth anniversary of the founding of the Delaware colony. Part of the celebration took place near Stockholm, at a church where Campanius had served as pastor. After the Indians had placed a memorial wreath on the minister's tomb, one in their number was so moved that he arose, raised his arms to heaven and to the four

corners in Indian fashion and recited a lengthy prayer in the
nearly extinct Delaware language. An eyewitness of the emotional scene wrote that among the congregation "not one eye
was dry when the little Delaware quietly retired to his seat." [2]

Long after their fortress and homes have disappeared, the
remaining monument to New Sweden in Delaware is a stone
church called Trinity, or more commonly "Old Swedes." Although it was not built until 1698, forty-three years after Swedish administration had ended on the Delaware, Old Swedes is
among the most ancient church buildings in the United States.
Tucked in among rows of nineteenth-century workers' homes
and bordering on the tracks of the Penn-Central Railroad, the
church must have looked very different to eighteenth-century
worshipers who approached the then quiet and secluded spot by
boat.

In the early days of New Sweden, the resident Lutheran
clergyman held services within the fort. When that practice died
out during the period of Dutch rule, some Dutch colonists
joined with the Swedes and Finns to build a wooden church at
Cranehook, along the Delaware River flats between the Christina and the town of New Amstel. Ministers from both Holland
and Sweden served the congregation until 1691, when the last
retired. In the meantime, the Dutch had built a Calvinist church
in New Castle, but the Swedish community of farming folk,
now subjects of the King of England and of the proprietor William Penn, sought a Lutheran clergyman from their homeland.
With the permission of the English, the Swedish government
responded by sending to them the zealous and capable Reverend
Mr. Eric Bjork, who built the present Old Swedes Church. The
dimensions of the church were sixty feet by thirty feet. The
walls were capped by a clipped gable roof. The original small
belfry was replaced in 1802 by a more substantial brick tower,
and in 1762 porticoes were added on either side to provide support for the building's bulging walls. Most of the construction
was done by a Philadelphia mason, assisted by a black man who

2. Weslager, *The Delaware Indians,* p. 27.

prepared the mortar, but some work was provided by members of the congregation.

The church became the mainstay of the Swedish community, but as the years passed, the younger generation learned English instead of the old language, and Swedish customs began to fall away. In the 1730s, English Quakers disrupted the rural quietude of the Swedes with their new commercial community of Wilmington. There was some intermarriage between the English and the Scandinavians, but just as important were the contacts gained through such practices as indenturing Swedish orphans into English-speaking homes or apprenticing Swedish youths to English masters. The influence of English law was also disruptive to the continuance of Swedish customs. For example, in Sweden, as in most continental countries, a marriage could not be contracted until banns were read in church for three successive Sundays. English law, however, provided the quicker route to marriage of buying a license from the governor in Philadelphia. Consequently, those who could afford the license fee ignored the old custom in favor of the speedier practice. That scandalized the resident Swedish clergyman Israel Acrelius, who wrote that, when the bridal pair received their license, "even if it be in the middle of the night or early in the morning, if they so please, with more or less company, then the marriage immediately takes place. The bride is in her usual dress, so that in that respect she cannot be distinguished from any of the company." [3]

Meanwhile, Trinity Church was itself following the trend toward Anglicization. From Bjork's tenure onward, the Swedish clergy maintained close ties with the local Anglican clergy, even to the point of filling in at Church of England ceremonies. The Swedish Lutheran and the Anglican churches had much in common. Both were national churches with similar liturgies, governed by bishops whose authority derived from the state. The ministers of these state churches were serving in a situation strange to them, in a land where dissenters, such as Quakers,

3. Acrelius, *History of New Sweden,* p. 357.

Congregationalists, Presbyterians, and others, were not only much more commonplace than at home but were, in fact, the majority. Pastor Acrelius complained of the difficulties inherent in maintaining church discipline in a country where the state-church relationship was so weak. In America, he found that "he who has no religion is just as much esteemed for it as though he thereby showed himself quite rational." [4] Some of the more free-thinking Swedes rejected Lutheranism and joined the Quakers, he noted, but when they discovered the difficulties in maintaining the Friends' strict morality, they often gave up churchgoing altogether.

As the descendants of the Swedish colonists became more conversant with English than with their mother tongue, their pastors began preaching in both languages. Acrelius attempted to reverse the trend in the 1750s. Appalled by the nearly total illiteracy that he found among the Swedes, he brought in a schoolmaster to instruct the children in religion and Swedish, but the master resigned because of inadequate pay. Acrelius then divided the congregation into study groups that he taught himself. During these sessions he found that "It could not be avoided that they had sometimes to be allowed to explain themselves in English, as their thoughts thus came most easily." [5] Although he tried to instruct the youth from the Swedish catechism, his efforts could not stem the tide of cultural adjustment that was to dissolve all formal bonds with the Swedish church and bring Old Swedes almost effortlessly into the Protestant Episcopal Church before the end of the century.

The last pastor sent from Sweden to Trinity, Lars Girelius, came in 1767 and served throughout the distressing days of the American Revolution, when for a time the church was commandeered as a barracks. One product of the Revolution was the rupture of the ties that had bound the American Anglican congregations to the Church of England. The Swedish government, instead of applauding that change, lost interest in maintaining

4. Acrelius, *History of New Sweden,* p. 352.
5. Acrelius, *History of New Sweden,* p. 303.

clergymen in the new United States if the pastors were no longer to be associated with the national church concept of ecclesiastical polity. Simultaneously, the congregation at Old Swedes amended the church's charter to permit the vestry to select its ministers from either the Lutheran or the new American Episcopal Church. Consequently, when Girelius resigned, about 1790, the vestry selected as his successor an Episcopalian who had served in Philadelphia's Swedish church, Gloria Dei.[6] In 1846, one hundred years after Acrelius's efforts to stem the tide of amalgamation, Benjamin Ferris, a local historian, wrote that the descendants of the Swedes had become indistinguishable from the predominantly British population. "Their language," he said, "is so entirely lost, that it is doubtful whether they possess a single individual who can read or speak it. But *there stands* their venerable *old church,* with solemn aspect, silently but expressively bearing testimony to the existence and piety of a generation that has passed away forever." [7]

The English migration into Delaware during the seventeenth century, although later than that of the Dutch and the Swedes, was larger and ultimately much more influential. Some Englishmen, such as Samuel Dickinson and John Dagworthy, came to the peninsula from the Chesapeake counties of Maryland or Virginia in response to land grants from the Maryland proprietor. Principally Anglican, these people created a life style in the southern part of the state that fell between the genteel agrarian ways of the Chesapeake tobacco plantations and the bourgeois world of Philadelphia. Another major group of English immigrants were Quakers, such as the founding families of Wilmington, the Shipleys, Canbys, and Tatnalls, who entered northern Delaware after sojourns in nearby Pennsylvania. They were part of the wave of Quakers who came to America to participate in Penn's Holy Experiment and to escape persecution at home. Their subsequent decision to settle in the "Three Lower

6. Nelson W. Rightmyer, *The Anglican Church in Delaware* (Philadelphia: The Church Historical Society, 1947), pp. 107–109.

7. Ferris, *Original Settlements On the Delaware,* p. 144.

Counties'' was prompted as much by Penn's control over that territory as by the economic opportunities that they perceived there.

The English were not the only settlers who entered Delaware from the British Isles. Almost equally numerous among eighteenth-century immigrants were the Scotch-Irish. Like the Quakers, they were fleeing from injustices that made life at home intolerable, and they found a haven in William Penn's colony, where freedom of religion was practiced as nowhere else in the English-speaking world. If the history of Ireland has been filled with scenes of man-made disasters, that of Ulster in the northeastern part of the Emerald Isle has been especially tragic. After the Elizabethan wars to subdue the Irish, the English government encouraged poor Lowland-Scot Presbyterians to colonize Ulster as a counterforce against the Catholic natives. Not surprisingly, that policy produced continual warfare in Ireland during the seventeenth century, punctuated by massacres, sieges, and pitched battles, the marks of which have yet to be erased. In spite of these difficulties, the poverty of their own land, joined with religious zeal, continued to bring Scotsmen to Ulster. Although England benefitted from the Scottish presence in Ireland, the English resented the economic accomplishments of their fellow-Protestant colonists. A law of 1670 stopped the Scotch-Irish from importing their most profitable commodity, woolens, into England. Other laws were directed at destroying the Presbyterian kirk and substituting an Irish branch of the Church of England. Beginning in the reign of Queen Anne, only those who belonged to the established church could hold public office. Everyone in Ireland, of whatever faith, was required to pay taxes for the maintenance of a religion that found few adherents on the entire island.

Faced with these unrelenting problems, both economic and religious, the Scotch-Irish left Ulster in droves and sailed for America. Many, lacking the money to pay for the voyage, signed papers of indenture that committed them to several years of servitude in the New World. Although they settled in all thirteen of the colonies, the greatest number landed in Philadelphia;

thus the region around that city was most affected by these twice-transplanted Scots. A great many came into Delaware, particularly to New Castle County, where their presence in those days before formal censuses can best be judged by the rapid spread of Presbyterian churches. Like some other groups who have emigrated in the face of persecution, the Scotch-Irish newcomers included many able, well-educated people who quickly moved into professional careers in the Presbyterian clergy, the law, and medicine.

The Welsh Baptists were another non-English group in Britain who came to Pennsylvania to escape religious persecution. William Penn set aside several "Welsh tracts" for these newcomers, where they might continue the use of their melodious Celtic language and maintain their congregational form of worship. Some Welsh miners, on hearing of the existence of ore-filled Iron Hill in western New Castle County, petitioned Penn for land there. In 1701, Penn granted them thirty thousand acres, including the hill that the settlers called Pencader, which means "the highest seat" in Welsh. There some became farmers, while others mined and forged iron. In the same year that Penn made his Pencader grant, a group of sixteen Baptists from the Welsh counties of Pembroke and Caermarthen resolved to go to America as a "church emigrant" under the leadership of their minister. After a short stay in Pennsylvania, they too took up land near Iron Hill, where they erected the first Baptist church in Delaware, a small wooden meetinghouse known as the Welsh Tract church.[8] The present church building was built on the same site, about a mile south of Newark, in 1746. The plain but well-proportioned brick structure, surrounded by a cemetery containing tombstones with weathered Welsh inscriptions, is a continuing reminder of the colonial ethnic community.

In terms of numbers and influence, the Welsh and the Swedes must take second place to the English and the Scotch-Irish in the

8. Richard B. Cook, *The Early And Later Delaware Baptists* (Philadelphia: American Baptist Publication Society, 1880), pp. 14–15.

history of the Three Lower Counties during the eighteenth century. Quakers, Anglicans, and Presbyterians were the major religious groups in the colony until the rise of Methodism during the years of the Revolution. In 1776—when the estimated population of Delaware was a bit in excess of 37,000, spread more or less evenly among the counties—there were twenty-nine Presbyterian congregations in the colony, seventeen of which were located in New Castle County. Second in terms of total number of congregations were the Quakers and Anglicans, with twelve each.[9] While the Quaker meetinghouses and Presbyterian churches were concentrated in New Castle County, the Anglicans were spread out nearly evenly among the counties.

To understand the interaction of these major groups, it is necessary to recall their intertwined historic and theological backgrounds. The Anglican Church, which grew out of Henry VIII's split with Rome, was the established religion of England during the colonial period, with the brief exception of the English Civil War and Cromwellian Interregnum, 1642–1660. Except for the absence of the pope, the Anglican Church was organized hierarchically in the Roman fashion under the authority of bishops who were appointed by the crown. The bishops in turn ordained the clergymen who served in the local parishes. The entire structure was maintained by taxes and was supported by laws that restricted participation in government and other favors to those who were within the church's communion. Theologically, Anglicanism was an uneasy compromise between Catholicism and Protestantism. Churchmen emphasized the sacraments and the efficacy of "good works," that is, the maintenance of church discipline, as means to salvation to an extent that drove more Calvinistic British Christians to seek alternative forms of worship. Numerous groups split off from Anglicanism in the course of the religiously troubled seventeenth century. The Pilgrims, Puritans, Presbyterians, and Baptists who came to America during those years were all part of the Calvinist per-

9. Elizabeth Waterston, *Churches in Delaware during the Revolution* (Wilmington: Historical Society of Delaware, 1925), p. 107.

suasion, which held that an omnipotent and omniscient God could not be coerced by man's feeble attempts at "good works." Salvation, they maintained, was a free gift from God to his predestined elect. The Calvinist doctrine required that its adherents reject the organizational structure of the established church along with its doctrines. In place of bishops they substituted a variety of polities: rule by the elect in the congregation, as in New England Puritanism; or, among the Presbyterians, rule by the clergy together with hierarchies of lay elders or presbyters elected by the congregations.

The Society of Friends differed from Anglicanism more radically than did the Puritans and Presbyterians. The society's founder George Fox aroused profound controversy throughout Britain with his teachings that God spoke to each man individually through an "Inner Light." Rejecting all signs of social distinctions, the early Quakers zealously adopted such egalitarian habits as refusing to tip their hats to social superiors and addressing every man with the familiar *thee* or *thou* instead of the more respectful *you*. To the further annoyance of non-Quaker society, the Friends refused to participate in warfare regardless of the provocation, and held that conciliatory understanding of others would render wars obsolete. William Penn, the highest-ranking and most important convert to the new faith, introduced the Society of Friends to America on a large scale. His policies of fair dealing with the Indians, together with his religious tolerance, dedication to representative government, and encouragement of colonization by non-Quaker dissenting groups such as the Welsh Baptists and German Mennonites, were the most conspicuous signs of his earnest effort to realize a Quaker Holy Experiment.

In an effort to stem the tide of religious dissent in their American colonies, the bishops and the government of England founded the Society for the Propagation of the Gospel in Foreign Parts in 1701. Until the Revolution abruptly terminated its role, the SPG sent missionary priests to America. The need for such an organization to maintain the Anglican faith in the colonies illustrates the church's most serious limitations abroad:

the necessity for its clergy to be ordained in England and the relatively weak sense of church affiliation among the Anglican colonists who, never having endured persecution at home, had come to America for economic reasons.

A number of SPG-subsidized clergymen came to Delaware, and the present-day Episcopal Church in the state rests upon the foundation of their work. The handsome colonial church buildings constructed for the society's chief missions in New Castle County—Immanuel Church in the town of New Castle and St. Anne's on the Appoquinimink—are still in use by Episcopal congregations. Immanuel, standing among other colonial buildings in the New Castle town green and distinguished by a graceful nineteenth-century tower and steeple, is the more famous of the two; Old St. Anne's, however, located just south of Middletown along the Appoquinimink, is more true to the original appearance of the Society's mission churches. Built in 1768, St. Anne's is a two-story rectangular brick structure. The churchyard includes a large, tree-shaded graveyard in which grows a magnificent oak dating from before the days of William Penn. Inside, the box pews supplied by early parishoners face a lofty canopied pulpit that dominates the room from its position midway along one side. The church also boasts an altar-hanging that was embroidered, at least in part, by Queen Anne.

The SPG missionaries believed that they were engaged in a contest for souls, especially in New Castle County, where the dissenting churches were strongly entrenched. In the town of New Castle, for instance, the earliest church had been the Dutch Reformed, a Calvinist denomination closely resembling English and Scottish Presbyterianism. The presence of the Reformed Church had attracted other Calvinists to the town, principally a group of French Huguenots who were among those expelled from France by Louis XIV in 1685. Later migrations of militantly Presbyterian Scotch-Irishmen strengthened the congregation still further. According to the first SPG missionary who served there, it was the apprehension of local Anglicans that the "Presbyterians were gaining Ground in the place by reason of their having a Preacher to promote their Interest" that had led them to petition for a clergyman of the Church of England. The same man related in a letter to his superiors in London that his first communicants at Immanuel consisted of about twenty families who were "generally low in their Condition but not indigent." Some were farmers from the surrounding area but others were townsmen employed in "retailing of Goods, Rum, Sugar, and Molasses together with some European Goods, some enjoyed posts in the Government and others got their living by their handy Crafts, as Carpenters-Smiths and Shoemakers." [10]

The competitive spirit in which some SPG ministers regarded the Presbyterians is evident in another letter written by a clergyman serving in Sussex County in 1728. He explained to the authorities at home that the inhabitants had been largely English with a few Dutch, until recently when the Scotch-Irish had become prominent. "They are Presbyterians by profession," and, he declared, "of the most bigoted sort." On the basis of the tax returns, the sheriff had estimated the population of the county to be 1,075 "Church people" (or Anglicians), 600 Presbyterians, and 75 Quakers. A missionary at the Appoquinimink Church was convinced that the success of the Presbyterians grew out of their ability to support local clergymen. Had the Anglicans been able to do likewise, he wrote, many of those who had become the "firmest Presbyterians" might have become part of the Anglican fold instead. [11]

The Appoquinimink region in lower New Castle County contained all the major religious denominations of eighteenth-century Delaware. In addition to St. Anne's parish, there were two other houses of worship in the area, both still standing. Old Drawyer's Presbyterian Church on Drawyer's Creek, just north of Cantwell's Bridge—now Odessa—is surely among the most elegant Presbyterian churches built in colonial America. Like its neighbor St. Anne's, Old Drawyer's is a rectangular building laid in Flemish bond, featuring two tiers of windows. But the entrance, midway along a five-bay side, with its columns and pediment, reflects a greater elegance, architectural sophistica-

10. Harold B. Hancock, "Descriptions and Travel Accounts of Delaware," *Delaware History* 10 (1962):127–128.
11. Hancock, "Descriptions and Travel Accounts," p. 138, p. 133.

tion, and costliness than can be seen at St. Anne's. That is not surprising, because the congregation of Old Drawyer's was very strong during the Revolutionary period, and the architect for the building was Robert May, who had already demonstrated his command of the Georgian idiom in his design of the nearby Corbit House.

The third place of worship along the Appoquinimink was a tiny Friends Meeting constructed in 1780 by a merchant of Cantwell's Bridge. A plain building, measuring only twenty feet by twenty feet, it may have been the smallest Quaker Meeting ever built. The diminutive meetinghouse has an interesting history. During the nineteenth century, it was used by its abolitionist members as a hiding place for runaway slaves. Later, the small congregation was reduced to just one person, an old gentleman who habitually unlocked the building on First Day to hold a "meeting" all by himself.[12]

On October 30, 1739, an event destined to reshape American religion occurred in Delaware when a young Anglican clergyman named George Whitefield disembarked at Lewes. Whitefield immediately began his campaign of itinerant preaching that marked the beginnings of America's first and most important revival, known as the Great Awakening. The Awakening touched every denomination, rousing ministers and laymen alike out of stale orthodoxy and bringing debate and division in its wake. Within the Presbyterian churches, "New Lights" confronted "Old Lights," while the Anglican Church was even more seriously split between its orthodox and Methodist elements. All of the colonies were affected by the fires of revival, Delaware no more than any other, and yet Delaware has special cause to recall the Awakening. Not only did Whitefield begin his preaching there, but also the colony was the center of early Methodist activity, and its state university traces its roots to the controversy that the revival inspired within the Presbyterian Church. Whitefield's call for people to experience conversion and his claim that many of the clergy were "unconverted"

---

12. Harold D. Eberlein and Cortlandt V. D. Hubbard, *Historic Houses and Buildings of Delaware* (Dover: Public Archives Commission, 1962), p. 127.

touched upon the most basic theological divisions within Protestantism. "Old Light" Calvinists, such as the Irish-born, Scottish-educated Reverend Mr. Francis Alison, who founded the New London Academy at New London, Pennsylvania, argued that the passionate enthusiasm inspired by the revivalists could neither induce nor guarantee salvation. But hordes of people who were less skilled in the niceties of theology, both among the unchurched and the churchgoers, were swept up by the movement. Thousands flocked to hear Whitefield wherever he preached, and even such a paragon of self-control as Benjamin Franklin was moved to make a sizable contribution to further the preacher's work.

Like John Wesley, Whitefield regarded all the world as his parish. When he began his first journey through America, he preached at the Anglican Church in Lewes, where he noted "Persons of different denominations were present; and the congregation was larger than might be expected in so small a place, and at so short notice." As his mission unfolded, however, and he became progressively more controversial, many of his fellow Anglican clergymen grew hostile, while some among the Presbyterian clerics welcomed his message. In New Castle County, Whitefield was invited to preach under a tent near the White Clay Creek Presbyterian Church. He optimistically estimated that ten thousand people, probably more than the total population of the county, came to hear him and that "many souls were melted down." At Wilmington, too, he attracted numerous enthusiastic listeners. In spite of his overwhelming preoccupation with religion, Whitefield took time to record in his journal his favorable impressions of Delaware and the Philadelphia area, a region which he found to be remarkably productive. "I have seen but very few poor objects since my arrival," he wrote. "Almost every one enjoys peace and plenty. The rich do not swallow up the poor as in other provinces; but there seems to be a proper balance." [13]

13. George Whitefield, *George Whitefield's Journals,* edited by William V. Davis (1905; Gainesville, Florida: Scholars' Facsimiles and Reprints, 1969), p. 336, p. 361, p. 422.

Some souls were indeed inflamed, but not all in the way that the Reverend Mr. Whitefield intended. The SPG ministers sent a chorus of letters of protest against the "mischievous Mr. Whitefield," that "indefatigable imposter in gown and cassock" who aroused "the flame of dissention" among the "Giddy multitude" in churches in the colony. One clergyman dared to write a direct challenge to the preacher accusing him of keeping a "Girl in Man's Cloathes during your Travels to sleep with you," and, in a more theological vein, criticized "your Inward feelings, wch are no evidence to any one (besides yourself) your Faith without good works, your want of Xn Charity & damning like a Pirate (in the Xn Ch), all but yourself & your crazy followers." [14]

The Presbyterian clergy could not reach nearly so much unanimity on the value of Mr. Whitefield's style of Christianity as their Anglican brethren. Some, like William Tennent, the minister at White Clay Creek, were thoroughly in accord with the "New Light" doctrines, while others had severe misgivings. Francis Alison, that highly intellectual Scotch-Irishman, feared that his church might soon be ordaining any uneducated man who claimed to have heard the "call." His academy at New London, Pennsylvania—later removed to nearby New-Ark, Delaware, where it became the precursor of the University of Delaware—was intended as a barrier to just such excesses of enthusiasm.

The later course of eighteenth-century American history has shaped historians' evaluations of the meaning and impact of the Great Awakening. Charles H. Maxson, in a major study of the revival, concluded that it set the stage for the Revolution. "It was more than wave upon wave of excitement; it was a transforming process in the nation's life," he wrote.[15] A unifying experience for all thirteen colonies, the Awakening put the individual and his soul before official religious authority figures. Its

---

14. Rightmyer, *The Anglican Church,* pp. 112–113, pp. 114–115.

15. Charles Hartshorn Maxson, *The Great Awakening in the Middle Colonies* (Chicago: University of Chicago Press, 1920), p. 139.

impact was to strengthen dissenting churches, such as the Baptists and the Presbyterians, at the expense of the Anglicans. Equally important was the movement's impetus toward the founding of new educational institutions that began providing home-grown American scholars. One such school, the New-Ark Academy, brought the light of learning into a colony that up to that time had shown little concern for education.

The most successful evangelists among eighteenth-century Delawareans were the Methodists, whose movement quickly grew to be the largest religious denomination in the state. English Methodism emerged from the same eagerness for inspirational religion that generated the Great Awakening. John Wesley, founder of the movement, was a devout Anglican clergyman who rejected the predestination theology of the Presbyterians in favor of the view that Christ would save everyone who turned to Him in faith, provided that their conversions were accompanied by a permanent purification of their lives. Wesley, like Whitefield, carried his message through outdoor sermons that attracted many people, especially among the poor who had lost the habit of church attendance. At its heart, his "method" consisted of forming local societies to help keep the converted in the path of righteousness. Originally, these societies were intended to supplement the work of the established church, not to replace it, and Wesley himself lived and died an Anglican.

Having served as a clergyman in the penal colony of Georgia at the beginning of his ministry, Wesley was familiar with the colonies and eagerly sponsored evangelical work there. His timing could hardly have been better. Following on the heels of the Great Awakening, Methodist ministers found many converts ready to hear their hopeful message of salvation and to accept their rigorous demands for piety. But the first Methodist preachers in America, such as Captain Thomas Webb of the British Army who preached in Wilmington in the late 1760s, lacked the prerogative to form Methodist societies. On the very eve of the Revolution, however, Wesley authorized several of his most capable lieutenants to go to America to form an American branch of the movement. One of these, Francis Asbury, known as the father of American Methodism, made Delaware the base for a career of itinerant ministry that took him to every part of the frontier and the settled regions of the United States.

The Revolution brought a great crisis to the fledgling Methodist movement in America. John Wesley, ever the loyal Englishman, wrote a tract entitled, *A Calm Address To Our Own American Colonies,* urging the colonists to seek reconciliation with the empire. His preachers, with the exception of Asbury, returned to England. Asbury continued his itinerant ministry until 1778, when his refusal to swear loyalty to the newly freed states forced him to seek asylum in Delaware, the only state that did not require loyalty oaths from preachers. Asbury stayed at the home of Thomas White, a Kent County judge and a Methodist convert. Revolutionary hotheads seized that pretext to imprison the judge briefly on a vague charge of Toryism, and Asbury spent some agonizing days hiding in a dreary swamp. In these severe straits, the harassed preacher gave way to some very human self-pity. He confided to his journal that "Satan has made several violent pushes at my soul, but he has not been able even to break my peace." And a few days later he admitted that "I was under some heaviness of mind. But it was no wonder: three thousand miles from home—my friends have left me—I am considered by some as an enemy of the country— every day liable to be seized by violence, and abused. However, all this is but a trifle to suffer for Christ and the salvation of souls. Lord, stand by me." Asbury spent the remainder of the war years in Delaware preaching and reading. Sometimes his forced confinement made him restive, but he brought the gospel to the most remote parts of the state, which was challenge enough. During a visit to western Sussex County in 1781, he wrote, "We have a society of more than twenty members, some of whom have found the Lord; but I think, for ignorance of God and religion, the wilds and swamps of Delaware exceed most parts of America with which I have had any acquaintance." [16]

16. Francis Asbury, *The Journal and Letters of Francis Asbury,* edited by Elmer T. Clark et al., 3 vols. (Nashville: Abingdon Press, 1958), 1:263, 1:263–264, 1:398.

Since the Methodists were still members of the Anglican Church, the outcome of the war put them into a quandary. While the Anglicans were in the process of forming their own Protestant Episcopal Church, the aged John Wesley dispatched Thomas Coke and several assistants to the United States for the purpose of founding a separate Methodist Church and ordaining its clergy. Coke and Asbury, the two leaders of the movement in America, met to discuss these plans at Barratt's Chapel in Kent County, Delaware, ever after called the "cradle of Methodism." Here in this unpretentious, nearly square brick structure built by Philip Barratt, a converted Methodist farmer and county sheriff, Coke for the first time administered the Lord's Supper in an American Methodist service. The pulpit-bench where Asbury and Coke sat has been carefully preserved as a relic of that historic occasion. Recently, the church has been restored to its original appearance, including the installation of a replica of the high pulpit where Coke and Asbury preached.

The Methodists harvested where Whitefield had sown. Their belief that men could renounce sin and be saved through the ever-willing aid of Christ captured the imaginations of hundreds, and ultimately thousands, of hearers in Delaware. Coinciding with America's political revolution, Methodism was a spiritual revolution that set the tone for religion in Delaware for a century and beyond. The new church, which quickly became the largest and most influential denomination in the state, was a force both for change and conservatism. The Methodists' insistence on spiritual equality weakened the concept of an immutable social hierarchy that had predominated in colonial days. On the other hand, their emphasis on pious self-control as expressed in their renunciations of alcohol, dancing, and other entertainments were restraints on individual behavior that turned people toward personal salvation rather than directing them toward consideration of broader social or economic problems. Methodism thus intermingled with geographic remoteness to produce the peculiar character of Delaware's down-stater, individualistic but fiercely conservative.

Of all the immigrant groups who came to colonial America, only the Africans came unwillingly, and only they came with no hope of improving themselves and raising their status in the new land. Historians can only partially reconstruct the evolution of the institution of Negro slavery in the early years of colonization on the basis of laws and legal proceedings. In Delaware, the task is unusually difficult, because the colony changed hands so often during its early years of development. We know, for example, that the Swedes purchased an African named Black Anthony during a trading cruise to the West Indies in 1639. Although that black man was among the very first colonists in Delaware, it is impossible to ascertain his legal status in the colony.[17] It seems likely, however, that, since the Swedes had had no previous experience with chattel slavery, he was treated much the same as those Finns and Swedes who, as employees of the New Sweden Company, were servants rather than freemen. The Dutch West India Company, which engaged in the slave trade between Africa and South America, was responsible for introducing slavery to the Delaware River, where the Dutch employed a few slaves to drain swamps.

But it was the more agrarian-oriented English settlers, many of whom came to Delaware from Virginia and Maryland, who really fastened the institution of slavery onto the little colony. While a few large-scale planters like Kent County's Samuel Dickinson employed large numbers of slaves, the failure of one-crop agriculture to take hold in Delaware as it had in tidewater Virginia, as well as Delaware's somewhat shorter growing season, limited the development of plantation-style, slave-oriented agriculture. As a result, most of those Delaware farmers who acquired slaves owned very few.

Slavery was superimposed on a labor system marked by reciprocal legal obligations that bound both masters and servants, in which masters had control over the person and not just the labor of their workers. The common means of learning a trade

---

17. Amandus Johnson, *The Swedish Settlements On the Delaware,* 2 vols. (Philadelphia: Swedish Colonial Society, 1911), 2:710.

was through an apprenticeship that bound a young man or woman to service in someone's household for a period of years. During that time the master was obligated to train the apprentice in his line of work. Another common form of servitude was the indenture, whereby a servant agreed to work for a master for a specified period, usually four to seven years, to pay off some debt or to secure capital. Many Americans who boast of their colonial ancestry are descended from poor English and Scotch-Irish settlers who indentured themselves to pay for their passage to America. The courts often resorted to indentures to place orphans, vagabonds, or criminals in useful work. The chief differences separating the slave from the indentured servant were that the master owed no reciprocal obligations to the slave, the slave served his master in perpetuity, the children of slaves automatically followed in their parents' footsteps, and only Africans were enslaved.

The obvious differences of color, culture, and religion that separated white colonists from blacks justified slavery, in the minds of some. Thomas Rodney, the younger brother of Caesar Rodney, for example, wrote an apology for the institution on the grounds that

> Nature formed the Negroes for slavery—that she stampts [*sic*] them
> with the radical colour of black to distinguish them from the
> children of light—that their native ignorance and dispositions
> disposes them to be 'Hughers of wood and drawers of water'—That
> they have such a native inclination and propensity to that kind of
> servile labour that it is impossible for them to rise above it.[18]

Others, however, attributed the Africans' alleged "propensity for . . . servile labour" to nurture, rather than nature. An SPG minister serving at St. Anne's, Appoquinimink, in 1748, who was charged with the task of bringing the gospel to the Indians and blacks as well as to the British inhabitants of his parish,

18. Thomas Rodney, "Essay On Negroes," Rodney Collection, Historical Society of Delaware, Wilmington, Delaware; quoted in "The Black American In Delaware History," by James E. Newton and Harold B. Hancock (manuscript, pages unnumbered).

wrote home that "the case of the Negroes among us is truly deplorable, and must excite the concern of every serious, considerate person." He blamed the situation on several factors. Many masters, he said, were "destitute of common humanity and differ in nothing but complexion and free estate from the most abject slave." "Their hearts," the minister charged, "are set upon nothing but gain." Coupled with that difficulty were cultural and linguistic differences that made it difficult for any white man to communicate to the blacks more than the most rudimentary orders. "They seem to be of a species quite different from the whites," he observed, "have no abstracted ideas," and besides "they have a language peculiar to themselves, a wild confused medley of Negro and corrupt English." Perhaps the most serious obstacle to their conversion was also the most cruelly pathetic, for many blacks, he discovered, persisted in their old religion "of superstition and idolatry" and sometimes killed themselves in the belief "that when they die they are translated to their own country, there to live in their former condition." [19]

By the Revolutionary era, slaveholders were on the defensive in Delaware, largely because of the Quakers' rising opposition to the institution. In 1758, the Philadelphia Yearly Meeting, having reached a consensus on the issue, began a new policy of excluding Friends who bought or sold slaves and urging manumission upon all slaveowners. Among Delaware Quakers of that generation, the most prominent opponents of slavery were Warner Mifflin and the patriot leader John Dickinson, both farmers in Kent County. Dickinson, who inherited many slaves from his wealthy father, freed them all when he became an active Quaker, late in life. Mifflin, reared in eastern-shore Virginia, declared that he first recognized the injustice of slavery when, as a boy of fourteen, "Being in the field with my father's slaves, a young man among them questioned me, whether I thought it could be right, that they should be toiling in order to

19. Harold B. Hancock, "Historical Records Relating to Delaware in the British Isles," *Delaware History* 10 (1963):351.

raise me, and that I might be sent to school; and by and by, their children must do so for mine." [20] As an adult, Mifflin lived near Camden, Delaware, and became a noted speaker in the cause of abolitionism at Quaker meetings throughout a wide region. He not only manumitted the slaves on his farm, but paid them for their past services.

Beyond these private attempts to weaken slavery, Delaware's lawmakers were beginning to set limits on the institution. In 1775, a bill prohibiting the importation of slaves into Delaware was vetoed by the proprietor John Penn, but the next year the convention called to write a constitution for the newly independent "Delaware State" inserted a similar provision into the organic law. A decade later, measures were passed in the legislature prohibiting the exportation of slaves from the state and forbidding the fitting out of slave ships at Delaware ports. These laws were by no means airtight, however, since slaveowners could petition the legislature to permit them to take their chattels into another state, usually Maryland, where many Delawareans owned other farms. But the laws did prevent slave auctions in Delaware and demonstrated the public's aversion to trading in human flesh.

The federal census of 1790, which provided the first hard data on Delaware's population, found 8,887 slaves and 3,899 free blacks in the state. Most of the free blacks were manumitted slaves or their children, living in Warner Mifflin's Kent County. While there were slaves in all three counties, nearly one-half of the total were concentrated in Sussex, especially in the Chesapeake-oriented Nanticoke River basin. [21] By 1860, the number of free blacks had climbed to nearly twenty thousand, while fewer than two thousand slaves remained in the whole state, mostly, as seventy years before, in Sussex County. It would be naive to assume that the many manumissions demonstrated by

20. John A. Munroe, "The Negro in Delaware," *South Atlantic Quarterly* 56 (1957):429.

21. John Gary Dean, "The Free Negro in Delaware" (M.A. thesis, University of Delaware, 1970), p. 18.

the striking shift in numbers from slave to free were prompted solely by moral and ethical considerations. Economic advantage was doubtless a more potent force for freedom. Because of Delaware's relatively short growing season, many farmers discovered that it was cheaper to hire farm workers during the summer than to maintain slaves year-round. In addition, it is clear that many slaveowners considered manumission a clever way to dispose of slaves who had become too old to work or were debilitated by illness. As early as 1740, the colonial Assembly passed an act requiring that a thirty-pound bond accompany each manumission to protect the colony from the cost of supporting former slaves at public expense. "It is found by experience," the lawmakers said, "that free Negroes and mulattoes are idle and slothful, and often prove burdensome to the neighborhood wherein they live, and are an evil example to slaves." [22]

It has often been said that slavery existed in its mildest form in Delaware. That was true, in some respects. For instance, Delaware was the only slave state in which the courts held to the doctrine that a black person was presumed to be free unless proven otherwise. On the other hand, the memoir of Mary Parker Welch offers a unique description of the institution in early nineteenth-century Sussex County that disputes that sanguine view. Although the author's opposition to slavery and her sympathy for the black people of her acquaintance no doubt influenced her reactions, the Welch narrative is particularly interesting because it describes two radically different types of slaveholders. Her parents, who had inherited slaves, took great care to make the lives of their charges as pleasant as possible, she claimed. Not being able to use or afford their many slaves, they considered manumission but decided that "to set them free was like abandoning a helpless clan." They therefore disposed "of most of them to their personal friends, with the proviso in the bill of sale that each was to be taught some useful trade whereby they could support themselves hereafter and each was to be manumitted when he or she had reached twenty-eight years of age." Following that description of her family's benign

22. Dean, "The Free Negro," p. 22.

actions as slaveholders, however, she recalled a series of incidents in which neighbors behaved hypocritically and made life nightmarish for their slaves. "I have heard many stories, told under the breath, of the cruelty of this or that master or mistress," she wrote, "whose faces wore a veneer of smiles and a gloss of courtesy when among their equals." She witnessed severe beatings of small black youngsters and knew of "a celebrated physician and his wife, people of beautiful Christian lives," who so overworked their slaves "that they became dwarfed in stature and prematurely old." Such stories demonstrate that even in its so-called "mildest form," slavery brutalized both slave and master.[23]

A predominantly Quaker abolition society, formed in 1800, regularly petitioned the state legislature in an effort to destroy slavery. "We deem it unnecessary at this day," they wrote in 1801, "to come before you with the arguments to prove that freedom is the natural and inalienable right of man; and that to deprive him of it is highly unjust, immoral, anti-Christian." In 1803, a bill "For the Abolition of Slavery" produced a tie vote in the state House of Representatives, with New Castle County solidly in favor, while all but one of the Sussex representatives opposed, and Kent's split. That was as close as the abolitionists ever came to victory in the state assembly, but many believed that no politically polarizing legislative action was necessary, since manumissions were already rendering slavery a dead issue in Delaware. Governor Caleb Rodney, a native of Lewes, claimed in his message to the legislature in 1823 that "slavery in every shape and form, and under any circumstances, is a blemish upon the fair fabric which we have erected in this country, to liberty." Predicting "greater evils" if the institution were ended too abruptly, he was pleased to note that, at the current rate of manumissions, the blemish would soon no longer besmirch Delaware.[24]

23. Mary Parker Welch, "Slave and Freedman," *Memoirs of Mary Parker Welch, 1818–1912*, edited by Dorothy W. White (Brooklyn: n.p., 1947); quoted in Newton and Hancock, "Black American."

24. Helen B. Stewart, "The Negro in Delaware to 1829" (M.A. thesis, University of Delaware, 1940), p. 76, p. 78.

The political wish to circumvent a controversial issue was not shared by the abolitionists, nor did they foresee such a happy outcome if matters were allowed to drift. In 1837, the American Anti-Slavery Society sent an agent to Delaware to ascertain the situation of the blacks there. His report, published in *The Emancipator* and *The Colored American,* pointed out that so-called free blacks in Delaware "enjoy but a mongrel liberty, a mere mock freedom." [25] Law and custom in Delaware had always conspired to "keep the Negro in his place" of inferiority. Blacks could not vote or hold office, nor could they testify in a court case unless there was no competent white witness. Following Nat Turner's bloody insurrection in Virginia in 1831, Delaware's whites experienced a new wave of fear that led to further limitations on blacks. Petitions to the legislature from Sussex County residents in 1831 and 1832 urged the adoption of laws to prevent free blacks from owning or carrying arms or assembling together at night, on the pretext that "black preachers that come into this state from other states are regular and constant preachers of sedition to our slaves and free blacks at the[ir] night meetings." [26] In truth, the only troublemakers were a group of whites who dressed up to look like blacks and staged a "shoot-out" along the Nanticoke River near Seaford at election time. Yet, the legislature responded to the wave of hysteria by passing more repressive measures against blacks.

The following year, the legislature received another petition, this one signed by twenty-nine free blacks, asking that the new laws be expunged because they had, in their words, "a demoralizing effect upon the People of Colour, for by placing them under suspicion—making them to feel that the eyes of the white people are continually over them. . . . takes from them one of the strongest inducements to virtuous actions." [27]

25. Harold B. Hancock, "William Yates's Letter of 1837: Slavery and Colored People in Delaware," *Delaware History* 14 (1971):208.

26. Delaware, Dover, Hall of Records, Petition from Sussex County to Disarm Negroes, 1832, Legislative Papers.

27. Delaware, Dover, Hall of Records, Petition to Free People of Colour Against Act to Prohibit Use of Firearms, 1833, Legislative Papers.

The petition was ignored by the state's politicians, who also ignored the advice of an Anti-Slavery Society agent who pointed out that Delaware was paying heavily for its efforts "to degrade, to crush, and to render them [blacks] ignorant and powerless." The farms in the state were in decline, white agricultural workers avoided Delaware because they would not compete with blacks, and so, he argued, "If then her laboring population are wanting in intelligence and are unskilful, who is the sufferer?" [28]

The single most important social institution among Delaware's black population in the nineteenth century was the Methodist Church. The ties of black people to Methodism go back to the days of the first itinerant preachers. "Black Harry" Hosier, Francis Asbury's illiterate right-hand man, was a spellbinding orator who captivated white audiences as well as black. The fact that the Methodists permitted blacks to preach must have attracted a great many black people who had previously felt culturally remote from Christianity. The early Methodist chapels organized in Delaware included blacks in their congregations. But after the first flush of conversion, white members began making distinctions based on racial prejudice. At Asbury Church in Wilmington, black members proudly left the church in 1805 rather than be relegated to seats in the gallery. They formed a new church called Ezion, but some among their number continued to be dissatisfied because the white-dominated conference dictated policy to them. Led by Peter Spencer and William Anderson, black lay preachers, the disaffected members at Ezion created yet another congregation in 1812, the African Union Methodist Church, which began its own conference. African Union, the first black-controlled incorporated body in Delaware and among the first in the United States, was the mother church to numerous black congregations in Pennsylvania, Maryland, and Virginia. Every August, Wilmington's black Methodists celebrated the birth of the conference at Big Quarterly, an event that uniquely blended reverence and

28. Hancock, "William Yates's Letter," p. 208, p. 215.

gaiety and attracted vast numbers of black people who came from as far away as Philadelphia and the Delmarva Peninsula, dressed in their best, most colorful clothes. On that one day each year, it was customary for masters to excuse their hired hands and even their slaves to join in the gathering of gospel singers, bands, preachers, and food hucksters that swirled along French Street, eating, listening, and showing off their finery to old friends.

In spite of the political, economic, social, and educational handicaps that held them down, Delaware's free blacks proclaimed their self-worth in various ways, such as their reaction to the creation of a chapter of the American Colonization Society in Wilmington. The society, formed by whites who purported to be the true friends of the Negro, argued that because "our laws do not and cannot permit them to enjoy the most important civil privileges," [29] the only humane and liberal course was to resettle the blacks in Africa.

In response, Peter Spencer called a meeting of free blacks at Wilmington's African Union Church in July 1831, where the group declared the intentions of the colonizers to be at variance with "the spirit of the Constitution and Declaration of Independence of these United States" and resolved to "disclaim all connexion with Africa; and although the descendants of that much afflicted country, we cannot consent to remove to any tropical climate." The meeting authorized a committee including Spencer and Abraham Shad, a mulatto shoemaker and an active member of several abolitionist societies, to prepare an address to the people of Wilmington, declaring that "we are natives of the United States; our ancestors were brought to this country by means over which they had no control; we have our attachments to the soil, and we feel that we have rights in common with other Americans." In contrast to the white colonizers who foresaw only a future of misery for blacks in America, these black men optimistically anticipated that their condition would be improved through education, which they declared "is

29. Delaware, Dover, Hall of Records, "The Wilmington Union Colonization Society Asks the General Assembly to Approve Its Objectives, 1827," Legislative Papers.

much better calculated to remove prejudice, and exalt our moral character than any system of colonization that has been or can be introduced." [30] It is worth noting that these black leaders living in a slave state were more convinced that race prejudice could be eliminated than were many contemporary whites.

Within a national culture that has been and is notoriously ambiguous concerning interracial relations, Delaware and her sister border states have been perhaps the most ambiguous of all. At no time was that more clear than in the years preceding the Civil War, when Delaware included within its borders both the notorious slavenapper and murderer Patty Cannon and the Quaker abolitionist Thomas Garrett, equally famed for his success in aiding slaves to escape to freedom. The grisly legends surrounding Patty Cannon point up what was in fact a frequent crime in Delaware, the kidnapping of blacks for sale in the South. Patty lived in the Nanticoke region along the Delaware-Maryland border in the early nineteenth century. Together with accomplices, she kidnapped numerous blacks, both slave and free, and sold them to unscrupulous slave dealers who transported them down the Chesapeake. Not content with that lucrative practice, she allegedly murdered traders, on occasion, for their money. The discovery of one such body in a farmer's field led to her arrest and imprisonment in Georgetown in 1829. Characteristically, she cheated the hangman by dying in her cell, although an alternative tale says that she escaped, leaving a dead woman in her place. The story of Patty's escapades has been told in fictionalized form in one of the few novels about Delaware life, *The Entailed Hat,* by George Alfred Townsend, a Civil War journalist from Georgetown.

Thomas Garrett, in every way the opposite of Patty Cannon, was the son of a Quaker farmer in Pennsylvania. When he was twenty-four years old, a black woman employed by his family was kidnapped. As Garrett pursued her captors, the evil of slavery struck him so strongly that he resolved to devote his life to its eradication. Having moved to Wilmington in 1820, he es-

30. W. L. Garrison, editor, *Thoughts On African Colonization* (Boston: Garrison and Knapp, 1832), pp. 36–40.

tablished himself as an iron merchant and began his work of deliverance that lasted until the Civil War. According to his own account, he aided more than two thousand escaped slaves, sometimes in conjunction with Harriet Tubman, herself an escaped slave known as the "Black Moses" for her repeated journeys into slave states to lead her people to freedom. Garrett's house was the last way-station in the underground railroad from the South before the free land of Pennsylvania. Sometimes slave owners came to his door and threatened his life with knives and guns, but he could not be intimidated. Although his house near Second and Shipley streets was closely watched by the police, he was caught only once. A U.S. District Court with Chief Justice Roger A. Taney presiding fined him so heavily that it cost him all his property, but, undeterred, he reopened his business at age sixty and continued his work of emancipation. Following the Civil War, Wilmington's black community honored Garrett with a parade. The old Quaker gentleman rode in an open carriage surrounded by the people he had sworn to help, who carried a banner inscribed "Our Moses." His funeral and burial in the yard of the Wilmington Friends Meeting in 1871 brought a large outpouring of people. Lucretia Mott, another well-known Quaker abolitionist, was the eulogist.[31]

It is ironic that Delaware, with its few slaves, many free blacks, and its core of active abolitionists, was among the very last states to end slavery; and the end came, not as the product of the state's own action, but rather through the adoption of the Thirteenth Amendment to the United States Constitution, an amendment that Delaware refused to ratify. President Lincoln's celebrated Emancipation Proclamation, a wartime measure designed to shore up northern support for continuing the struggle and to weaken the Confederacy's ability to continue the war, touched only those slaves who were in the rebellious South. Slaves held in the loyal border states were unaffected. Emancipation by presidential proclamation was a drastic step that Lincoln had sought to avoid but ultimately embraced, in part because of political actions in Delaware in 1862.

31. *Wilmington Daily Commercial*, January 25 and January 30, 1871.

The key to Delaware's politics amid the swirl of conflicting emotions and events that brought on the Civil War and Reconstruction was stubborn conservatism. The majority of the state's voters could be swayed by fears of secessionism and abolitionism alike. Their futile hope was for a restoration of the lost world of the past. Nowhere are these views more evident than in Delaware's rejection of Lincoln's compensated-emancipation plan.

Lincoln formed his plan as a means to end the war and to deal fairly with both slaves and slaveholders. Recognizing that the latter had invested considerable money in acquiring their human capital, he proposed that the federal government purchase the slaves from their owners and free them. The president reasoned that if he could get the plan to work in one loyal slave state, then others would adopt it, and the states of the Confederacy would lay down their arms and embrace the plan also. It is hardly surprising that he chose Delaware as the most likely starting point for this idea. The Diamond State was the smallest of the border states, with the fewest slaves, and her citizens bore a high degree of loyalty to the Union; further, by 1860, most of the remaining slaves in Delaware were the property of Sussex County farmers who were unable to sell their property out of state because of state law, and they were too poor to suffer the loss of private manumission. In November 1861, a few months after the outbreak of war, President Lincoln called to the White House George P. Fisher, Delaware's lone representative and an administration supporter. There the president outlined his plan and asked Fisher's help in presenting the measure to the Delaware legislature. At Fisher's suggestion, the president also sounded out Benjamin Burton, a prominent Republican slaveholder of Millsboro. As Burton later recalled the interview, Lincoln earnestly told him, "I am satisfied that this is the cheapest and most humane way of ending the war. If I can get this plan started in Delaware I have no fear but that all the other border states will accept it." [32]

32. H. Clay Reed, "Lincoln's Compensated Emancipation Plan," *Delaware Notes, Occasional Papers,* 7th series (1931), p. 38.

The presidential plan rested upon two legislative enactments, first an enabling act by the Delaware Assembly, then an appropriation by Congress. Despite his initial optimism that Delaware would accept the plan, Fisher faced a difficult job of persuasion, because too few politically active people in the state were willing to use the war as an excuse for improving the position of blacks. As one careful scholar on the subject has put it: "Although the war in the last analysis was being fought *over* the Negro, it certainly was not being fought *for* him, by Delawareans, at least." [33] The legislature, truly representing the state's intense yet contradictory political views, was split exactly halfway between Democrats sympathetic to the South but not to secession and the Peoples' party, which favored the Republican administration, yet claimed to be nonabolitionist. The politically charged compensation plan attracted the support of the Peoples' party legislators but failed to win the Democrats. Caleb S. Layton, a prominent Sussex County lawyer-politician and a long-time supporter of a plan to affect gradual emancipation by freeing slaves when they reached adulthood, published a letter condemning the Lincoln proposal as an unconstitutional use of federal powers. Together with many of the measure's opponents in Delaware, he perceived it as interference by the federal government into the state's internal affairs. Tainted by its enemies' use of the catch-word *abolitionism* in a state that lacked strong proadministration leadership, the president's plan was defeated without ever coming to a formal vote. Delaware thus lost the chance to initiate a plan to end slavery that just might have saved thousands of lives, as Lincoln himself believed. Whether the plan could have been made workable is questionable, however, since the states of the Confederacy would probably have perished in their war for independence rather than relinquish the doctrine of states' rights that the plan itself seemed to violate.

The Union's military victory hardly clarified the status of Negro Americans in Delaware. Unlike those states that had

---

33. Reed, "Lincoln's Emancipation Plan," p. 51.

seceded, the First State was not subjected to military interference. Nonetheless, national Reconstruction played a role in the unfolding of the state's race relations in several important ways: the Thirteenth, Fourteenth, and Fifteenth amendments promised black males the suffrage and other civil rights, and beginnings were made in providing education for blacks.

As we have already seen, nineteenth-century black leaders looked upon education as a panacea. Through education, they believed that they could successfully cure the ignorance, poverty, and other ills that they acknowledged to be common to their race. In looking to education as their major weapon in the war against racial bigotry and as the primary means to set blacks upon America's promised road to success, they were echoing the beliefs of those educational reformers who a generation earlier had created public school systems throughout the northern and midwestern states. Delaware, again revealing its peculiar status as a border state, responded to the public school movement and to the later movement for black education in its characteristic Januslike style.

Education systems and goals reflect the needs and aspirations of the societies that create them. In the early colonial period, when most people received their vocational education through apprenticeships, and the Bible and the catechism were the only frequently read books, it is hardly surprising that book-learning was left in the hands of religious authorities. The efforts of Swedish minsters such as Acrelius to school their congregations was closely associated with their desire to continue the use of the Swedish language among the colonists and to maintain religious orthodoxy. But a succession of Swedish clergymen discovered that their flock was content to farm and to slip slowly into the words and ways of a predominantly English culture. As the colonial economy grew, the need for education shifted from religious and cultural goals to commercial purposes, and the trade-minded Dutch at New Amstel made a greater effort to increase literacy at New Amstel than did the farm-oriented Swedes.

The English, by contrast, represented both of these tendencies simultaneously. Many English settlers were small landowners or servants whose meager educational interests and accomplishments mirrored their lifestyles and limited ambitions. Respect for education and for the educated was slow in coming, as indicated by an appalled SPG minister at New Castle, who wrote, in 1727:

> There are some private schools within my reputed district, which are put very often into the hands of those who are brought into the country and sold for servants, some schoolmasters are hired by the Year, by a Knot of Families, who in their Turns entertain him monthly, and the poor Man lives in their Houses, like one that begged an Alms, more than like a person in Credit and Authority. When a ship arrives in the River it is Common Expression, with whose who stand in need of an Instructor for their Children—'*Let us go and buy a Schoolmaster*'; the Truth is, the Office and Character of such a person is generally very mean and Contemptible here; and it cannot be otherways, till the publick takes the Education of Children into their mature Consideration.[34]

Larger landowners who made up the gentry sent their sons to Philadelphia or beyond to be educated above the low level that was available at home. Nicholas Ridgely of Dover, for example, sent his thirteen-year-old son Charles to the Academy in Philadelphia in 1751, where the boy studied the classical languages in preparation for apprenticeship to a prominent Philadelphia physician. Similarly, the Ridgelys' neighbor John Dickinson went to the Inns of Court in London to prepare for a legal career. Dr. Francis Alison's New London Academy, later moved to Newark, was the most conveniently located classical academy for Delawareans. Two of the state's three signers of the Declaration of Independence, Thomas McKean and George Read, both lawyers, studied with Alison. The Scottish-trained doctor was an excellent scholar who instilled in his predominantly Scotch-Irish students such character-building traits as strenuous hard work and simple living along with the Latin and Greek syntax that were intended to improve their writing and

---

34. Hancock, "Descriptions and Travel Accounts," pp. 129–130.

speaking. By the early nineteenth century, there were a number of private schools in Delaware of various types of distinction, centered mostly in the larger towns. The Wilmington Academy, opened in 1765, offered a curriculum that included both the English language and literature and the classics, in keeping with its purpose of providing training for those young men who planned to attend college as well as those who did not. Several women kept schools, where they taught needlework to well-bred young women. It was not until 1818 that a school was opened in Wilmington to give girls training equivalent to that received by boys at the academies, although the girls studied French instead of the more intellectually demanding ancient languages. The Wilmington Friends School, begun in 1748, grew from a simple curriculum featuring the three Rs to include the classics as the Quakers became more firmly established.

The idea that the specific goals of education should be narrowly vocational or should make one a gentleman conflicted with the egalitariansim of the early nineteenth century. In New England, especially, reformers argued for the creation of more broad-based concepts of the purposes and forms of education. They declared that schools must be made available to all if American society was to achieve true democracy. Willard Hall, a Massachusetts-born graduate of Harvard College, known as the father of public education in Delaware, shared those ideals. Hall came to Delaware as a young lawyer in search of a promising place to begin his professional career. Committed to the views of educational reformers in his native state and made powerful by political appointments in his adopted state, Hall set about to create a public school system.

When Hall came to Dover in 1803, he was horrified by the poor schools near the state capital. Little had changed since colonial days. "Neighbors or small circles united and hired a teacher for their children," he wrote, "the teachers frequently were intemperate, whose qualification seemed to be inability to earn anything in any other way." [35] The state legislature had

---

35. Lyman P. Powell, *The History of Education in Delaware* (Washington: Government Printing Office, 1893), p. 142.

adopted a measure in 1796 whereby the fees from marriage and tavern licenses went into a fund to establish schools, but the income from the fund accumulated so slowly that it could only provide instruction for the children of paupers. Not surprisingly, few people wished to be stigmatized in that fashion, and the fund went virtually unused. By 1820, public support was growing for a state-supported school system in Delaware. Governors regularly included references to education in their annual messages to the legislature, but it took Hall's determined efforts to achieve success. As a leading attorney in a state that had a small bar, he was ripe for political office. He had served in the U.S. Congress and as Delaware's secretary of state and as a member of the state senate before President James Monroe appointed him to the federal bench in 1823. Drawing upon his faith in Jeffersonian popular democracy, his Massachusetts upbringing, and his knowledge of Delawareans, Hall crafted a plan for state-supported free schools that passed the legislature in 1829. The law divided the state into many small school districts, all very loosely administered by county superintendents. The voters of each district were to decide how much they would be taxed for their school and then to apply for a matching grant from the state. That practice, which allowed for considerable variation in the quality of education, was in keeping with Willard Hall's belief that "It is not that the state shall educate the children; But that the people shall educate their own children, and the state confer upon them power to effectuate this purpose." If the plan were properly administered, Hall trusted that "the poorest child may be trained to have a fair chance for honor, wealth, and usefulness, as the child of the most affluent." [36] He might have added—so long as the child was white, for the law specifically excluded black youngsters from the state school system.

In operation, the school law of 1829 was but a feeble first step toward adequate public education. Some rural districts refused to tax themselves even the tiny amount necessary to

36. Report of The Annual School Convention of New Castle County, February 12, 1849, Historical Society of Delaware, Wilmington, Delaware.

operate a school, and many of the schools were underfinanced. There were no standards for teacher competence, and there was no uniform series of textbooks, so that teachers were forced to use the time-wasting system of instructing each child individually. A Methodist minister who attended school in Delaware during the 1830s and forties later recalled that learning by rote was carried to ridiculous extremes. Pupils were required to master the spelling of the most difficult words imaginable before they were given any instruction in reading. In the interest of discipline, the children were subjected to repeated floggings, whether they had broken any rules or not. The wonder is that, in such generally miserable surroundings, anybody was educated at all.

The education of black Delawareans has pursued a course very different from that of the whites. Excluded from the public school system until after the Civil War, Delaware's few literate blacks were either self-taught or had attended one of the few charity schools operated on their behalf by Wilmington's Quakers. The contrasts between the availability of educational opportunities for blacks and whites and between the concepts of popular control versus paternalism that marked the educational experiences of these two groups persisted through Reconstruction. Delaware was among those rare former slave states that produced an indigenous postwar movement to aid the black man. Both white and black reformers of the Reconstruction era believed that education was the most effective kind of aid, because it would both raise black peoples' self-esteem and remove the chief causes of white prejudice. In that spirit, a group of prominent white Republican businessmen and clergymen—many, but not all, Quakers—met in Wilmington in 1866 to found the Delaware Association for the Moral Improvement and Education of the Colored People.

With the aid of private donations and contributions from the federal government's Freedmen's Bureau, the association built and maintained primary schools for black children and adults throughout Delaware. Black people co-operated enthusiastically with the effort. The teachers were blacks educated in the North;

their salaries were paid by the association, but they depended on the local black community for their housing. Blacks also demonstrated their support for the association's objectives through donations and by their eagerness to enroll in classes. Between 1867 and 1876, the association established thirty-two schools, which at their height were training twelve hundred pupils in the rudiments of the three Rs.[37] Although the association's leaders were gratified by such a response, their ultimate goal was state support for the black schools they had begun.

Judging from postwar election returns, most Delawareans deeply opposed efforts to achieve racial equality. The Democrats, the majority party in the state, went on record to say that "the immutable laws of God have affixed upon the brow of the White race the ineffaceable stamp of superiority and . . . all attempts to elevate the negro to social and political equality are futile and subversive." [38] Democrats suspected the association of consciously serving partisan interests, and vigorously protested any suggestion of state aid to education for blacks on the grounds that that was merely a first step toward the integration of the public school system. In some places in southern Delaware, the association's teachers were ostracized and threatened, and in at least one instance a schoolhouse was burned. Meanwhile, enthusiasm for aid to the blacks diminished as the war receded in people's memories, and by the mid-1870s, the association was experiencing difficulties in financing its schools. To show just how resistant the opposition to black education was, a bill that was introduced in the state legislature in 1873 to empower local government officials to tax blacks for the support of their own schools failed. It was only when other southern and border states assumed responsibility for black schools in the face of threatened federal intervention that a similar measure passed in 1875. The law created a dual school system that not

37. Jacqueline J. Halstead, "The Delaware Association for the Moral Improvement and Education of the Colored People: Practical Christianity," *Delaware History* 15 (1972):28.

38. Halstead, "The Delaware Association," p. 22.

only segregated the children, schools, and school districts, but also created two distinct school funds. The black schools were bound to be inferior because they depended upon a relatively poorer tax base. Furthermore, in Wilmington, which had its own elected school board, the law was used to exclude blacks from participation in school affairs on the grounds that the support for their schools did not come from the citywide school tax. Delaware was the only state in the union to maintain this inequitable system of school support based on race.

When the First State entered the twentieth century, its schools and school laws had been only slightly modified in seventy years. Outside of the city of Wilmington and a few other incorporated towns, the typical Delaware school was a one-room, ungraded clapboard building, where one teacher taught ungraded students. The schools suffered from years of neglect; they were dark, poorly heated by potbellied stoves, and the sanitary facilities consisted of a usually decrepit outhouse. Teaching materials such as books, charts, and maps were generally lacking. The teachers were scantily paid and untrained, following a policy laid down by Willard Hall, who during his long life had opposed suggestions for a state normal school on the grounds that "The art of teaching lies in the heart." [39] The landowners who controlled the state legislature kept the school tax low and arranged that it fall most heavily on their tenants, on the grounds that tenants sent more children to the public schools than landowners did. The same landowners long resisted pressures from Wilmington to insure that all children attend school. Delaware did not adopt compulsory school-attendance legislation until 1907, when a weak compromise bill was passed requiring that children in rural districts attend a minimum of only three months a year.

With the new century came the quickening effects of change. Wilmington, long the hub of the state's industry, was just entering into its new role as a corporate center, and the city was now

39. Stephen B. Weeks, *History of Public School Education in Delaware* (Washington: Government Printing Office, 1917), p. 47.

more closely linked to the rest of the state by the Du Pont Highway. In addition, the ideas of the Progressive movement gradually touched even the slow-to-change rhythms of a pre-dominantly agrarian population. The movement was an effort by urban-middle-class Americans to reorganize and reform a soci-ety that seemed to be breaking into two camps, the rich and the poor. The Progressives used many of the same words used by the Jeffersonians a hundred years earlier—democracy, popular sovereignty, equality—yet they used some new words as well: professionalization, organization, Americanization. In Dela-ware, the leading Progressive was also the state's premier indus-trialist: Pierre S. du Pont.

P. S. du Pont has had more impact on his fellow Delawareans and their descendants than has anyone else in the state's history. Like Judge Hall before him, du Pont's ideas on education were shaped by his own time and experience. Born and reared along the Brandywine, educated at the Massachusetts Institute of Technology, Pierre du Pont soon left the stodgy family firm for more invigorating business opportunities in the Midwest. He be-came the protégée of Tom Johnson, Cleveland's Progressive mayor. Exposure to Johnson's social philosophy and business techniques helped shape the career of the brilliant but shy young man who was destined to play the most important role in the massive reorganization of the Du Pont Company after 1902. In common with other Progressives, du Pont saw public education as a key social institution and was appalled by the low level of schooling in much of his native state. The findings of a scien-tific survey of Delaware's public schools in 1919, which unsen-timentally denounced the "little red schoolhouse" in favor of modern comprehensive schools, made a deep impression on du Pont. The report argued for the necessity of good lighting, ven-tilation, and sanitation as prerequisites for good learning. Of Delaware's few quaint octagonal schools, for instance, the sur-veyors wrote that: "At a time when it was considered essential to one's educational development that he be within easy reach of the master's rod, an octagonal room may have had peculiar advantages, but in the present era when the angle at which the light falls upon the pupil is regarded as more important than the angle at which the rod falls, the eight square is out of place as a school building.'' [40]

Not surprisingly for a man whose principal vocational preoccupations dealt with organization to achieve concrete results, P. S. du Pont's chief contributions to improving public education in Delaware fell into two areas: replacing antiquated one- and two-room schools with modern consolidated buildings, and creating a well-financed, professional, statewide board of education that could establish and maintain improved standards for instruction. Toward those ends, he used his enormous wealth not only to build new buildings but to generate public support for a tax structure that could maintain them.

P. S. du Pont's famed largess to public education in Delaware was not undertaken in a political vacuum. He carefully enlisted the support of numerous prominent citizens of both political parties, mostly from urban New Castle County, but including as well representatives of the rural areas of Delaware. With their help, he formed Delaware Service Citizens, a professionally staffed organization through which du Pont funneled millions of dollars to build and equip new schools and to lobby for school-related measures in the state legislature. Delawareans, particularly in the rural parts of the state, were prone to look a gift horse in the mouth. Recognizing that his opponents were especially likely to denounce any increased state support for black schools, du Pont shrewdly stole their thunder by providing all the money needed to build new schools for black youngsters throughout the state at no expense to the taxpayers. He was also concerned about the unfairness of the tax structure, which fell more heavily upon the rural poor than on the rich. A solution to that difficulty was absolutely necessary if the state was to improve teacher salaries and maintain the new buildings. Here again, Delaware Service Citizens persevered and eventually won acceptance for a new tax law that replaced the property tax

40. *General Report on School Buildings and Grounds of Delaware,* Bulletin of the Service Citizens of Delaware, edited by George D. Strayer et al., 1, no. 3 (1919):73.

with a more fairly distributed income tax. To insure that the law was properly enforced, P. S. du Pont got himself appointed state tax commissioner. Another problem was the short supply of trained teachers. To fill that need, du Pont and his reformers worked with women's clubs throughout the state to create a women's college, in conjunction with Delaware College, where young women could prepare for teaching careers. The college, a land-grant institution that had arisen out of the remains of Alison's old Newark Academy, united with the women's institution in 1944 to form the present University of Delaware. Subsequent changes in state law have superseded the tax structure of P. S. du Pont's day, but the basic changes that he ushered in—consolidated school districts, professional control under a hierarchical statewide board, buildings designed to the specifications of modern school architecture, and adequate tax support—have been the hallmarks of public education in Delaware ever since.

In the course of the nineteenth century, Wilmington developed social characteristics that set it apart from rural Delaware. Downstate, nearly all of the people were of either British or African background, and many families proudly traced their land holdings back to an original grant from Calvert, Penn, or the Duke of York. In that conservative society, the same gentry families dominated politics, the professions, and agriculture, generation after generation. By contrast, Wilmington's people included many newcomers, not only from the surrounding farmlands and villages of the peninsula and southeastern Pennsylvania, but from Europe as well. By 1900, 14 percent of the city's 76,508 people were foreign-born. Wilmington had fewer foreigners than the nearby cities of Trenton, New Jersey, and Philadelphia; but by Delaware standards, the city's diverse ethnic and religious mix was unique. The largest group among these nineteenth-century immigrants were the Irish, followed by Germans and English, but Italians and Poles were beginning to make an impact on the city as the new century began.

The story of the vast Irish migration to America in the wake of overpopulation, unendurable hardship, and famine in the 1840s is a familiar one, but the earlier movement of Irishmen to America is less well known. Decades before the potato-rot ca-

DELAWARE

A photographer's essay by Bruce Roberts

Photos in Sequence

tastrophe, ships bearing Irish immigrants docked at New Castle, and Irish names began appearing among the workmen at industrial sites on the Brandywine as early as the 1790s. When E. I. du Pont built his extensive powder mills in 1802, he imported Irish workers at the company's expense. Recognizing the importance of maintaining the loyalty of his employees on a site that was quite literally a powder keg, du Pont not only supplied housing for his workers but his sons also built a Roman Catholic church, St. Joseph's-on-the-Brandywine, which served as a religious and social center for the mill hands and their families. Thus, Delaware's first substantial Irish settlement was not made up of jobless migrants packed into dockside slums, but rather was a sequestered, close-knit community located a few miles away from the city. Likewise, the many Irish workers employed on the construction of the Chesapeake and Delaware Canal and the New Castle-Frenchtown Railroad spent most of their time in work camps relatively remote from population centers. In the 1840s, that pattern underwent change, as Irish migration accelerated and the city of Wilmington industrialized. By the end of the Civil War, there was a substantial Irish presence in the city, including two Catholic churches, each with its parochial school, one Catholic orphanage, and a short-lived college. In the city the Irish congregated in the more low-paying, low-skilled jobs, such as domestic service, day labor, and the strenuous, monotonous tasks offered by the city's foundries and tanneries. As elsewhere, the Irish also demonstrated a flair for ward-level politics and adhered to the Democrats, the party that united the urban white working class with rural landowners against the more dynamic capitalism of the Republicans. The Irish were by far the largest single immigrant group in Wilmington throughout the nineteenth century. Their members hovered around 3,000 for several decades and peaked in 1900, when 4,870 Wilmingtonians representing 6 percent of the city's people and 38 percent of its foreign-born were Irish.[41]

The Germans were Wilmington's second-largest immigrant

41. U.S. Census, 1900, *Population* (Washington: Government Printing Office, 1902), 1:741.

group. Many of them came to the city with skills, and some had money to begin businesses. Germans predominated as painters, upholsterers, and wood-workers at the city's carriage, car, and shipbuilding shops. Others became tradesmen, especially saloon-keepers and brewers. In spite of many instances of relative economic success among them, the German immigrants met with some cultural resistance. The usually liberal-minded *Wilmington Every Evening,* for example, printed an unflattering portrait of German workers in 1881, claiming that they were contentious, litigious, and uncommonly prone to petty lawlessness, such as leaving a landlord without paying the bill. "They have the faculty for contracting what seems to them to be great grievances, and . . . jabbering and chattering like so many monkeys and about as intelligibly. . . . Two or three families living in the same house will fall out and will do anything that occurs to mind that can annoy each other." [42] Politically, the Germans were split between the major parties, but some were attracted to socialism and labor militancy. That tendency towards radicalism, together with other cultural differences from the natives, helps to explain antagonism against German workers in the Delaware area.

Some Palatinate Germans came to Delaware before the Revolution as part of the Pennsylvania Dutch settlement encouraged by the Penns, but the major thrust of German immigration began in the 1850s, when Germans who had settled in Philadelphia or Baltimore began moving to Wilmington in search of employment. In addition, Wilmington firms sent representatives to Castle Garden, the docking point for immigrant ships in New York harbor, to hire skilled workers. The Protestants among them re-established the Lutheran faith in Delaware with the formation of Zion Lutheran Church on Wilmington's east side in 1848. German Catholics were at first assigned to Irish parishes, but as the German community grew, in both size and wealth, they demanded a church of their own, and in 1873 the German Catholics built Sacred Heart Church in a middle-class westside neighborhood. They could not have picked a worse time to

42. *Wilmington Every Evening,* December 9, 1881.

build, in some respects, for the country was suffering a serious depression, and many in the congregation were out of work. But the construction went on, because the many skilled men in the congregation, although unable to give much financial support, gave their labor free of charge, and the church was completed rapidly.

Like the Irish, with their Hibernian Society and St. Patrick's Day celebrations, the Germans clung tenaciously to cultural elements from their native land. A Sängerbund choral society founded in 1853 is still flourishing, as is the Turnverein, one of Wilmington's pioneer athletic clubs. The German community also supported the *Freie Presse,* the city's only foreign-language newspaper; a German library; and an annual Volksfest that attracted large crowds of Wilmingtonians. In spite of all such efforts, however, the Germans, like the Swedes so many years before, slowly lost their ties to the Fatherland. The immigrant generation labored in vain to maintain the German language through special schools and Sunday school activities, for they could not match the exposure of their children to English. At Zion Lutheran Church, the shift to English came in two stages. In 1879, the Young People's Society was permitted to hold services in English, but the main service was still conducted in German until 1912, when the congregation voted to conduct most of its activities, including Sunday school, in English. By that time, few of the Sunday school teachers spoke German as their native language, and most of them admitted that they could express themselves more easily in English.[43]

The percentage of foreign-born people in Wilmington reached its height immediately before World War I, when among the city's 87,411 people, 15.6 percent were immigrants, compared with 73.9 percent native whites and 10.4 percent blacks.[44] Among the immigrants, more than 3,000 had been born in Ireland, nearly 2,000 in Germany, and about 1,000 in England. Most noteworthy, however, was the extremely rapid rise of two

43. *Wilmington Sunday Star,* September 27, 1908.

44. U.S. Census, 1910, *Population* (Washington: Government Printing Office, 1913), 1:215.

new groups—the Italians, who numbered more than 2,000; and the Poles and the Russian Jews, whose exact numbers cannot be determined, since Poles were incorporated into the census statistics for Germany, Austria, and Russia. Jews were not listed as a separate group because religion was not designated in the city's census figures. The fact that the number of Russian-born people in the city exceeded the Irish is, however, an important clue to the shift in immigration patterns that was in progress.

Italians first appeared in Wilmington in the 1880s as construction workers on the Baltimore and Ohio Railroad. They lived in boxcars, which a local reporter described as "dirty, ill-smelling, [and] badly ventilated." Their food consisted of a steady diet of macaroni and hard bread, with an occasional sausage. In spite of these dreary conditions, the newspaperman found that "they evidently do not consider their lot a hard one." Through hard work, the men earned thirty dollars a month, much of which they sent to families in the old country. "As labor they are cheap and easily controlled and that is the reason they are here," the writer concluded.[45] Like the blacks and earlier unestablished immigrant groups, the first Italians in Wilmington were perceived as a threat to the position of the local working class. Only two months after the newspaper article about them was printed, the Wilmington city council, in a rare show of unanimity, adopted a resolution condemning the employment of Italians and Hungarians on public works. Nonetheless, in the years that followed, Italian workmen were frequently hired to lay trolley tracks, dig sewer lines, and pave the city's streets. Skilled Italian masons readily found work in the construction trades, which became a leading field for Italian-born entrepreneurs.

The new wave of immigrants clustered into newly built rows of working-class houses on the far west side of the city. Although their community, called "Little Italy," appeared homogeneous to outsiders, its people had come from various parts of Italy and spoke an array of dialects that were hardly intelligible to one another. At first, the Italians had no cultural institutions

45. *Wilmington Every Evening*, July 18, 1888.

to bind them together. Few of them attended church because there were no Italian priests in Wilmington. It was not until the 1920s, when the Roman Catholic diocese created an Italian parish, that a real community spirit began to emerge.

St. Anthony's Church, a large, light-colored stone structure built in Italian-basilica style, together with its campanile, dominates Wilmington's Little Italy today. The church was the lifetime work of Father J. Francis Tucker, an indomitable Wilmington-born Irish priest. In 1924, the bishop had appointed Tucker, then a young priest, pastor of the Italian people of Wilmington, and he was well prepared for the role. Having studied in Rome and served as a U.S. Army chaplain in France during World War I, Tucker spoke both French and Italian fluently and was familiar with European customs. He galvanized the Italian people in support of the church project by involving the community's leading builders and suppliers in its construction and by creating church-related social clubs for people of all age groups. The church sponsored carnivals, football teams, spaghetti dinners, and similar activities that served both to raise money and to expand St. Anthony's role in the neighborhood. Outstanding among this plethora of organizations that mushroomed as a demonstration of the priest's understanding of his parishoners was St. Anthony's Catholic Club for boys. Tucker, an outspoken foe of prohibition during the 1920s, applied for and got the state's first postprohibition license to operate a taproom in the club's headquarters in the church basement, so that the boys could drink beer under spiritual supervision, rather than in speakeasies. The club was responsible for the erection of a large hall adjacent to the church, which still serves as a community center for meetings, concerts, and dinners. Tucker was a strong force for Americanization among his parishioners. The success of his efforts was demonstrated in World War II, when Wilmington's Italians strongly supported the war effort against Fascist Italy, and a great many of Father Tucker's "boys" served in the American army.[46]

46. Joseph A. L. Errigo, *History of St. Anthony's Church* (Wilmington: Lithographed by Hambleton Co., 1949), pp. 95–96.

Like the Italians, the Poles have maintained their ethnic identity while establishing a strong community identification in Wilmington. Anyone passing through the city on I-95 is likely to see the impressive twin Gothic spires of St. Hedwig's Church in a southwest section of Wilmington called Browntown, for a pre-Polish-era landowner. Near the church is an amazing array of other Polish institutions, including a library society, political clubs, veterans' groups, and the Polish Falcons. As in the Italian section to the north, there is a good deal of local ethnic color in Browntown, such as special parades and festivals associated with saints' days and national holidays of the old country and many specialty shops supplying ethnic foods.

During the nineteenth century, Poland, divided by its stronger neighbors Austria, Russia, and Prussia, had ceased to exist as a nation-state. Its largely agrarian people, dislocated by economic shifts that affected all of Europe and laboring under the additional burdens of foreign occupation, began a large-scale flight to America during the 1880s. Farm workers from the German-occupied western section of Poland settled in Wilmington as early as 1882, where they obtained factory jobs, associated with the German community, and attended Sacred Heart Church. As the incoming number of Poles grew, their eagerness to establish a separate national identity found support with the Bishop of Wilmington. In 1890, the bishop brought to Wilmington a Polish priest who organized St. Hedwig's Church, which became the community's principal social institution. Within a few years, the church spawned the Mutual Aid of St. Stanislaus Society and the Polish Library. During the decade of the nineties, immigrants from the Russian zone in eastern Poland joined the community. These people spoke no German and would have been in great difficulty without the assistance of those who had come before. Unable to secure many industrial jobs because the English- and German-speaking foremen could not communicate with them, the new wave of Polish immigrants were relegated to heavy, low-paying jobs primarily in the railroad and leather industries. As Poles rose to become foremen in the leather factories, they, in turn, hired their countrymen, and the leather industry in particular came to be associated with Polish ethnics. Wilmington's Poles are justly proud of their patriotic responses to America's demand for men to serve in the first and second World Wars. During World War II, the Polish community raised enough money in just one of several bond drives to purchase an entire bomber, which was aptly named "Polish Avenger from Delaware." [47] Since the war, some Delawareans of Polish descent have moved away from the old neighborhood, with its thrifty, well-scrubbed houses, to farms or homes in the suburbs, but they still return to southwest Wilmington to participate in the community's many organizations and to celebrate Polish holidays.

Another important group of immigrants from Central Europe were the precursors of Wilmington's sizable Jewish population. Although we generally associate the first visible presence of a Jewish community in Wilmington with this late nineteenth-century migration, Jews had been present in the Delaware region as early as 1655, when the Dutch West India Company granted permission to Isaac Israel and Benjamin Cardoso, Sephardic Jews of Iberian origins, to trade on the South River. Jews have lived in Delaware ever since, but their numbers were so small in the state's early history that Delaware was the last among the original thirteen states to hold Jewish religious services. Not until 1879, when the number of Jews in Wilmington approached one hundred, did the community form its first organization, a mutual-aid society named in honor of Sir Moses Montefiore, the internationally known Jewish philanthropist. The society sponsored a Hebrew school; and, through a highly successful Purim Ball, it raised funds to begin a synagogue. Most of the Jewish families in Wilmington at that time were of German origin. Eschewing factory labor in favor of being self-employed, many of them made a living in the retail trades, especially as clothing merchants, or as tailors and barbers. Their homes, often includ-

47. Vincent J. Kowalewski, "A History of the Polish Colony in Delaware," in *Delaware, A History of the First State,* edited by H. Clay Reed, 3 vols. (New York: Lewis Historical Publishing Co., Inc., 1947), 2:633–638.

ing a shop or work-room, clustered around the city's principal retail center on lower Market Street.

During the 1880s, the migration of Russian Jews fleeing from czarist pogroms enlarged Wilmington's Jewish population and led to the split of the reform-oriented Germans and the orthodox Russian Hasidim into several congregations. By 1900, Delaware's population included about twelve hundred Jews, centered largely in Wilmington but also scattered throughout the towns of the state.[48]

The self-help societies and social organizations that characterized the immigrants' adaptation to America were part of more general developments in American society precipitated by the growing complexities of urban and industrial life. One of the best indices of social change has been in the area of care for those who cannot maintain themselves, such as orphans and the elderly. "The poor you always have with you" has been the American experience since early colonial times. Even the Swedish colonists, who certainly needed every able hand they could get and never experienced unemployment, found it necessary to establish a charity fund for the assistance of unfortunates such as "Karin the Finnish woman," probably a widow, who had been reduced to begging.[49]

The English introduced two forms of relief to America that are often labeled *indoor* and *outdoor*. The Elizabethan Poor Law of 1601, which required each county in England to maintain a workhouse for its indigents, was the precursor of *indoor* relief. *Outdoor* aid, by contrast, did not require that the recipient be confined to an asylum. Although the English poor-law system was considered the best modern remedy for poverty in colonial times, Delaware, with its small population and penchant for cost-cutting, adhered to the more ancient practice of outdoor aid long after most other colonies had built almshouses. Delaware's orphans were bound out as indentured servants, to

48. Elihu Schagrin, "The Jews of Delaware," in *Delaware, A History of The First State,* 2:623.

49. Johnson, *Swedish Settlements,* 2:547.

be reared in private households until they were old enough to work on their own. Similarly, the colony's overseers of the poor supplied wool for spinning to poor women and wood for cutting to men, and the recipients' income depended upon their success-ful completion of these assigned tasks. In an effort to lower the relief rolls, those receiving public charity were required to wear large letters on their clothing announcing their poor condition. Vagrants were disposed of more cheaply yet by whippings and commands to quit the colony.

Not until 1791 did Delaware's lawmakers order each county to tax itself for the construction of an almshouse to provide in-door support for the poor. The primary reason for the change in policy was not humanitarian, but rather the notion that the cost of caring for the poor could be further reduced if they were made to work steadily under the constant eye of attendants. In practice, however, the county almshouses became catchalls for many unfortunate people who were incapable of work, such as the senile, the chronically ill, the insane, and those with con-tagious diseases. Since most of the inmates required health care, the almshouses resembled hospitals more than workhouses. One means the lawmakers used to reduce the tax burden of welfare was to continue the practice of selling the services of certain classes of each county's wards. Poor orphans continued to be bound out for service as in colonial times, until that practice was finally prohibited in 1921. Indigent blacks were especially subject to servitude, including black unwed mothers, but the state refused liability for destitute manumitted slaves unless they had been freed in good health, between the ages of ten and thirty-five. Otherwise, their former masters were judged to be responsible for them.[50]

By the early twentieth century, welfare reformers had become disenchanted with indoor relief because of the overcrowding, poor sanitation, and idleness that characterized most asylums. These reformers maintained that the state should adopt a bal-

50. Elizabeth H. Goggin, "Public Welfare in Delaware, 1638–1930," in *Delaware, A History of The First State*, 2:793–819.

anced program, including both indoor and outdoor aid. In many cases, they argued that outdoor help was the most humane and socially beneficial, since the recipients could remain in their own homes to be cared for by friends or relatives.

Delaware, however, which had been slow to adopt the asylums, was now slow to give them up. Urban New Castle County provided the state's best welfare facilities, including Delaware's first insane asylum, built in 1885. The other counties, with many fewer poor to look after, still housed the insane, the sick, and the indigent together; yet the rural counties were suspicious of plans for statewide consolidation, since their taxes would then be helping to pay for the urban county's welfare problems. During the 1920s, various measures for reform were brought forward, only to go down in defeat. Alfred I. du Pont, wealthy leader of a powerful political organization and newspaper, grew so exasperated with the failure of the state legislature to reform the state's welfare system that he personally sent pension checks to elderly Delawareans all over the state in 1929 and 1930. Finally, in 1931, the legislature passed the Old Age Pension Act that removed responsibility for welfare from the counties and placed it on the state. The state took over Mr. du Pont's pensions and immediately laid plans for the erection of a well-equipped welfare home to serve as both hospital and refuge.[51] The new law closed the doors of the old county almshouses, but it left many problems unsolved. Eligibility for state aid was narrowly conceived, so that, for example, anyone with a criminal record could be denied admission unless he satisfied the authorities that he had been thoroughly reformed.

The enactment of the Old Age Pension Act was independent of the Great Depression that had settled across the nation a year earlier. The depression came more slowly to Delaware than to many regions of the country, and its effects were not felt equally throughout the state. The farming region that comprised most of the state's land mass but little more than one third of its

51. B. Ethelda Mullen, "The Development of Welfare Services in Delaware since 1930," in *Delaware, A History of The First State,* 2:839–840.

people had been in an economically depressed state since farm prices fell at the end of World War I. Nonetheless, the farmers were fiercely independent people who neither asked for help nor expected to give any. The diversity of industries in the Wilmington area softened the initial blow for a year or two, but by the early 1930s, many hundreds of Delawareans were out of work.

At the beginning of the depression, the only relief agencies in Delaware were the county almshouses, the Mothers' Pension Fund—which, since 1917, had provided aid for morally fit but destitute widows with children—and the Family Society, a privately financed organization in Wilmington. The Family Society was the outgrowth of the Associated Charities, an organization created in the 1880s by a group of well-to-do, socially concerned Wilmingtonians for the purpose of co-ordinating and improving the charitable efforts of the city's churches and welfare groups. From the beginning, leaders of the Associated Charities stressed self-help and thrift. Whenever possible, they provided work for applicants, while their volunteer "friendly visitors" checked up on recipients and gave them advice on how to live more economically. In time, the organization broadened its activities as its members learned about the plight of the poor at first hand. One of the most dedicated Associated Charities' workers, Emily P. Bissell, became so incensed by the deplorable health conditions she witnessed in the homes of poverty-stricken tuberculosis patients that she helped to organize the Delaware Anti-Tuberculosis Society. In 1907, in an effort to raise funds to build a sanitarium near Wilmington, she introduced to America the Danish practice of selling Christmas seals.

By 1930, the friendly volunteer visitors had been replaced by trained professional social workers, and the name of the organization had been changed to the Family Society, but it still depended solely upon private donations for support. Late in 1931, the Family Society found that private funds were inadequate to aid the thousands of jobless families in New Castle County who had turned to them for help. The society then asked the city government for money to tide such families over the winter. Responding to the need, the mayor formed a committee that launched a well-publicized appeal for additional private donations. The committee raised $1,612,000. The money was administered by the Family Society in a program that provided temporary jobs on local highway construction and maintenance. The work-relief philosophy emphasized that, unlike the state's wards in the Welfare Home, the recipients of emergency relief were able-bodied and eager to work.[52]

Finally, in November 1932, Governor C. Douglass Buck acknowledged that the depression had become a statewide problem and called the legislature into special session to deal with the crisis. The legislators were badly split on the relief issue, since those from the lower counties opposed any plan that would force them to pay for the economic dislocations of the industrial north. After much debate, the legislature compromised on a weak measure that created the Temporary Relief Commission. The TRC was to subcontract for work with both state and private agencies, using a combination of state and local funds that required a minimum of 20 percent local donations to qualify for state aid.[53] Modeled on the Family Society's program, the TRC emphasized work, it paid cash only for wages, and provided direct unearned relief in the forms of food, shelter, clothing, and fuel. The life of the commission was to be only one year, by which time the legislators hoped the emergency would be over. Instead, 1934 found the depression as deep as ever, with eleven thousand families in Delaware without working breadwinners. Once more, Governor Buck drew attention to the crisis and suggested that the state postpone construction projects that put a premium on costly materials in favor of relief projects that would put as many people to work as possible. But the farmers would have none of it. Granges from all over the state

52. Elizabeth Godwin Goggin, ''The History of Poor-Relief Administration in Delaware'' (M.A. thesis, University of Chicago School of Social Service Administration, 1938), p. 262.

53. Goggin, ''History of Poor Relief,'' p. 264.

barraged the legislature with demands that state-financed relief be curtailed. They pointed out that 93 percent of those on the relief roles were in New Castle County, 75 percent in Wilmington alone. Furthermore, the farmers were having trouble competing with the TRC, which paid better than the fifteen cents per hour that farmers paid their workers. One New Castle County Grange declared that ''Unemployment in Delaware will not improve as long as they [the recipients] have this invitation.'' [54] Politics exacerbated the controversy still further, as Republicans and Democrats accused one another of foot-dragging and each demanded control over the relief commission. Incredible as it may seem, the ultimate result of the debate was a total deadlock that ended state-supported relief efforts in Delaware in the very middle of the depression.

Fortunately for the thousands who were still out of work in New Castle County, the state gave the county the legal right to tax its own citizens for welfare needs. A new Temporary Emergency Relief Commission was authorized for the county, and the new organization worked closely with the professionals of the Family Society. The commissioners, including a judge, the Episcopal bishop, and P. S. du Pont, who had become an implacable foe of the Roosevelt administration, disassociated themselves ideologically from the New Deal. ''Low standards of living must exist among a limited number of persons in every community, generally those of no ambition,'' they wrote at the beginning of their first report. ''Some of these have undoubtedly found easy living during the recent years of distress; they may be undeserving but they cannot be wholly separated from the more important class for whom 'relief' was instituted.'' [55] In that cautious spirit, the new TERC continued the earlier TRC program.

In 1938, a professional welfare group surveying Delaware's care for the needy concluded that the Diamond State, which

54. Goggin, ''History of Poor Relief,'' p. 272.

55. Temporary Emergency Relief Commission for New Castle County, ''Interim Report,'' Wilmington, Delaware, March 1, 1935-March 31, 1936.

ranked fourth in the nation in per-capita income, was notably stingy in its welfare policies. "In spite of its natural advantages—smallness of size and population, density of population, high income—Delaware has been slow to accept responsibility for public assistance and welfare services," they announced, "and the standards of assistance and service are in some programs on a par with the economically hardpressed states of the South." [56] The recently built State Welfare Home was already badly overcrowded, as was the state mental hospital at Farnhurst, while the amount of outdoor relief for depression victims was little more than half that of the national average. Only six states, all in the South, paid less. Delaware also had the dubious distinction of being the only state lacking a vocational-rehabilitation training program for the handicapped. Delaware's lawmakers had failed to meet the test of the greatest economic catastrophe of modern times because of upstate-downstate antagonisms and political rivalries. The crisis that might have brought the state together and reformed its welfare system served instead to enlarge the division between rural and urban areas without appreciably improving the welfare system.

The story of penal reform in Delaware demonstrates the same conservatism, intrastate antagonism, and missed opportunities that have haunted the state's slow progress in welfare. At a busy intersection in the suburbs southwest of Wilmington there stood, until quite recently, a large, forbidding-looking brick structure surrounded by a wall capped by towers and turrets. This grim old edifice, which was for nearly seventy years the New Castle County Workhouse, had the infamous distinction of being the last place in the United States where a sentence of flogging was executed. Although toward the end of its career the workhouse had become a symbol for Delaware's backwardness in penology, it was considered a major step toward progress when it was first opened in 1901.

In the colonial period, Delaware's criminal code reflected Eng-

56. Fred K. Hoehler, "Public Welfare Survey of the State of Delaware" (Chicago: American Public Welfare Association, 1938), p. 1.

lish practice, which favored punishments that inflicted immediate pain and humiliation—the exacting of fines, ear-cropping, branding, whipping, hanging, standing in the stocks, and selling into servitude. In the eighteenth century, leaders of the European enlightenment took issue with these age-old practices that put revenge ahead of rehabilitation. The Quakers eschewed blood-letting and were among the first Americans to adopt the idea that incarceration in solitary confinement at hard labor would cause criminals to repent, to reflect upon their lives, and to improve themselves. For a short time, William Penn was able to soften the laws that the Three Lower Counties had inherited from the Duke-of-York period, but as his personal influence waned, Delawareans reverted to their old ways.

While nearby Pennsylvania led the country in prison reform after the Revolution, Delaware clung to its old criminal code, which emphasized corporal punishment. As one student of Delaware's penology put it, the state's record in penal reform during the nineteenth century was "a dismal story of failure and stagnation" that ultimately left Delaware the last state in the union to maintain the whipping post.[57] One would not necessarily have anticipated such a reactionary course of events in the early nineteenth century. In 1810, a commission appointed by the state legislature reported most enthusiastically on the merits of a penitentiary as the capstone of a revised criminal code. Governor Joseph Haslet of Sussex County denounced the state's antiquated "laws, the offspring of a corrupted monarchy, [which] are suffered to exist in the bosom of a youthful republic." He lectured the legislators on their duty to alter such laws as Delaware's statute inflicting the death penalty for forgery, which, he said, "ill befits a state under the influence of reason and humanity." [58] In spite of that and other vigorous gubernatorial messages on the question, the legislature in session after session fell a few votes short of enacting penal reform, because

57. Robert G. Caldwell, *The Penitentiary Movement in Delaware, 1776 to 1829* (Wilmington: The Historical Society of Delaware, 1946), p. 64.

58. Caldwell, *Penitentiary Movement,* pp. 102–104.

downstaters were, on the whole, satisfied with the old, inherited ways. When the state finally did revise its criminal code in 1829, the changes were slight. Pillorying, hanging, whipping, and servitude were retained as standard punishments. Each county was required to maintain a jailhouse where people awaiting trial, those locked up overnight, and some convicted criminals were jumbled together in idleness and filth, freezing in winter, sweltering in summer.

In the late nineteenth century, the Associated Charities initiated a movement to replace those wretched jails with a workhouse, after their representatives visited the incarcerated husbands of aid recipients and found men and boys mixed in together in overcrowded cells, idly smoking and playing cards. Following the traditional upstate-downstate split, Kent and Sussex refused to participate in the movement to modernize the jails, and when the bill authorizing the construction of a modern workhouse was adopted in 1899, it applied to New Castle County only. The workhouse with its farm and its segregation of inmates by age and sex was a move toward the type of penology that had become commonplace in urban, industrial states.

The whipping post, however, was not allowed to die. By the early twentieth century, the post was a long-forgotten historical relic in most of the United States, but in Delaware it remained a much-used tool of punishment. Between 1900 and 1942, 1,604 prisoners—22 percent of Delaware's total prison population—received whippings with the cat-o'-nine-tails; 66.2 percent of those whipped were blacks.[59] Arguments against whipping were still heard, from time to time, but while most Delawareans were apathetic, many others felt the need to defend their state's eccentricity. Claims that the post kept criminals away from Delaware or helped dissuade the state's would-be criminals from illegal acts were countered by factual, rational proofs to the contrary, but as one crusader against whipping learned, its defenders did not primarily care about rationality.

59. Robert G. Caldwell, *Red Hannah: Delaware's Whipping Post* (Philadelphia: University of Pennsylvania Press, 1947), pp. 69–70.

"The whipping post . . . is more than an instrument of punishment. Encrusted with tradition, it has become a legend . . . a totem pole . . . an expression of Delaware's right to punish her prisoners as she thinks best." [60] Last used in 1952, as punishment for breaking and entering, the post was not officially cast aside by the Delaware code until 1972.

In the twentieth century, the size, location, and composition of Delaware's population has changed dramatically. Most significantly, the state has experienced large in-migrations of people from other parts of the country. These new residents come from very different backgrounds—poor, uneducated blacks from the rural South, Puerto Ricans, and highly trained whites, mostly from the northeast corridor and the Midwest, scientists, engineers, and business managers. These groups have settled in New Castle County, the blacks and Puerto Ricans in the city of Wilmington, and the whites in the suburbs. Although the demography of Delaware has changed, race relations have continued to dominate the state's social history, and as in the days of Reconstruction and P. S. du Pont, education has remained the principal focus of black efforts to achieve equality.

In 1952, Ethel L. Belton was a fifteen-year-old schoolgirl who lived in Claymont, an old railroad suburb of Wilmington and Philadelphia, located in Delaware's extreme northeast corner. Although her home was close to the campus of Claymont High School, Ethel did not attend Claymont. Instead, on every school day, she rose early to catch a public bus for a nine-mile ride into Wilmington, where she was enrolled at the Howard High School. Ethel was black; and under Delaware law, she was not part of the Claymont School District, but of a special district for Negroes only. The state provided four high schools for blacks, one each in Kent and Sussex counties, both only recently opened, and two in New Castle County—Howard in Wilmington and a much smaller school to serve the rural area south of the canal. The NAACP, convinced that the educational resources of these schools were demonstrably lower than those available to whites, brought suit in the state's court of chancery on behalf of Ethel and another suburban black student. In spite of pleas from the State Board of Education that Delaware was not "ready" for integration, the court concluded that Delaware's schools were separate but quite unequal. "The application of constitutional principles is often distasteful to some citizens, but," the chancellor pointed out, "that is one reason for constitutional guarantees. The principles override transitory passions." [61]

Although Delaware's courts agreed with Ethel Belton and other Negro litigants that segregation was in itself a denial of constitutional rights, the state courts were reluctant to enforce desegregation without a similar finding from the United States Supreme Court. Consequently, in 1954, Ethel Belton's suit, together with similar cases from several other states, came before the Supreme Court as a group action headed by the now-famous *Brown* v. *The Board of Education of Topeka, Kansas*.

When the Supreme Court's desegregation decision brought shouts of defiance from politicians in the Deep South, Delaware's leaders voiced reluctant submission to the "law of the land" and predicted that there would be acceptance of the law in the Diamond State. A few black children were quietly admitted to formerly all-white schools in the Wilmington area. But when the school board in Milford, a country town straddling Kent and Sussex counties, initiated a small experiment in integration, the town and the state of Delaware were suddenly catapulted into national headlines. "We don't want to ram anything down anybody's throat," the president of the Milford board announced; "we're the people's representatives—but we've got the law to uphold." Believing that they should "get a little experience in the matter of integration before we are forced to change our whole setup," the board disclosed in September 1954 that it had accepted eleven blacks into the Milford High School.[62] Immediately after that announcement, a crowd es-

61. Belton v. Gebhart, DELAWARE CHANCERY REPORTS, 43 vols. (St. Paul, Minn.: West Publishing Co., 1954–), 32:349.

62. *Wilmington Journal–Every Evening,* September 18, 1954.

timated to be fifteen hundred strong met to protest the board's decision. In the debate that followed, it soon emerged that the local board had failed to get the approval of the state school authorities before admitting the blacks. A potentially explosive matter was now placed in a thicket of overlapping jurisdictions, contradictory laws, and human emotions. Sensing that they had the upper hand, those who opposed integration organized a boycott by the white students at Milford High School.

The boycott precipitated one of the stormiest periods in Delaware history, as many people in Milford and the surrounding area lashed out at integration, and the community teetered on the verge of serious lawlessness. No sooner had the protests and the boycott got under way than an out-of-state professional racist named Bryant Bowles, creator of an organization called the National Association for the Advancement of White People, stormed into Milford and began distributing hate-filled literature and staging rallies in which he denounced the Supreme Court and state officials as communists, proclaimed the superiority of the white race, and vowed to maintain segregation "no matter if this means bloodshed." [63] He attracted a large following, and many paid him five dollars per person to join his organization. Bowles's tactics exacerbated a tense situation. The national press carried stories of mass hysteria as sympathy boycotts nearly closed other schools in lower Delaware, and a cross was burned in Milford. Under intense pressure, the Milford school board resigned, and the state courts allowed the new board to withdraw the Negro students, pending the creation of a statewide desegregation plan. Bowles claimed credit for the "victory" in these actions, but his star fell as rapidly as it had risen. When a state police investigator revealed that he had a criminal record in other states for fraud and bad checks, those who had paid dues into the NAAWP suddenly realized that they had been duped; and with the immediate cause for the agitation removed, Bowles and his NAAWP retreated into oblivion.

In the years that followed, Delaware moved cautiously toward full integration. Not until 1965 did the state board end the

---

63. *Wilmington Journal–Every Evening,* September 28, 1954.

separate Negro school districts and close the all-black segregated schools. The following year, without fanfare, black students were peacefully integrated into schools throughout the
state, including Milford High School, which is now 29 percent
black, a percentage that is about average in lower Delaware
towns. A new era in the state's social history was beginning.
Today, race relations at Milford High School are generally
friendly and relaxed. Not only have there been no major racial
incidents in their first decade of integration, but Milford students casually and unselfconsciously have elected blacks to such
positions as student council president and homecoming queen.

Delaware's historic consistency with national trends on race-
related issues continued through the 1960s, when tensions were
relaxing south of the canal and simultaneously rising in the city
of Wilmington. Demographically, Wilmington has been part of
a syndrome that is familiar to many old American industrial cities. Since its population peaked in the World War I period at
about 120,000, the city has been losing people to its suburbs. In
Wilmington, that trend has been accelerated by dramatic shifts
in the employment pattern, expanding the number of white-
collar jobs in the city, principally in the areas of chemical research and management. Meanwhile, blue-collar jobs have disappeared, or, as in the case of automobile-assembly plants, have
been moved to the suburbs. Superimposed on the pattern was
the migration of thousands of blacks to Wilmington during the
industrial boom of the war years, which expanded Wilmington's
black population from nine thousand to seventeen thousand between 1910 and 1950.[64] More recently, Spanish-speaking
Puerto Ricans, some directly from the island, others from New
York or Philadelphia in search of a better environment in which
to live and rear their families, have swelled the city's proportion
of people who are both poor and unskilled. Wilmington faces a
dilemma as an increasing number of its people are unprepared
for the technical, scientific, and managerial positions that pre-
dominate in the city's large downtown office buildings.

---

64. Charles Tilly, Wagner D. Jackson, and Barry Kay, *Race and Residence in Wilmington, Delaware* (New York: Teachers College, Columbia University, 1965), p. 105.

In the 1950s, when federally funded urban renewal was the most popular panacea for urban ills, Wilmington's leaders plunged into a program that resulted in the destruction of many whole blocks of old working-class houses in the city's major black neighborhood. When the destruction ceased, much of the city's east side had been reduced to brick-littered fields that remained as a glaring sign of the city's inability to generate new construction for more than a decade. Some former east-side residents were relocated in a new government housing project in a depressing-looking and remote area at the northeast edge of the city. Others moved westward into the neighborhood where the state and federal governments were already condemning rows of homes, stores, and churches along a two-block path through the heart of the west side in anticipation of highway construction for Interstate 95. White homeowners who could afford to do so reacted to these developments by selling out to blacks and moving to the suburbs, leaving only their oldest and poorest behind. By the early 1960s, the area between center city and the freeway known as the Valley had become solidly black. Between 1960, when these changes were in progress, and 1970, the number of black children enrolled in Wilmington's schools rose sharply from 45 percent of the total to 79 percent.

In the mid-1960s, while civil-rights demonstrations in the South and riots in northern cities captured national attention, Wilmington was experiencing frightening increases in crime, including warfare between gangs of young people in the city's black neighborhoods. The assassination of the Reverend Martin Luther King, Jr., in the spring of 1968 proved to be the culminating event in a decade of growing racial tensions. In an effort to avert the rioting, looting, and burning that were reported from nearby Washington and Baltimore, Wilmington's mayor, John E. Babiarz, attended an emergency meeting with a number of young black adults who demanded jobs, better housing, and an end to police brutality. Apparently unsatisfied that the mayor could or would solve their problems, the young men later broke out in a rampage of burning and looting that centered on a few blocks in the West Side Valley. The city presented an odd scene, as thousands of frightened white office workers created a monumental traffic jam as they fled to their suburban homes beneath a backdrop of billowing smoke. Governor Charles Terry, exaggerating the situation somewhat, accused the blacks of attempting "to destroy the city" and ordered the entire contingent of the state national guard to the scene.[65] Terry's reaction rather than the riots themselves raised the status of the Wilmington disorder from a local incident to an event of national interest as he stubbornly kept guardsmen on duty for many months afterward. It was not until January of 1969, nine months later, that his successor, Governor Russell Peterson, removed the guard patrols that had not only become an acute embarrassment to many Delawareans, but were also a symbolic focus for racially inspired fears and resentments.

At present, in the middle of the 1970s, the social problems that plagued the last decade are far from solved. The city continues to become more and more a big ghetto for the poor, the old, the Spanish-speaking, and—most of all—the blacks. In 1975, the percentage of black students in the Wilmington public school system reached an all-time high of 84.7 percent. Meanwhile, nearly all of the suburban school districts that surround the city have remained almost exclusively white. The United States Supreme Court recently ordered that New Castle County's schools, including those in the city, be desegregated. Busing has replaced integration as the key word in a confrontation of people and issues that has moved from rural southern Delaware to northern suburban developments. The one element that has not changed in the twenty-three years since Ethel Belton waited each norning for a Delaware Coach Company bus to take her into Wilmington is the Supreme Court's insistence that separate education is by its very nature unequal. At this stage, we can only hope that, if busing is enforced, New Castle County will integrate its schools as gracefully and successfully as her sister counties to the south.

65. *Wilmington Journal–Every Evening,* April 9, 1968.

Part III

The First State

$\mathscr{G}$OVERNMENT began in Delaware nearly 340 years ago with the charter of the New Sweden Company. It passed through periods of autocratic control by the Dutch and the Duke of York before entering into an important evolutionary phase under the liberal-minded leadership of William Penn, who introduced a legislature. The Revolutionary War furthered the development of representative government, and subsequent generations have expanded the franchise, thus bringing the state, as Professor H. Clay Reed once wrote in an article descriptively entitled "From Dictatorship to Democracy." [1]

Although Delaware, in common with her sister states, now possesses broad suffrage and a representative government, not everyone is convinced that the state is a model democracy. The history of political power in the First State has not been a simple growth from colonial autocracy to modern mass rule. A few years ago, Ralph Nader attacked Delaware in his usual pugnacious and provocative style, charging that "Du Pont dominates Delaware as does no single company in any other state," and a group of his associates concluded from a brief but intense study of the state's power structure that "Du Pont in Delaware is the prototype of the large corporation in an American community." [2] The influence of the du Ponts, both as company owners and as a family, has complicated Delaware's history in a way

1. H. Clay Reed, "From Dictatorship to Democracy," in *Delaware, A History of the First State,* edited by H. Clay Reed, 3 vols. (New York: Lewis Historical Publishing Co., Inc., 1947), 1:251.
2. James Phelan and Robert Pozen, *The Company State* (New York: Grossman Publishers, 1973), p. ix, p. 409.

that illustrates political and economic themes whose importance transcends the boundaries of the second-smallest state. The following pages explore the evolution of politics and government in Delaware from colonization to the present.

When Peter Minuit landed two small shiploads of settlers at "the Rocks" in 1638, he embodied the authority that the Swedish government had granted to the New Sweden Company. He and his successors ruled as autocrats, restrained only by their commissions from the company. In the face of the potential danger of hostile Indians and European rivals, the tiny group of Swedish and Finnish settlers found cohesion in the leadership of their military governor. Johan Printz, who ruled New Sweden for ten of its seventeen years, was the colony's most effective and most tyrannical ruler. His instructions gave him the power to carry on trade, erect forts, and to try criminal and civil cases according to Swedish law, which required that his judgments be made in consultation with assistants selected from the leading men of the colony.

In 1653, twenty-two colonists accused Printz of arbitrary administration in such matters as passing judgments against the opinions of the court assistants and profiting personally from illegal commerce. Printz responded characteristically by executing the instigator of this opposition; but soon afterward, he retired from the irksome problems of colonial administration and returned to Stockholm.

The last Swedish governor, Johan Rising, attempted to allay further disorders by involving leading colonists in drawing up a set of explicit ordinances covering "people, land, and agriculture, forestry and cattle." [3] Unfortunately, the ink was hardly dry on the new popularly established regulations when the Dutch engulfed New Sweden and established a new jurisdiction based on the chartered privileges of the Dutch West India Company.

The Netherlands was, at that time, a loosely strung republic of cities, each ruled by its merchant aristocracy. The company,

3. Johnson, *Swedish Settlements,* 2:505.

reflecting the same political organization, was controlled by a council representing the various cities of the republic. The council appointed the director-general of New Netherland and provided him with near-dictatorial powers in colonial management. Peter Stuyvesant, who held the post during the years when Fort Casimir and New Amstel were part of the Dutch empire, was like Johan Printz—a headstrong man used to the absolute power of military rank. It was he who had insisted upon the costly expedition that eliminated the Swedish presence on the Delaware at a time when the company's finances were low. His unilateral action forced the company to cede their newly acquired lands on the South River to the city of Amsterdam. The city in turn undertook the cost of developing the town of New Amstel, but without withdrawing the town from Stuyvesant's administrative authority.

Government in New Amstel reflected the division of jurisdictions. Because the city of Amsterdam was eager to induce immigration, the city fathers were determined to give the colonial townsmen some say in civil affairs. Once the town had grown to include two hundred families, it was to adopt the same governmental structure that prevailed in Amsterdam itself, including an elected common council. In the meantime, however, the chief executive authority in New Amstel was vested in the director. Under him was an officer called the *schout,* who was primarily a court official comparable to a modern prosecuting attorney, sheriff, and judge rolled into one. The director was assisted in the government by several burgomasters selected by the townsmen from their "honest, fittest and richest" neighbors and *schepens,* or magistrates, chosen by the peculiarly Dutch device of double nomination.[4] Under this plan, a group of people, be they burghers, magistrates, or whatever, selected two nominees for a post from which the director-general chose one. The history of New Amstel was too brief to see the town develop the representative form of government that its projectors had intended. In-

4. Jeannette Eckman, "Life among the Early Dutch at New Castle," *Delaware History* 4 (June 1951):277.

stead, life in the little Dutch community was marked by administrative ineptness and wrangling. The last director of the colony, Alexander D'Hinojossa, was a vengeful, greedy, and childish man, whose downfall at the Duke of York's conquest could not have been mourned even by the most ardent Dutch patriot.

The duke's government introduced English common law to Delaware, but did nothing to further the nascent movement toward self-government that the city of Amsterdam had promised its colonists. The duke, whose autocratic nature and notorious insensitivity to popular politics was later to cost him his throne as King James II, was hardly the man to encourage popular participation in government. From 1664 until 1682, when the duke ceded his territories on the Delaware to William Penn, Delaware was governed by magistrates appointed by the royal proprietor's governor in New York. The English moved slowly to abolish Dutch ways, however; their seeming generosity in initially permitting the Dutch judicial officers to "use and exercise their Customary power in administration of justice within their Precincts" [5] emanated, no doubt, from their own meager resources in trained personnel. In time, Englishmen were appointed to these posts, and English replaced Dutch as the language of the court records. As the population along the Delaware increased, two new courts were established, one along the St. Jones River in central Delaware and one at Lewes, near Cape Henlopen. Thus William Penn referred to his newly acquired territories in 1682 as "the three lower counties on the Delaware."

The uniqueness of Delaware's colonial status from 1682 until 1776 is one of the most intriguing, yet perplexing, aspects of the state's history. Delaware was neither a proprietary nor a royal colony, but was, rather, a legal patchwork-combination of both types. Just how such an odd jurisdiction came about is a story of considerable complication, which began with the

5. H. Clay Reed, "The Early New Castle Court," *Delaware History* 4 (June 1951):237.

weakness of Penn's claim to the "lower counties" or "territories." As we have seen, Penn asked his friend the Duke of York for his lands along the Delaware River so that the new colony of Pennsylvania might enjoy control of the western bank of the river from its mouth northward. The duke's claim to the land was, in turn, based upon his conquest of the Dutch, and was already disputed by the Calverts, who contended that the entire Delmarva Peninsula was included in their grant of 1632. To help clarify matters, the English government awarded the duke a charter for the territory dated March 22, 1682, just before he relinquished the land to Penn. That handsome and impressive document, complete with a meticulously drawn likeness of Charles II, has for many years been on display at the Delaware State Archives, where it is described as the Royal Charter for Delaware. In spite of this formidable document, however, the legality of the duke's grant to Penn was questioned by the Maryland proprietor. King James attempted to make things right for Penn with yet another charter, but his hurried abdication in 1688 occurred before he could sign it. Through this truly weird fate, Penn was denied the clear title he sought and was subjected to years of seemingly endless litigation.

William Penn conceived of his colony as a refuge for persecuted Quakers and other Protestants from both the British Isles and continental Europe. Imbued with Quaker principles concerning human relations, he eagerly set about creating a plan of representative government that was to encompass both the province of Pennsylvania and the territories along the Delaware in one governmental unit. To balance the three counties in the latter, he initially created three counties for Pennsylvania proper so that neither section could dominate political affairs. The qualifications for voters, at first defined as freeholders owning one hundred acres of land or its equivalent, were later reduced to fifty acres or fifty pounds a year. The freemen were to elect two bodies: the council, which, together with Penn himself, would legislate and execute policy; and the assembly, which, as originally conceived, could not propose legislation but could accept or reject bills sent to it from the council. This rather cumbersome constitution produced vigorous antagonisms between the two bodies. Eventually the assembly won the right to initiate legislation, thus making Pennsylvania one of the most democratic of the English colonies.

Amid the interminable debates that swirled around Penn, involving land claims and the rivalries of his two houses of government, came the additional and not unrelated problem of the status of the Delaware counties. From the first, it was apparent that the Delawareans, far from being appreciative toward the proprietor for introducing representative government, were instead vigorously attempting to dissolve their political bonds with Pennsylvania. They had a number of reasons for dissatisfaction. For one thing, they resented and feared the rapid growth of the province, while their own region, although settled earlier, grew more modestly. Most glaringly, Penn's newly laid-out town of Philadelphia swiftly surpassed New Castle in size and usurped the older town's river trade. The people of the lower counties recognized that their initial political equality with Pennsylvania could not last for long, and they feared the dominance of their northern neighbors.

A major cause of that fear lay in the reluctance of the Quaker majority in the province to protect the farms and towns of the lower river from armed attack. The Glorious Revolution, which brought William and Mary to the throne in 1688, thrust England into war with France. In America, the conflict was appropriately called King William's War, and it raged during the final decade of the seventeenth century. Unlike later wars against the French, in which Indian attacks made the western frontiers of Pennsylvania the most exposed flank of Penn's lands, this first Anglo-French war included privateering, which placed the lower counties on the Delaware in a most vulnerable position. While the Pennsylvania Quakers hesitated, for the sake of their consciences, to provide defenses, the people along the Delaware were in constant danger. In 1697, fifty armed men from a French privateer rampaged through the town of Lewes, plundering the houses and killing livestock. The marauders made off with money, plate, clothing, and bedding, leaving the terrified inhabitants with "scarce anything in the place to cover or wear." [6]

No issue was better calculated than was defense to arouse the sympathy of persons in powerful positions in England for the plight of the three lower counties. From the time of the Restoration in 1660, there had been a growing desire within the English government to bring the American colonies under closer control by the crown. It was something of an anomaly, therefore, that the government agreed to give William Penn a proprietorship at all, although the grant was hedged with innumerable restraints to insure that Pennsylvania could not deviate from royal policy on important issues such as trade policy. King William III intensified the English government's concern with colonial affairs, most particularly in the area of defense. Penn recognized, therefore, that a succession of bad reports from the lower counties to London might cost him his charter not only for the three counties but even for Pennsylvania itself. In 1698 Edward Randolph, the surveyor-general of customs in America and an advocate of increased regulation from the crown, gave the Council of Trade and Plantations just such a report when he claimed that the inhabitants of the three river-front counties were under the control of an "arbitrary Quaker Government," and were "in no wise secure in their estates, lives and liberties." [7] The Delawareans themselves made it plain that they were reluctant partners in the proprietary colony. They continuously drew attention to the weakness of Penn's claim to the three counties and to his lack of charter rights to rule them; and they insisted that they would accept Penn's government only at the behest of the king, to whom they owed prior allegiance.

A formal breach in the union of the province and territories

6. J. Thomas Scharf, *History of Delaware,* 2 vols. (Philadelphia: L. J. Richards & Co., 1888), 1:100.

7. Robert W. Johannsen, "The Conflict between the Three Lower Counties on the Delaware and the Province of Pennsylvania, 1682–1704," *Delaware History* 5 (September 1952):123.

finally came in the first decade of the eighteenth century. In October 1700, Penn personally convened a joint assembly at New Castle in an effort to assuage the counties. Instead of bringing reconciliation, however, the meeting only increased the rupture. The Pennsylvanians demanded that their greater numbers should permit them a larger share of membership, a position to which the representatives of the counties would not agree. There was also disagreement on the matter of taxation, especially since the less populous counties were not so well off as the province. In short, the Delawareans were demanding an equal voice in a government that they were not willing to support on an equal basis. After much haggling, the meeting adjourned without reaching an accord, and one weary Pennsylvania delegate wrote that he was relieved to leave that "Frenchified, Scotchified, Dutchified place." [8] To make matters worse, the Pennsylvanians questioned whether any of the measures adopted in New Castle were valid in the province, since they had been passed outside its boundaries. That was the final straw for the Delawareans: if legislation adopted in the counties was invalid in the province, then laws passed in the province could not be enforced on them. With stubborn determination, they refused to attend future assembly meetings in Pennsylvania and left the reluctant proprietor with no recourse but to grant them the right to a separate assembly. Thus, after little more than two decades, the union with Pennsylvania was dissolved, although the lower counties on the Delaware and Pennsylvania continued to share the same governor until the Revolution. The Delawareans, weak and ethnically dissimilar though they were, shared a distinct history that had enabled them successfully to resist envelopment into a larger, more unified colony.

The strange anomalies that characterized Delaware's political situation in the seventeenth century continued until independence. For one thing, the colony had no name. Because it had no charter from the crown and thus fell between the stools of proprietary and royal control, its affairs were little supervised. The crown was unwilling to relinquish its claim to the counties, although it acknowledged Penn's rights *de facto*. Therefore, although successive monarchs reserved the right to veto any governor Penn or his heirs might select for the three counties, the crown never sent any special instructions to the governors of Delaware, nor was the colony obliged to send its laws to England for review. Delaware even lacked its own file of papers in the colonial bureaucracy. It is little wonder, then, that when independence came, the Delawareans proudly, if somewhat self-consciously, declared themselves to be the "Delaware State."

The Old Court House that faces Delaware Street from the green in New Castle, just a short block from the wharves of the Delaware River, is one of America's most venerable public buildings. Built long before Philadelphia's Independence Hall or Boston's Faneuil Hall, it was Delaware's first state house and served as the New Castle County Court House from the days of the Penns until 1881, when the courts were moved to Wilmington. The Court House consists of three sections, a handsomely designed central building, capped by a balustrade and cupola, and two smaller wings. Because the early records of the building were either destroyed by a fire in 1722 or were stolen by the British during the Revolution, little was known about the exact history of the Court House until 1936, when the WPA undertook its restoration. The yellow stucco that had covered the entire building during living memory was removed, revealing colonial brick masonry. Inference from existing records suggests that, about 1732, the colonists built the large central portion, fashionably laid in Flemish bond with darkly glazed header-bricks alternating with red stretchers. The central portion is entered through an elegant classic doorway flanked on either side by two tall windows on the second floor. Wings were added in 1765, and the east wing was extended to its present size in 1802. The west wing was demolished and replaced in 1845. The building remained the State House until 1777, when fears of British naval attacks impelled state leaders to seek an inland capital at Dover. The Court House, now restored to its eighteenth-century appearance and open to visitors, remains the most important visual symbol of the unbroken history of government in Delaware, going back to its colonial beginnings.

In the period immediately following the rupture with Pennsylvania, relations between the two colonies, still connected like Siamese twins by their single governor, continued to reflect antagonism. John Evans, sent by Penn to be his lieutenant-governor in 1703, played upon these feelings in a way that exacerbated mutual jealousies. Determined to comply with the crown's desires to improve colonial defense, Evans issued calls for the organization of militia units in 1704. The lower counties responded by raising seven companies and authorizing the erection of a fort at New Castle, while in Pennsylvania the Quakers obstructed action. When the counties' assembly imposed a duty on all ships passing their fortress, Philadelphia merchants charged that the defense plan was designed to sacrifice their trade to New Castle rather than to protect the towns and commerce of the river. Declaring that Evans had interfered with their charter rights to free passage on the Delaware, the Philadelphians raised such a fuss that Penn recalled the governor in 1708.

Thereafter, relations between the proprietor's colonies slowly mended, but the depredations of pirates and privateers continued intermittently through the 1740s. In one well-documented case in the summer of 1747, a party of nineteen Spaniards attacked two families south of the Appoquinimink on a remote point of land near the river. The armed assailants landed from an open boat and captured a Negro girl who had been crabbing, then accosted Edmund Liston, a Quaker farmer who lived nearby. While holding Liston at gunpoint they plundered his house, stealing clothing, bedding, furniture, and Negroes, and then, according to Liston's deposition, forced him to direct them to the nearby plantation of James Hart, where they repeated their thefts and wounded Hart's wife. The privateers got away and continued their pillaging along the coast throughout the summer, aided by a treasonous river pilot. Aside from the written record, the two houses still standing alone and vulnerable on the edge of the marshlands at Liston Point are the only remaining material evidence of that privateering venture. The Liston house, built in 1739 with a quaint, double-pitched gambrel roof, exemplifies Delaware's pre-Georgian domestic architecture. Originally, the main floor consisted of one large rectangular room with a fireplace to one side and a winding stairway that led to the attic sleeping rooms. The Hart house, built in 1725, has a single pitched-gable roofline, but is otherwise similar to its neighbor in arrangement. These two substantial brick structures recall the dangers as well as the prosperity that were the lot of Delaware's yeomen farmers during the colonial wars.

In the first three-quarters of the eighteenth century, the population of the Delaware counties rose from a few hundred families to an estimated 37,000 people in 1776. Growing numbers brought the need for increasingly complex local government and courts. In the Duke-of-York period, the English anglicized the Dutch *schouts* and *schepens* into justices of the peace, who were appointed by the colonial governors from the ranks of the most prosperous and trustworthy colonists. Singly, they each heard minor law cases, while all the justices in a given county constituted the court sessions that dealt with more serious crimes. From that court, cases could be appealed to the Court of Assizes in New York under the duke or, in the Penn period, to the proprietor, his council, and the Provincial Court. In the early days, the justices also served in a variety of administrative capacities, such as tax assessors, fence-viewers, coroners, and overseers of the highways. Delaware's unique, antiquated local divisions, called hundreds, which are roughly comparable in size to the townships of Pennsylvania, originated as tax assessment districts. The levy courts, long the governing bodies of Delaware's counties, likewise date back to that early period when the justices of the peace in each county met as a "levy court" to adjudicate cases involving tax payments and to administer laws relating to the counties.

In the course of the eighteenth century, the assembly increased the number of law courts and created new administrative posts, such as coroner and assessor, thus reducing the duties of the justices of the peace until they eventually became mere magistrates in the lower courts. Following Delaware's break with Pennsylvania, the joint Provincial Court was dissolved, and the lower counties created a Supreme Court that tried all serious cases and received appeals from the justice of the peace and the county courts. Later in the century, a court of common pleas, county courts of quarter sessions, and an orphan's court were added to the colony's judicial system, their judges appointed by the governor. A special court was authorized for the trial of Negroes and mulatto slaves, to enforce the special legislation governing them, such as the law that required the county to reimburse slave owners whose chattels were executed and another requiring owners to make reparation for property stolen by their slaves. In those days, before the separation of church and state, the officers of all these courts were required to take an oath, or, if Quakers, to affirm their faith in the Trinity and to acknowledge "The Holy Scriptures of the Old and New Testament to be given by divine inspiration." [9]

The only elected officials were the county sheriffs and coroners and the six assemblymen, chosen at large from each county. In the early part of the century, voters were defined as freemen who were citizens of Great Britain, Pennsylvania, or the local counties, twenty-one years of age, resident in the counties for two years, and owners of a freehold estate of at least fifty acres of land of which twelve acres were cleared or who possessed fifty pounds sterling, cash. That provision was in keeping with the eighteenth-century view that only those who had a financial stake in the community should participate in its government. But since most people owned their own farms, it did not exclude many, according to one student of the period, although servants, tenants, blacks, and, of course, women could not vote. In 1734, the assembly revised the legal qualifications for voting downward to an estate of forty pounds sterling. The new law also fined qualified voters twenty shillings for failure to

9. Jeannette Eckman, "Colony into State," in *Delaware, A History of the First State,* 1:274.

exercise the franchise. Elections took place annually on October 1 at each county court house, and the assembly met two weeks later at New Castle. The governor generally came down from Philadelphia to address the assembly from an inn or a private home where he stayed. He did not attend assembly meetings, and although he could veto any of its measures, the governor could not prorogue the assembly nor interfere with its selection of its own officers.

Generally speaking, the proprietary governors found the people of the lower counties much more amenable than those of Pennsylvania, particularly in the important area of defense. For instance, while Pennsylvanians were seriously split over the issue of military spending during the French and Indian War of the late 1750s, the response of the lower counties was a very model of enthusiastic patriotism. When General Edward Braddock undertook his ill-fated march to western Pennsylvania, the counties sent him a load of provisions and a herd of cattle. Several times during the war the assembly voted funds for the king's use through new taxes and loans for which the colony was later partially recompensated by Parliament. In addition, each county raised and drilled numerous companies of militia, altogether comprising about four thousand men.

The colonists' vigorous reaction against the Stamp Act must be seen in light of their pride, recalling their recent sacrifices for king and empire in the war. The Stamp Act of 1765 appeared as an aberration in the continuing political relationship between the mother country and her colonies, because it raised for the first time the question of Parliament's right to tax the colonies for the benefit of the empire. The act galvanized the heretofore disparate colonies into united action, and a Congress was called in New York to protest Parliamentary interference in the exclusive right of each colony to tax itself through its own assembly.

Two of the delegates from the Lower Counties to the Stamp Act Congress, Caesar Rodney and Thomas McKean, were destined to play leading roles in the Revolutionary drama. Both then young men in their thirties, they served in a variety of elected and appointed offices in colonial Delaware. Rodney, grandson of an Anglican minister, was a third-generation planter in Kent County and chief representative in his generation of a prominent political family. McKean, the Presbyterian son of Scotch-Irish parents, had received the better education of the two at the Reverend Francis Alison's New London Academy. Born in Chester County, Pennsylvania, McKean read law with his uncle in New Castle, where he later began his own practice. Throughout a very active and ambitious life, he continuously took advantage of the rights of dual citizenship in Delaware and Pennsylvania that remained the vestige of the proprietorship until the 1780s.

Parliament's speedy repeal of the offensive Stamp Tax provoked gratitude throughout the colonies. The Assembly of the Lower Counties appointed Rodney and McKean, who so recently had championed American rights at the Stamp Act Congress, to write an address to the king expressing their thanks. The address beginning, "We cannot help glorying in being the subjects of a king that has made the preservation of the civil and religious rights of his people . . . his chiefest care" so pleased George III that he read it twice. The Delawareans' optimistic belief that "The clouds which lately hung over America are dissipated," and their promise to "at all times most cheerfully contribute to your majesty's service to the utmost of our abilities" [10] was soon dissolved, however, in the crisis over the Townshend Duties.

These duties, betraying Parliament's continued intention to tax the colonies, were the impetus for John Dickinson's famous "Letters of a Pennsylvania Farmer," which appeared serially in the *Pennsylvania Chronicle* and were reprinted throughout North America. Dickinson, like McKean, held positions in both Penn colonies throughout the Revolutionary period. His farm on Jones Neck made him one of the largest landowners in Kent County. He also owned houses in Wilmington and Philadelphia, which were more convenient for his many legal and political obligations. Dickinson trained for the law at the Inns of Court in

10. Scharf, *History of Delaware,* 1:144.

London for four years before entering practice in Philadelphia in 1757. A scholarly man, undoubtedly the most intellectually gifted Delaware politician of his age, he possessed a remarkable grasp of the constitutional and economic relationships inherent in the British common law and in England's imperial policy. While Dickinson's belief that liberty must be guarded and controlled by law was later to make him a reluctant revolutionary, he felt himself to be on firm legal ground in his attacks on the Townshend Duties. Writing with an air of judicious reason in an effort to affect a reconciliation with Britain, his letters served instead to solidify colonial resistance to Parliament. "No free people ever existed or can exist without keeping . . . the purse strings in their own hands," he argued. "When this is the case they have a constitutional check upon the administration, which may thereby be brought into order without violence." [11] In Delaware, as throughout the colonies, committees were formed to enforce a boycott of British goods in the name of American liberty.

In 1773, the crisis suddenly deepened when the British ministry once again announced a tax on the colonies, this time on tea. Caesar Rodney's brother Thomas later recalled that "this diabolical measure, like another electric shock, rouzed [*sic*] the Americans again, as the arrival of the Stamps had done eight years before." [12] When some Bostonians threw the hated tea into the harbor, the British responded forcefully with a series of new laws designed to punish the Yankee city. Throughout the colonies, the plight of Boston, alive with English soldiers, its port closed and the Massachusetts charter suspended, became a symbol for the exercise of arbitrary and abusive power. At a meeting in July 1774, more than five hundred freeholders of New Castle County resolved to form a committee to collect

11. Charles J. Stille, *The Life and Times of John Dickinson,* 2 vols. (Philadelphia: The Historical Society of Pennsylvania, 1891), 1:89.

12. Harold B. Hancock, "County Committees and the Growth of Independence in the Three Lower Counties on the Delaware, 1765–1776," *Delaware History* 15 (October 1973):277.

money for the relief of Boston and to recall the Assembly to New Castle to elect delegates to a Continental Congress. A similar meeting in Kent County, which attracted more than seven hundred people, demonstrated an equivalent patriotic zeal but showed displeasure that the representatives of the upper county had named the place for the assembly to meet to suit their own convenience. In spite of even more grumbling from Sussex, the assembly did meet at New Castle, for the first time—not at the request of the proprietary governor, but rather in answer to a call from the speaker, Caesar Rodney. They chose Rodney, McKean, and George Read, a New Castle lawyer and assembly-man, to represent the Lower Counties at the Continental Congress in Philadelphia.

The Congress brought together outstanding men from all the colonies. Friendships were formed and alliances forged. Thomas McKean grew close to John Adams and became a supporter of the Massachusetts man's radical politics, while the more moderate Read formed a circle with the Virginians. Writing to an acquaintance in May 1775, Read described his life in Philadelphia.

> I prepare in the morning for the meeting at nine o'clock, and often do not return to my lodgings till that time at night. We sit in Congress generally till half-past three o'clock, once till five o'clock and then dine at the City Tavern, where a few of us have established a table for each day in the week, save Saturday, when there is a general dinner. Our daily table is formed by the following persons, at present to wit: Messrs. Randolph, Lee, Washington, and Harrison, of Virginia, Alsop of New York, Chase of Maryland, and Rodney and Read.[13]

At that time, one month after the battles at Lexington and Concord, as the colonies were rushing toward outright war with Great Britain, Congress wrestled with the problems of defending a continent. In Delaware, as elsewhere, militia companies were being organized and drilled and officers elected to protect

---

13. William T. Read, *Life and Correspondence of George Read* (Philadelphia: J. B. Lippincott and Co., 1870), p. 106.

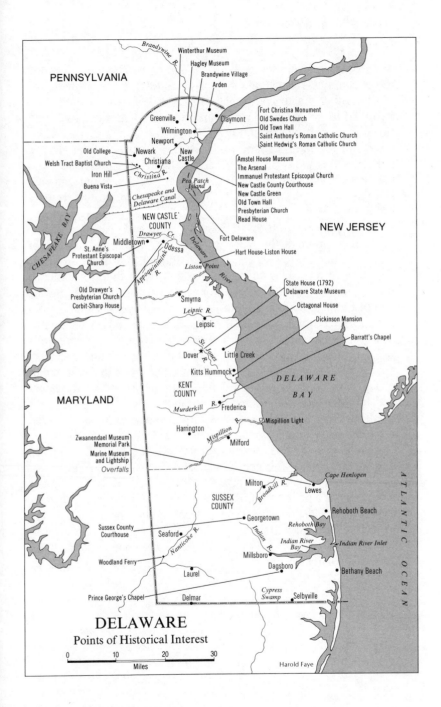

PENNSYLVANIA

Brandywine R.

Winterthur Museum

Hagley Museum

Brandywine Village

Arden

Greenville
Wilmington
Newport

Claymont

Fort Christina Monument
Old Swedes Church
Old Town Hall
Saint Anthony's Roman Catholic Church
Saint Hedwig's Roman Catholic Church

Old College
Welsh Tract Baptist Church
Iron Hill
Buena Vista

Newark
Christiana

Christina R.

New Castle

Amstel House Museum
The Arsenal
Immanuel Protestant Episcopal Church
New Castle County Courthouse
New Castle Green
Old Town Hall
Presbyterian Church
Read House

Pea Patch
Island

Chesapeake and
Delaware Canal

NEW JERSEY

NEW CASTLE
COUNTY

Drawyer Cr.

St. Anne's
Protestant Episcopal
Church

Middletown

Odessa

Fort Delaware

Hart House-Liston House

Appoquinimink R.

Liston Point

Delaware River

CHESAPEAKE BAY

Old Drawyer's
Presbyterian Church
Corbit-Sharp House

Smyrna

Leipsic R.

Leipsic

State House (1792)
Delaware State Museum

Octagonal House

Dickinson Mansion

Barratt's Chapel

St. Jones R.

Dover

Little Creek

MARYLAND

Kitts Hummock

KENT
COUNTY

DELAWARE
BAY

Murderkill R.

Frederica

Harrington

Mispillion R.

Milford

Mispillion Light

Zwaanendael Museum
Memorial Park
Marine Museum
and Lightship
Overfalls

ATLANTIC OCEAN

Milton

Broadkill R.

Cape Henlopen

Lewes

SUSSEX
COUNTY

Rehoboth Beach

Sussex County
Courthouse

Seaford

Georgetown

Nanticoke R.

Indian R.

Rehoboth Bay

Indian River
Bay

Indian River Inlet

Millsboro

Woodland Ferry

Dagsboro

Laurel

Bethany Beach

Prince George's Chapel

Delmar

Cypress
Swamp

Selbyville

DELAWARE
Points of Historical Interest

0   10   20   30
Miles

Harold Faye

their local areas. In September of 1775, representatives from the three counties formed a Council of Safety to co-ordinate the militia units, which had already raised five thousand men "determined to defend their rights and liberties with their lives and fortunes." [14] In the meantime, Congress was organizing a Continental army in anticipation of a British invasion. John Haslet, a Kent Countian who accepted a colonel's commission from Congress, expressed the feelings of many reluctant but patriotic soldiers when he wrote that "it would be Infamy to refuse, rather than Virtue to Accept." [15]

The people of the Lower Counties were not nearly so unanimous in support of the Revolution as the words and actions of these leading patriots might suggest. Indeed, the question of independence and subsequent fears of a British invasion aroused internal discord to a high pitch. The move toward instituting an independent colonial government exacerbated jealousies between the counties, reopened old political wounds, and created new alignments. Those who figured in Delaware's colonial politics were drawn from among the country gentry and the merchants and lawyers of the few towns. Politics within that small group was necessarily highly personal. Many of its members had intermarried, and, since the number of elective offices was small and the powers of the assembly limited, factions revolved around family alliances and private interests as much as issues of public policy. The Revolution altered that basis for politics but did not unseat the gentry's leadership. Much was at stake, and while men such as Rodney, Haslet, and McKean eagerly accepted the challenges of independence, others were reluctant to throw off all ties with Britain. Because the nature and extent of that reluctance varied, it is misleading to adopt the terminology of the patriots, or Whigs, as they called themselves, who, in the intensity of the moment, labeled all their opponents as Tories.

14. Hancock, "County Committees," p. 285.
15. Harold B. Hancock, "Letters to and from Caesar Rodney," *Delaware History* 12 (April 1966):65.

Religion and ethnicity were important factors in Delaware's political scene during these crucial years. The Quakers generally remained aloof from the conflict, although in some instances they supported one side or the other by means short of taking up arms. But in Delaware the Quakers were far fewer than in Pennsylvania and not so important politically. Of the two most significant religious groups in the Lower Counties, the Presbyterians were generally ardent Whigs, while the Anglicans were divided. Some Anglicans saw the war as a cleverly disguised effort by hyperambitious Scotch-Irish Presbyterians to take over the colony. In addition, a few Anglican clergymen refused to give up the prayer for the king on the grounds that their oath required them to say the established Prayer Book services in their entirety. Some evaded that responsibility, however. On at least one occasion the rector at Immanuel New Castle, the Reverend Mr. George Ross—a relative by marriage of Betsy Ross—allowed a visiting Methodist preacher to recite the controversial prayer. Among Delaware's leading political figures, McKean was a Presbyterian, while Rodney and Read, both Anglicans, were closely related to Anglican clergymen.

The most provocative and enlightening contemporary document concerning the colony's wartime factions was an exaggerated newspaper attack on George Read, entitled, in the then popular style of classical allusions, "Timoleon's Biographical History of Dionysius, Tyrant of Delaware." [16] Written in the 1780s, the work has been attributed to Dr. James Tilton, a Scotch-Irish Presbyterian physician of Dover. The doctor alleged that Read, whom he referred to as the "tyrant of Delaware," was secretly a Tory sympathizer. The vehemence expressed in the piece suggests the nature of Revolutionary politics in Delaware, where strong groups opposed independence.

In May 1776, responding to an act by the king in Parliament that excluded the colonies from the protection of Great Britain,

16. John A. Munroe, editor, *Timoleon's Biographical History of Dionysius, Tyrant of Delaware* (Newark, Delaware: University of Delaware Press, 1958).

156   DELAWARE

Congress requested each colony to assume independence and alter its government accordingly. The measure aroused the fears of conservative-minded Delawareans, many of whom subscribed to a petition urging the assembly to refrain from changing Delaware's constitution:

> We beg leave to observe that the present unhappy disputes in which
> the colonies are involved were begun for the defence and
> preservation of the chartered rights and privileges of the colonies,
> and their then forms of government. And we humbly apprehend that
> the changing of the constitution at this critical period would be
> acting contrary to the avowed principles on which the opposition
> was made to the oppressive measures of the British ministry, would
> tend very much to disunite the people, and be productive of the
> most dangerous consequences.[17]

The fears expressed in the conservatives' petition were indeed prophetic, as Thomas Rodney acknowledged, when he later wrote that it inspired "all the Whig and Tory feweds [sic] that have reigned in Kent and Sussex since . . ." In Dover, John Clark, a member of the Kent County Committee of Inspection, but according to Timoleon "a noted bully, who, on all occasions, cursed the Bostonians as rebels and traitors," was attacked by a mob who put him in the town pillory and pelted him with eggs for his advocacy of the petition. In light of that experience, it is hardly surprising that he "fortified his house with loop-holes and guns, for his defense against Whigs and committees." Soon afterward, an alleged plot of the Tories to revenge themselves on the Whigs and burn Dover was discovered and thwarted.[18]

Worse disorders followed soon after in Sussex County, where Thomas Robinson, a politically powerful plantation owner from the backwoods of the Indian River region, raised an insurrection against the Whigs. Fifteen hundred men gathered at Lewes, determined to prevent the change in government, but their efforts

17. Munroe, editor, *Timoleon's Biographical History*, p. 11.
18. Munroe, editor, *Timoleon's Biographical History*, p. 72, p. 20, p. 21.

proved ineffectual. When the commander of the HMS *Roebuck,* a British man-of-war then cruising in the Delaware Bay, refused to supply the insurgents with arms because of his own short supply, the men were easily dispersed by a contingent of three thousand Pennsylvania militiamen sent by Congress. Robinson later fled to a British warship in the bay, co-operated with the British army and then settled temporarily in Nova Scotia. When he died in 1786, however, he was back in his native Sussex County petitioning for his permanent return, and he was buried in the churchyard at Prince George's Chapel, where he had once served on the vestry.

Delaware's peninsular position made the state vulnerable to British sea raids, especially along the coast of Sussex County. That helps to explain the feeling there that the rebellion could not possibly succeed against English power on both land and sea. Conversely, fears were weakest in New Castle County, where armed patriots in galley boats pushed British ships downriver in a hotly contested action in the spring of 1776. George Read, who witnessed the action, informed his fellow members of Congress, McKean and Rodney, that "I suppose it will be thought that too much powder and shot have been expended by the galleys in these attacks; but I am well satisfied they have produced a very happy effect upon the multitudes of spectators on each side of the river; and in that part of the colonies where this relation shall be known, British ships of war will not be thought so formidable." [19]

In light of the disturbed public mood in the Lower Counties during the spring of 1776, it is not surprising that the colony's representatives in Congress, together with those from the other Middle Colonies, were more conservative than those of Massachusetts and Virginia. When the vote on independence was put before Congress, Timoleon's nemesis, George Read, declined to vote for it on the grounds that it was premature. Thomas McKean, however, embraced the resolution, and since Rodney was temporarily away at his farm in Dover, the little

19. William T. Read, *George Read,* p. 158.

colony's two delegates would have negated each other's votes had not McKean sent posthaste for Rodney to return to Philadelphia. Rodney's ride, probably the best-known event in Delaware history, is also one of the most obscure. Rodney himself wrote that he rode through the "thunder and rain" of a typical summer storm on the night of July 1, but he failed to say whether he traveled in a carriage, as some have claimed, or whether he was exposed to the elements, as depicted in the equestrian statue in Wilmington's Rodney Square. In either case, his arrival must have been dramatic, since it insured Delaware's acceptance of the resolution for independence. Read, seeing that his fears were not shared by the vast majority of his congressional colleagues, agreed to sign Jefferson's Declaration adopted July 4, and thus accepted equal responsibility for that momentous action.

With American independence being declared throughout the world, Delaware could no longer hesitate to reorganize its government, and the assembly resolved to hold elections for a constitutional convention. The election of representatives to the convention was hotly disputed between the more conservative men, such as Read, who wanted only minor modifications in the government, and the Whigs, who demanded a more complete break with the past. During the election in Kent County, the Whigs indulged in a publicity event designed to build support for their cause. The Whig-dominated Committee of Inspection secured a portrait of George III, with which they marched at slow time around the Dover Green, followed by the Light Infantry militiamen. They then ceremoniously burned the portrait, as their leader intoned, "Compelled by strong necessity, thus we destroy even the shadow of that King who refused to reign over a free people." As three cheers went up, Thomas Rodney noted "the greatest joy in every countenance except a few long faces." [20]

In spite of their most assiduous efforts, the Whigs lost control of the convention's membership to the conservatives, whose

20. Leon deValinger, "Rodney Letters," *Delaware History* 3 (September 1948):109.

imprint is strongly evident in Delaware's constitution of 1776. The thirty men who gathered in New Castle in September of that year faced the unusual task of creating a sovereign government for a very small yet independent country. Determined to be free from dominance by Pennsylvania, they dropped the title of Lower Counties on Delaware for the more emphatic name of the Delaware State. Echoing the majority's conservative political views, the convention fashioned a document that adapted their former colonial government to the new political situation. There were some notable changes, however. In common with the other states that were wrestling with constitutions at the same time, the Delawareans feared a strong executive and consequently increased the power of the legislature. The legislators were empowered to choose the new executive officer, to be called the president. Less powerful than the proprietary governor, the president could not veto legislation, nor did he have so much appointive power as the executive officer held in the past. His role was more than honorary, however, for he retained control over some offices and was to be commander-in-chief of the militia. He was also to preside at the state supreme court, which thus replaced the colonial king in council as the highest court for Delawareans.

Delaware's Revolutionary constitution shifted power from the executive to the legislature, but it was by no means "revolutionary" with respect to who might share in legislative authority. The constitution makers left undisturbed the colonial property qualifications for voting, limiting the suffrage in their declaration of rights to those "having sufficient evidence of a permanent common interest with, and Attachment to the Community." [21] On that issue the Delawareans showed themselves to be more conservative than their neighbors in Pennsylvania, who had recently eliminated property qualifications for the suffrage. A religious test was also maintained, excluding non-Trinitarian Christians from holding public office.

21. H. Clay Reed, "The Delaware Constitution of 1776," *Delaware Notes,* Occasional Papers, 6th series (1930), p. 32, p. 30.

The most progressive feature of the constitution was its declaration against the slave trade, which read, "No person hereafter imported into this State from Africa ought to be held in Slavery under any Pretence whatever, and no Negro, Indian or Mulatto Slave, ought to be brought into this State from any port of the World." [22] That article, unique in state constitutions of the period, grew out of the earlier frustrations of Delaware's lawmakers who, just a year before, had passed a similar measure only to see it vetoed by Governor John Penn. Ending the slave trade did not, of course, end slavery; in fact, it probably increased the value of the slaves already in Delaware. It seems likely, however, that the lawmakers contemplated the move as a first step in ultimate eradication of the slave system from the state.

Independence had been declared and new constitutions written, but the American states still had to wage a long and at times bitterly discouraging war to insure the continuity of their new governments. The year of independence was also the year in which the English began expensive and massive efforts to restore control over their former colonies. That summer, Sir William Howe landed 32,000 British and Hessian troops on Staten Island, where they faced George Washington's largely untrained and ill-equipped force of 19,000 across the bay on Long Island. Conspicuous among the Americans was the Delaware regiment of about 550 men, handsomely uniformed in blue coats faced with red, white waistcoats, and buff breeches. Their black leather hats were inscribed "Liberty and Independence, Delaware Regiment" and ornamented with the Delaware crest, depicting a full-rigged ship and a sheaf of wheat. From the day when they first came under fire at the Battle of Long Island, these troops displayed such outstanding courage and tenacity that General Washington exclaimed, "Good God! What brave fellows I must this day lose!" Their colonel, John Haslet, described as "a large, athletic, handsome man . . . in courage and impulse a typical Irishman," was born in Ulster and edu-

22. Reed, "Delaware Constitution," p. 30.

cated for the Presbyterian ministry. On emigrating, he became a physician in Dover and gained a bit of military experience in the local militia before the Revolution.[23]

Following Washington's uninterrupted series of defeats in the New York campaign and the Americans' discouraging retreat across the Jerseys in December, most of the men went home, because their enlistments ran out at the end of the year. Haslet alone stayed on, without troops to command, and thus was a participant in Washington's successful strikes at Trenton and at Princeton, where the colonel was killed while rallying the fallen General Hugh Mercer's brigade of Continentals.

One of the most exasperating aspects of the Revolution for General Washington was the fluidity of army personnel. The Delaware Regiment, as reconstituted by Colonel David Hall, Jr., in 1777 was part of the Continental Army recruited and paid by the Continental Congress and thus subject to orders from the commander-in-chief to go and fight anywhere, at any time. Unfortunately for Washington, the state militia units that made up most of his army were not subject to that discipline. Not only were their enlistments for short durations, but they were also unwilling to venture far beyond their local soil. That system, awkward though it was, sometimes produced victory when militia units joined with the Continental Army at moments of maximum danger. Such a moment came in the last days of 1776, when the enemy, having taken New York City and overrun New Jersey, stood poised to invade Pennsylvania and capture Philadelphia, hampered only by the Delaware River and Washington's exhausted, defeated army. At that juncture, which later historians have identified as the major crisis of the whole war, militiamen from surrounding communities flocked to swell the depleted army, and thus gave Washington the fighting strength he needed to launch his surprise, morale-saving drive back into New Jersey.

Among those that rallied to the cause during "these times

---

23. Christopher L. Ward, *The Delaware Continentals* (Wilmington, Delaware: The Historical Society of Delaware, 1941), p. 41, p. 7.

that try men's souls" as Tom Paine had just proclaimed, were companies from Delaware led by Caesar Rodney's energetic younger brother Thomas, whose diaries and letters offer splendid insight into the campaign. Captain Rodney marched out of Dover on December 15 with thirty-four men and reached Philadelphia three days later, to find the congressional city "looking as if it had been plundered," its streets empty, and its citizens fled in panic. He dined with some Tory-leaning relatives there who were understandably pessimistic about American chances to maintain the rebellion much longer. Rodney told them, with more confidence than the situation warranted, that some circumstances still favored America, "and concluded by assuring them that I should not change my determination, that I knew my business and should not return until the British were beaten." On Christmas night, Rodney's company crossed the Delaware south of Trenton. "The river was very full of floating ice, and the wind was blowing very hard, and the night was very dark and cold, and we had great difficulty in crossing." After such arduous hardships, the troops were angered to learn that General John Cadwalader, their commanding officer, had ordered a retreat because they could not land their artillery on the icy shore. Rodney and his men acquiesced only when the commander pointed out that if Washington's contingent farther upstream "should be unsuccessful and we also, the cause would be lost, but if our force remained intact it would still keep up the spirit of America." [24]

Two days later, they returned to New Jersey, and in the wake of their comrades' victory at Trenton, joined the march to Princeton. Everywhere Rodney saw signs of the Hessians' quick flight. The foreigners had devastated the land, and the Hessian general's headquarters at Burlington "looked more like the headquarters of a swineherd." [25] At Princeton, the Kent County

24. Caesar A. Rodney, editor, "Diary of Captain Thomas Rodney, 1776–1777," *Historical and Biographical Papers,* 7 vols. (Wilmington, Delaware: The Historical Society of Delaware, 1888), 1, no. 8: 17, 16, 22, 23.

25. Caesar A. Rodney, editor, "Diary of Captain Thomas Rodney," 1, no. 8:26.

militiamen got into the thick of the fight, but none were killed, although their neighbor John Haslet fell on another part of the field. As the patriots later hastened to escape the wrath of Lord Cornwallis's superior force, Washington placed the Delaware men at the rear of the American army to destroy bridges and create obstructions. Once the army was safely quartered in Morristown, Thomas wrote to his brother Caesar, "I thank God that the American cause is now safe," [26] and when his men's brief enlistments ran out, he returned with them to Dover, "where I found all well on the 28th of January 1777." [27]

The year 1777 proved to be a year of mixed successes for the American cause. At Saratoga, New York, General John Burgoyne surrendered his entire army to the patriots, but meanwhile Washington's forces were unable to prevent a British invasion of Delaware and Pennsylvania. In July, Howe embarked with a formidable army of more than fifteen thousand men, together with horses and artillery, which set sail from New York for an unknown destination. A week later, that armada of more than 230 ships was sighted off Cape Henlopen. The Americans assumed that the British planned to sail up the Delaware and attack Philadelphia and were surprised when the fleet left the capes and vanished for a time before it reappeared in the Chesapeake. After thirty-two days at sea in their hot, cramped quarters, the British and the Hessians finally disembarked at Head of Elk in late August. The reason for such a time-consuming and circuitous approach to Philadelphia seems to have been Howe's fear that the quicker route up the Delaware was too dangerous, since the river's narrow channel would force the British to arrange their ships in a vulnerable single-file line.

Once the British intentions were clear, Washington marched his army southward from its base north of Philadelphia and established his headquarters in a house on Quaker Hill in Wilmington on August 25, the very day that the British landed. The

---

26. George H. Ryden, *Letters to and from Caesar Rodney, 1756–1784* (Philadelphia: University of Pennsylvania Press for the Historical Society of Delaware, 1933), p. 155.

27. Caesar A. Rodney, editor, "Diary of Captain Thomas Rodney," 1, no. 8:50.

next day, the Continental commander-in-chief reconnoitered the region from Iron Hill, south of Newark, Delaware. Howe's army, hungry after an ordeal at sea, were in no hurry to march, however, and the enemy spent several days rounding up all the livestock and other provisions they could find in a wide swath around their encampment at Elkton. Washington organized a corps of light-infantry riflemen under the command of Brigadier General William Maxwell, with orders "to be constantly near the Enemy and to give them every possible annoyance." [28] On September 3, the king's troops began moving up the road from the vicinity of present-day Glasgow, Delaware. As they marched through a densely wooded area just south of the Christina, Maxwell's men opened fire. The invaders fired back with musketry and small field pieces and then charged with bayonets. The badly outnumbered Americans fell back across Cooch's Bridge, while keeping up their fire to harass the enemy and make good their escape. Although there are no firm figures on the skirmish, known to Delawareans as the Battle of Cooch's Bridge, both sides probably lost between thirty and forty men.

Washington, assuming that the British were heading toward Wilmington, to reach the only bridge over the Brandywine, drew up the main van of his army at Newport, intending to give battle when Howe forded Red Clay Creek. Washington also ordered the millers at Brandywine Village to dismantle their millstones and hide the runners, in anticipation of an enemy advance. Instead, the British moved to the west. Early in the morning of September 8, they marched through Newark and headed for Kennett Square, Pennsylvania. Thus Cooch's Bridge turned out to be the only battle fought within Delaware, as Washington quickly marched north to Chadds Ford on the Brandywine, just above the Delaware line, to interpose his army between the enemy and their ultimate objective, Philadelphia. The stage was set for the Battle of the Brandywine.

On September 11, the residents of Wilmington heard the ominous sounds of cannon fire moving down the deep hills of the

28. Ward, *Delaware Continentals*, p. 190.

Brandywine valley. Early the next morning, one sleepy-eyed Wilmingtonian looked out and "saw three red-coats and supposed them prisoners, but soon found the scene was the reverse, and greatly alarmed were we all." [29] A regiment of Scottish Highlanders and another of Hessians occupied the town, captured the state president, Dr. John McKinly, and a mass of county documents that had been sent up from New Castle on the mistaken notion that they would be in safer hands. The British army's main interest in Wilmington, however, was as a storehouse of wheat and flour and as a hospital for troops wounded in the battle.

In October, the British admiral, General Howe's brother Richard, easily sailed a large fleet up the Delaware and anchored his ships from Reedy Island northward past Wilmington. The admiral's secretary, who visited the riverfront towns, reported that Wilmington's Quakers "though decent and passive have not escaped Distress from the Hands of the Rebels . . . They feel very deeply the Horrors of this unnatural War, wch the Wickedness and Wantonness of some of their principal People have brought upon them." The region around New Castle appeared to him "by far the most pleasant and the most fertile Lands I have yet seen in America." But the town itself, largely abandoned by its frightened residents, was "small, and its Buildings mean and scattered; . . . inferior in size and every other Respect to Wilmington." [30]

With the state's chief executive a captive and Vice-President George Read attending Congress, civil authority in the unoccupied portions of the state fell to Thomas McKean, Speaker of the Assembly. McKean established a temporary capital at Newark and attempted to round up militiamen to harass the British and drive them away. Washington begged him to send the American army shoes and blankets, since many of his men had lost everything they were not carrying in the battle of Chadds Ford. The hard-working Speaker found the situation very exas-

29. Ward, *Delaware Continentals,* p. 212.
30. Ward, *Delaware Continentals,* pp. 522–523.

perating. New Castle County had been looted of its sheep, and no blankets or shoes could be found. He informed Washington that Continental troops would be needed to keep independence alive in Delaware. "The people were dispirited and dispersed; and the Tories, and less virtuous part that remained, were daily employed in supplying the British troops, both in Wilmington and at New Castle, on board the ships of war, with all kinds of provisions." [31] Things were little better in the unoccupied southern portion of the state.

> The Whigs in Sussex County are said to be rather too few to keep the Tories there quiet. The same is said of Kent County, and the militia there absolutely refuse to march out of the county. In New Castle County, the lower class of the people have got an opinion that, by remaining quiet, they will not be molested, and seem unwilling to join their officers. . . . There are so many virtuous and brave men in the State, who will be sacrificed to their inveterate enemies, by leaving them in their present situation, that my blood runs cold at the reflection. [32]

The chief stimulus to McKean's fears removed itself, however, when Howe, no doubt fearing another Trenton, pulled his troops out of Wilmington after only a few weeks and sent them to join the main body of his army in Philadelphia.

The British withdrawal did not end serious threats to the peace in Delaware. The next year, Cheney Clow, an English-born Kent County Tory farmer, built a blockhouse and collected a band of partisans with the apparent intention of marching on Dover, the new state capital. His plot was uncovered, and when the militia charged the fort, they found it abandoned. Many of the insurgents were later captured, and some were punished by being sent off to enlist in the American army.

In March 1778, the legislature elected Caesar Rodney president to fill the post of the captured Dr. McKinly. Rodney, who was suffering from debilitating and painful asthma and skin can-

31. Ward, *Delaware Continentals*, p. 514.
32. Ward, *Delaware Continentals*, pp. 514–515.

cer, faced the formidable task of making the state government work under wartime conditions. His government proved unable to prevent coastal raids by Tory refugees that recalled the piracies of the French wars, nor was Delaware capable of raising enough revenue to pay its soldiers in the field or keep them adequately supplied. In August 1781, a party of sixteen Tory raiders descended upon John Dickinson's home on the St. Jones River and made a shambles of it, stealing silverware, china, clothing, liquors, and other goods amounting to fifteen hundred pounds sterling. They had escaped back to their boats before the Kent County militia could organize a counterattack. That escapade, one sign of the serious lethargy in state affairs, brought Dickinson from his Philadelphia home down to Kent County to put matters aright. Pursuaded to accept the Delaware presidency when the ailing Rodney's term expired, Dickinson proved to be a vigorous administrator, in contrast to the more radically democratic Rodney, who had purposely subordinated himself to the will of the assembly. Dickinson, who believed in a strong executive power, reformed the state's creaky judicial system, improved the collection of taxes, and paid the soldiers in the Delaware Regiment during the one year he served as president of Delaware.

By the time these reforms were made, the war was nearly over, and the Delaware Continentals, so long treated like stepchildren by their state, were soon coming home. Their regiment, which had the longest service record of any in the American Revolution, marched and countermarched through forests and swamps, slept out in all manner of inclement weather, often without tents or blankets, and fought and died for seven years with only one brief interruption in the early days of 1777. Men from the regiment fought in every major engagement of Washington's army, from Long Island to Monmouth. When the major theater of the war shifted to the south, they joined Generals Horatio Gates and Nathanael Greene there and played an important role in the numerous battles against Cornwallis, leading up to the final campaign at Yorktown. Although the fine uniforms in which they began their service had long since become threadbare and ragged, the Delawareans acquitted themselves like the veteran soldiers they were. "The State of Delaware furnished one regiment only; and certainly no regiment in the army surpassed it in soldiership," [33] said Colonel Henry Lee of Virginia, who fought with them during the arduous southern campaign. Their American comrades dubbed the Delaware men "the Blue Hen's Chickens," because, it was said, they fought with the tenacity of the blue-tinted game cocks that they carried with them.

In 1783, when the regiment made its final tedious march homeward, many of the men suffered from a lingering, debilitating illness. They returned to a state that was itself just recovering from ills of an economic, social, and political nature. The war had thoroughly disrupted Delaware's economy. River traffic on the Delaware, the state's commercial bloodstream, had long been seriously interrupted by British ships of war and Tory raiders. While the state suffered from depression, inflation raged from the indiscriminate printing of increasingly worthless Continental money. In addition, the war had left Delaware seriously scarred by intense political feelings that had to be reconciled under an untried state constitution and an equally untried national confederation. The cessation of hostilities marked only the beginning of the little state's recovery from these serious problems.

After Rhode Island, Delaware was the smallest state, but unlike the tiny New England commonwealth, Delaware had no ports like Newport and Providence to secure control over her own trade. Delawareans were, instead, dependent upon Philadelphia, an out-of-state port that was free to penalize their trade under the Articles of Confederation. Questions of trade and tariffs weighed heavily on the minds of the state's leaders. What sort of future could landowners, manufacturers, and merchants look forward to, in light of Delaware's vulnerability? Thus, when Virginia proposed a meeting at Annapolis, Maryland, in 1786 to discuss how Congress might alleviate the problems of

33. Ward, *Delaware Continentals,* p. xiii.

interstate commerce, Delaware's leaders responded with alacrity. The state's delegation, including George Read and John Dickinson, supported the call for a second convention to meet in Philadelphia in the summer of 1787. On Read's urging, the Delaware Assembly passed an act instructing the state's delegates to the Philadelphia meeting to discuss "such alterations and further provisions, as may be necessary to render the Federal Constitution adequate to the exigencies of the Union," [34] with the single restriction that Delaware demand a continuation of the policy of equality among the states within the confederation.

The convention at Philadelphia decided to scrap the Articles and undertook to write a wholly new constitution. One of their most vexatious problems was the battle between the large states and the small states over the composition of the proposed federal legislature. Delaware's delegation, in response to their instructions, stood firmly for the rights of the small states. At one point, John Dickinson, again a delegate from the Diamond State, warned James Madison of Virginia that his state would seek a foreign alliance before it would be dominated by its larger neighbors. Yet, that same Dickinson later saved the day and the hopes for a new, stronger federal government by sponsoring the compromise that preserved the equality of the states in the Senate, while making population size the criterion for each state's membership in the lower house.

The Delaware delegation returned home with the completed document and presented it to the State Assembly. The assemblymen, seeing in this matter "the most important consideration, involving in its adoption not only our prosperity and felicity, but perhaps our national existence," [35] called for an election to choose delegates to a convention that would decide the question of state ratification. When the convention met in Dover on December 3, 1787, Delaware was largely free of the factional disputes that swirled about the ratification issue in most other states. Whatever their political differences, Dela-

34. Munroe, *Federalist Delaware,* p. 105.
35. Munroe, *Federalist Delaware,* p. 108.

wareans recognized that their state could not survive as an autonomous entity tied only loosely into confederation with much more powerful states. In five days, on December 7, the convention decided to ratify, thus making Delaware the first state to accept participation in the constitution's promise of a more solid union.

The year that saw beginnings of the American experiment in national self-government under the constitution—1789—also witnessed the outbreak of revolution in France. It was a time of questioning of the political faiths of the past on both sides of the Atlantic. Although the war was over in America, the revolution was still in progress. Throughout the country, there was growing sentiment in favor of broader class participation in government within the checks and balances of state and national constitutional systems. These views were amply demonstrated in Delaware's new constitution of 1792, which removed all property qualifications for the suffrage but retained them for some offices. Henceforth, the franchise was to be open to any taxpayer who was a "white free man of the age of twenty-one years, having resided in the state two years." [36] The extension of the suffrage may have been more symbolic than real, however, according to one researcher who discovered that more people had voted in the last election under the old law than did in the first contest after 1792.[37] But many factors can influence voter turnout, so we must accept such findings with caution. The new state constitution also restored to the executive some of the power that had been taken from him in the heat of the conflict with England. Fear of a monarchical executive had dimmed, and it no longer seemed important to make the state's chief executive officer a creature of the legislature. Indeed, in the fashion of the checks-and-balances concept written into the federal constitution, it appeared to be far better to give him a wider share of power within the government, subject only to the

36. Munroe, *Federalist Delaware,* p. 196.
37. David P. Peltier, "Border State Democracy: A History of Voting in Delaware, 1682–1897," (Ph.D. dissertation, University of Delaware, 1967), p. 75.

will of the people. Consequently, the governor, as he was re-titled, was to be elected by the voters, rather than by the legislature.

Delaware also bowed to the prevailing notion among political philosophers that saw the two houses of the legislature checking one another: the upper house as spokesman for the well-to-do, versus the more popular lower house. The state constitution required that candidates for the state senate possess a much more considerable estate than those for the House of Representatives.

In 1792, while the convention was writing a state constitution, Kent County was building a new courthouse on the Dover green, providing the state legislature with its first permanent home since it had left New Castle in 1777. The combination statehouse-courthouse was designed as a two-story, rectangular brick structure with a gambrel roof capped by a cupola. Its most distinguishing features included a semicircular bay window in the middle of the rear wall and the first documented geometrical staircase built in America. The building contained a county courtroom, offices for county officials, and, on the second floor, the chambers for the two houses of the legislature. Victorianized beyond recognition in the 1870s, the building has recently undergone a complete restoration as part of Delaware's bicentennial effort. The legislature, now housed in Legislative Hall, built in 1933, does not plan to return, but a state court will use the building, and it will also function as a museum.

In the course of the 1790s, national issues dominated local politics, as Jefferson and Hamilton offered the country contrasting visions of its future. Generally speaking, the Hamiltonians, or Federalists, wished to promote American trade and manufactures and favored policies such as a strong federal government, a national bank, and close commercial ties with Great Britain. Their opponents, the Jeffersonian Democrat-Republicans, were, by contrast, sympathetic to the French Revolution and inclined toward states' rights and agricultural interests. In Delaware, those who had been conservatives during the war—men like George Read—gravitated toward Federalism, while their former radical opponents, like Thomas Rodney and Dr. James Tilton, joined with the Democrat-Republicans. The new political configuration thus perpetuated old divisions between anti-English, Presbyterian Scotch-Irishmen, whose power was concentrated in New Castle County, and Episcopalians, who dominated the southern counties. Politics really does make strange bedfellows, as the saying goes, and the allegiance of men is unpredictable. John Dickinson, for example, who was a political ally of the Read faction during the war, became a resolute Jeffersonian. More striking still is the fact that, in Delaware, Federalist strength lay in the rural areas, while the Democrat-Republicans were most powerful in the most mercantile and industrial part of New Castle County. E. I. du Pont, who came to Delaware in 1801 and became a leading manufacturer, was a personal friend of Thomas Jefferson and a supporter of his party. In that instance, as in many others, the apparent political anomaly can best be explained on the basis of ethnicity and cultural background. Du Pont, a Frenchman reared by a father who was a leader in the Age of Enlightenment, was a natural antagonist for the conservative-minded, pro-English Federalists to whom the Enlightenment was an anti-Christian intrusion likely to lead to social anarchy.

In spite of new directions in economic development and the existence of a strongly based Jefferson party, many Delawareans, especially in the southern counties, persisted in their allegiance to the Federalist party through the second decade of the nineteenth century, long after it had disappeared everywhere else except in New England. Delaware's Federalism, based upon the old social values of the state's agrarian landed gentry and the closely allied Episcopalian and Methodist religions, prompted Thomas Jefferson to typify Delaware as "a county of England." But as John Munroe persuasively argued, in his book *Federalist Delaware,* the longevity of Federalism in the First State also owed a great deal to the state party's willingness to bend with the times and copy their opponents' increasingly democratic party machinery. Like the Democrat-Republicans and unlike their partisans elsewhere, Delaware's Federalists abandoned the method of choosing the party's slate of candidates by the narrowly aristocratic method of the caucus in favor of the more liberal means of the nominating convention, which permitted the party rank and file to participte in the selection of their leaders. The Federalists successfully appealed to what Munroe called the "stand-pat" doctrine popular with downstaters "who faced none of the new conditions which bred radicalism on the frontier or in the city." [38]

During the first decade of the new century, Britain and Napoleonic France were locked in a life-and-death struggle that overflowed from Europe to the high seas and to the very shores of the United States. Foreign-policy matters became the most disconcordant issues in American national politics. Delaware's greatest statesman in that period was James A. Bayard, a Federalist senator who had entered the practice of law in New Castle in 1787. The descendant of a Huguenot family that had settled in nearby Maryland in the 1690s, James A. was the first in a long line of Bayards destined to play leading roles in Delaware's political history. His fame as a national figure rests upon two incidents: his decision, during the political crisis that followed the election of 1800, to desert his party and support Jefferson over Burr for the presidency; and his participation as the sole Federalist in the United States's delegation that secured a peace treaty with Great Britain in 1814.

During the United States Senate debates that preceded the declaration of war against Great Britain in 1812, Bayard no doubt spoke for the majority of Delawareans when he warned that such a challenge was folly. He argued that the United States should take all measures short of war to protect her shipping, but—as the representative of a coastal state—he was apprehensive of the sea power of such a mighty adversary. The senator's fears proved prophetic, for shortly after the war commenced, the British blockaded major American coastal ports from New York southward. A squadron of British ships, including a formidable seventy-four-gun man-of-war bigger than any ship in

38. Munroe, *Federalist Delaware*, p. 213, p. 239.

the American navy, appeared in the Delaware Bay early in 1813. The enemy ships, under the command of Commodore John Beresford, remained to bottle up the shipping of Philadelphia, Wilmington, New Castle, and the other river towns for more than a year. The squadron's presence was a constant menace to counties Sussex and Kent shore folk, who endured intermittent raids of British sailors in search of cattle and other food.

The most serious of the enemy assaults occurred in April 1813, when Beresford threatened to level the town of Lewes unless the townspeople supplied his ships with provisions. Colonel Samuel Davis, the dashing and experienced commander of the little town's paltry defenses, defiantly refused the British demands. After some delay, which allowed Davis time to augment his forces with militiamen from around the state and to secure gunpowder from the du Ponts, Beresford commenced his bombardment. The British had overwhelming artillery superiority. In addition to their 241 cannons, they fired numerous incendiary Congreve rockets, whose "red glare" was, on a similar occasion, made famous by Francis Scott Key. In response, the defenders had only two serviceable eighteen-pound cannons and two nine-pounders. Yet, ironically, the fortunes of war favored the meagerly equipped townsmen. Most of the British rockets overshot the town and landed harmlessly in the fields beyond. One that did come down in Lewes failed to explode. Because the bay was shallow near the shore, the British could not bring their ships into cannon range of the town, and their rain of cannonballs fell in the low swampland that separated Lewes from the bay. Throughout the day-long siege, small boys collected the spent balls so that the militia could keep up its equally ineffectual return fire. When Beresford realized the futility of his cannonade, he attempted to land a force of marines, but the militia drove them off. Finally, the commodore of the world's mightiest navy concluded that his squadron could not destroy an isolated little fishing town, and to the relief of the townsmen, he gave up the fight and sailed farther out into the bay. When the jubilant people of Lewes surveyed the destruction, they discovered that, although a few houses had been hit by stray cannon-balls, none was seriously damaged. No people had been harmed either, but a few head of livestock were wounded and a chicken was killed, prompting a town wit to say of this inglorious naval action: "The Commodore and all his men, shot a dog and killed a hen." [39] No foreign power has attacked Delaware since that day.

The War of 1812 produced several other Delaware heroes in addition to the courageous Davis and permitted old Revolutionary veterans to take up arms once again. Two important naval commanders came from Delaware. Jacob Jones, born near Smyrna, and a veteran of the war against the Tripoli pirates, thrilled Americans early in the war when his sloop *Wasp* defeated the H.M.S. *Frolic* in a spirited action fought in heavy seas off Cape Hatteras. Commodore Thomas McDonough of St. George's, Delaware, won a more significant battle on Lake Champlain in 1814 against a superior British force. The victory of his fleet, consisting of thirteen small vessels, destroyed British hopes for an invasion of the northern United States that might have cost the Americans land in the Great Lakes region at the peace talks. Another Delawarean, Dr. James Tilton, the Revolutionary pamphleteer, was selected by the Madison administration to be surgeon-general of the United States in recognition of his Democrat political principles as well as his former experience as a wartime doctor.

Politically, the war highlighted troubling difficulties in Delaware that presaged nationwide problems concerning immigrants, the relationship of factory owners to their employees, and the role of industry in society. In 1810, during the period of preparation for the possibility of war, a group of New Castle County manufacturers petitioned the state assembly to absolve their workers from militia duty. In support of their request, the industrialists pointed to the need for manufactured goods to spark Delaware's flagging agricultural economy and declared that mi-

39. William M. Marine, "The Bombardment of Lewes," *Historical and Biographical Papers,* 7 vols. (Wilmington: The Historical Society of Delaware, 1901), 3:27.

litia service by only one man in a work gang could gravely injure productivity. In addition, the factory owners claimed that their workers would learn dissipating habits of intemperance and slothfulness from contact with militiamen. E. I. du Pont and his brother Victor, a textile manufacturer, who both supported the petition, employed largely foreign-born laborers, especially Irishmen. It seems reasonable to conclude that they were eager to keep their employees isolated from life away from the tight-knit community at the Brandywine mills. After some lobbying by the du Ponts in Dover, the legislature passed a bill in 1811 that exempted workmen from military service in several industries, including powder-making and textiles.

When war was declared and the British blockaded the Delaware and Chesapeake bays, the du Ponts, fearful of an enemy attack on their property, requested the governor's permission to form their employees into military companies for the purpose of protecting the mills. The governor complied. E. I. and Victor were commissioned as captains, and the "Brandywine Rangers" began drilling with federally supplied weapons during their rare breaks from work. The du Ponts' actions were not kindly regarded by their Federalist farmer neighbors, who accused them of circumventing the state militia law and "raking the gutters of Philadelphia . . . to form a body of men to defend their own private property." [40]

The ill will engendered by the manufacturers' actions culminated on election day in 1813, when Victor du Pont marched the company's workers to the polls to vote the Democratic ticket under banners proclaiming "Domestic Manufacturers—Bees in peace, hornets in war." Their Federalist opponents countered with handbills stigmatizing the workmen as "Alien Enemies—Friends to Bonaparte, Marat, and Robespierre." [41] In the overheated political atmosphere, the confrontation soon disintegrated from name-calling into stone-throwing and fist fights.

40. Native Citizens of the State of Delaware, "To The Farmers and Citizens of the State of Delaware" (Wilmington: W. Riley, Printer, 1813 [?]).
41. Munroe, *Federalist Delaware*, p. 225.

After the election, the victorious Federalists repealed the law that had given the manufacturers their special military exemption on the grounds that the factories had become a refuge for draft-dodgers. The du Ponts bitterly denounced the action as politically motivated and told their workers that it was "a chastisement for your patriotism." [42] E. I. du Pont predicted that Federalist-leaning, poorly equipped downstate militia companies were "friends of England" who would never defend the upstate manufactories.[43] In another blow aimed at the industrialists, the Federalist-controlled assembly increased the penalties to be levied against aliens who attempted to vote. Thus, very early in the nineteenth century, Delaware was already split between its industrial north and rural south.

In the shifting political alignments of the postwar years, new national issues came to the fore in Delaware, and new leaders arose who played significant roles on the broader stage of the federal government. Louis McLane, son of Revolutionary hero Allen McLane, emerged as Delaware's chief Jacksonian Democrat, while John M. Clayton became the state's leading Whig. Both men served Delaware in the United States Congress for numerous terms and both rose to occupy seats in presidential cabinets.

Louis McLane originally entered politics in Delaware as a Federalist follower of James A. Bayard, whom he served as law clerk. He married into the wealthy Milligan family, who owned extensive lands along the Bohemia River in nearby northeastern Maryland. As a young Federalist congressman, McLane supported the Missouri Compromise of 1820, which attempted to remove slavery from national politics by defining its geographical limits. In the battles over the presidency in the 1820s, McLane aligned himself with Jackson against the John Quincy Adams-Henry Clay faction and became the most powerful Jackson supporter in Delaware. He served twice as minister to Eng-

42. Munroe, *Federalist Delaware,* p. 226.

43. B. G. du Pont, *Life of Eleuthère Irénée du Pont,* 11 vols. (Newark, Delaware: University of Delaware Press, 1925), 9:173.

land and filled the important posts of secretary of the treasury and secretary of state in President Jackson's cabinet. As secretary of the treasury during the president's famous war on the Second Bank of the United States, McLane demonstrated his independence of thought by refusing to acquiesce in Jackson's plan to bleed the bank dry by withdrawing federal funds into selected state-chartered banks. For that apostasy, he lost his standing in the Democratic party and ultimately left politics for a very successful career as president of the Baltimore and Ohio Railroad.

John Middleton Clayton was reared in Milford, Delaware, where he studied at local academies and assisted in his father's farming, milling, and tanning operations. He graduated with honors from Yale College, studied law, and returned to Delaware to practice in Dover. A large man, standing more than six feet tall, Clayton was gracious, friendly, and a good speaker. In politics, he supported Jackson's rival, Henry Clay, who favored a national bank, protective tariffs, and a strong union. Clayton's party, called the Whigs, arose in opposition to Jackson and became the dominant party in the state during the 1830s. The new party attracted support from two groups that had once been antagonists, the old Federalists among conservative-minded farmers and the New Castle County manufacturers. Clayton himself attributed much of the Whigs' success in Delaware to the liberal donations of the du Pont family, who, he asserted in 1851, "have spent a fortune for the Whig Party, and have never received a favor from it, for they never desired any." [44] For the powder makers, it was enough that the Whigs stood for policies designed to increase their markets and income, such as sound money and credit, high protective tariffs, and the expansion of transportation.

Disappointed at not receiving a federal post from William Henry Harrison, the first Whig president, Clayton later served as secretary of state in the brief administration of Zachary Tay-

44. John A. Munroe, "Party Battles, 1789–1850," in *Delaware, A History of the First State*, 1:153.

lor in 1849. In that role, he is best remembered for securing the Clayton-Bulwer Treaty with Great Britain, which prevented a rather nasty international dispute over access to the site for a possible isthmian canal in Central America.

In the late 1840s, Clayton built, on his farm southwest of New Castle, an elegant Greek-Revival mansion, which he named Buena Vista, in honor of the Whig General Taylor's Mexican War victory. There he introduced a number of improvements that increased the productivity of his lands and made his farm a model for other Delaware farmers. The house remained in the statesman's family until recently. It is presently owned by the state, which uses it as a conference center—a fitting memorial to the man who, when on his deathbed, implored James A. Bayard, Jr., "Don't let anyone abuse Delaware. I care not what else they may say." [45]

In the 1850s, as the crisis that ultimately led to civil war unfolded, Delawareans watched national politics in horror and fascination, unable to avert the catastrophe that they all feared. The vast majority of the little state's people damned all extremists, be they secessionists or abolitionists, who threatened to destroy the Union that Delaware had been first to join. Although the Diamond State ultimately emerged from the Civil War physically unscathed, it long bore scars from that tragic time. Not surprisingly, loyalty to the Union was most strong in New Castle County, while sympathy for the Confederacy was more commonly found in Kent and especially Sussex counties.

The political crisis of the 1850s destroyed the ties of Democrat and Whig that had been formed in the political battles of the Jacksonian age. The Whig party was split asunder by abolitionism and the temperance issue. Many former Whigs joined a new local party called the People's party that represented the interests of manufacturers. With the collapse of their opposition, the Democrats emerged as the state's major party. But since they combined two disparate groups, conservative farmers and the urban working-class immigrants, they were themselves easily

45. Munroe, "Party Battles," p. 150.

divided. At the outset of the Civil War, the leaders of the state's dominant party were the three Saulsbury brothers, Willard, Eli, and Gove, of Sussex County; and the Bayards of Wilmington, James A., Jr., and his son Thomas F. The two families led rival factions, each trying to take command of the state party. The Bayards, who had the support of the national party leadership, controlled federal patronage in Delaware during the Democratic administrations of the 1850s. The Saulsburys, with their strong local ties downstate, had considerable power over state government. Both factions were anti-Negro and consistently opposed both emancipation and citizenship for the blacks.

The election of 1860 was the most momentous and hard-fought in the history of the state and the nation. There were four candidates for the presidency. Stephen A. Douglas, the choice of the northern and midwestern Democrats, appealed for a compromise on the devisive issue of slavery in United States territories on the basis of his popular-sovereignty concept that would give each western territory the right to decide whether it should be slave or free. John C. Breckinridge, the choice of the southern Democrats, stood by the Supreme Court's ruling in the Dred Scott Case that slaves could be taken into a territory in the same way as any other property. Abraham Lincoln, candidate of the Republican party, opposed the extension of slavery into U.S. territories; and James Bell was the candidate of the short-lived Constitutional Union party, whose adherents hoped that, by ignoring the slavery issue, they could make it go away. Delaware's Democratic factions were for once together in their support of Breckinridge and opposition to Douglas, whom both the Bayards and Saulsbury regarded as a self-serving political trickster. Very few Delawareans were Republicans, because the party was tainted by the issue of abolitionism. In 1856, the new party received only 307 votes in the entire state, every one from New Castle County. In 1860, the People's party served as an umbrella for most people who opposed the Democrats.

The campaign was as colorful as it was vitriolic. The parties outdid themselves in staging huge torchlight parades, rallies, and fireworks displays that kept emotions at a high pitch. Meanwhile, the partisan newspapers issued blast after blast against the opposition, as each party claimed that the victory of any other would lead to rupture and civil war. The Democrats, especially, pilloried the Republicans and their cousins in the People's party as "nigger-lovers" who would amalgamate the races. Election results gave a clear victory to the Breckinridge forces, which received 7,323 votes to 3,833 for Bell, 3,811 for Lincoln and 1,001 for Douglas. Put another way, however, the Democrats' triumph was not so impressive: 8,324 people voted with the Democrats, while 7,644 voted against them. But the Democrats carried every county including New Castle, which they won by 173 votes. Of the meaning of that important contest, Harold Hancock concluded in his study, *Delaware During the Civil War,* that "The Democrats won the election by playing upon the fears of Delawareans that the Republicans were enemies of slavery, believers in Negro equality, and dissolvers of the Union." [46]

As the cotton states began their parade toward secession in the wake of the Republican national triumph, representatives from the Confederate States journeyed to Delaware and to the other border states to urge them to join with the South. That, Delaware's state legislature made clear, it would never do. "As Delaware was the first to adopt, so will she be the last to abandon the Federal Constitution," the assemblymen told a Georgian representative. Yet, many Delawareans believed that their sister slave states should be allowed to withdraw from the Union peacefully, if that was their wish. When the newly installed president sent a relief expedition to the Federal troops at Fort Sumter in the Charleston harbor, Senator Bayard declared that Lincoln would be remembered "in after ages as a monster" if he led the nation into war. [47]

The outbreak of hostilities magnified the intense excitement and suspense that hung over not only Delaware but the whole

46. Harold B. Hancock, *Delaware during the Civil War* (Wilmington, Delaware: Historical Society of Delaware, 1961), p. 37.

47. Hancock, *Delaware during the Civil War,* p. 46, p. 54.

nation. Union supporters flocked to the Wilmington railroad station to bring food and first aid to soldiers from Massachusetts and Pennsylvania, who had been wounded by Confederate sympathizers in Baltimore en route to Washington. The Unionists feared that the state's Democratic militia units might prove disloyal and held mass meetings throughout Delaware to stiffen support for the Union and to raise loyal militia companies. A Wilmington lady confided to her diary,

> All at once the flames of Civil War seem raging around us—we hear of our friends and acquaintances enlisting in various places and feel an anxiety and dread that we never dreamed of before.—The telegraph wires have been cut, Railroads torn up and Mails from the South suspended, and we are all the time agitated by alarming and conflicting rumors. We seem threatened not only with war but anarchy, as the Capital and the Government are in great danger . . . Baltimore is in possession of the mob . . . and everybody is absorbed by the anxiety prevailing for the welfare and existence of our country.[48]

Delawareans were bitterly divided over the war. Probably a majority agreed with the state's Democratic senators, Willard Saulsbury and James A. Bayard, Jr., in their belief that the South should be allowed to go in peace. Democratic politicians accused the administration not only of flagrant assaults on constitutional liberties, but of plotting Negro equality. Their opponents responded with cries of treason. In Camden, a typical, formerly peaceful country town south of Dover, a resident recalled that, after the Battle of Bull Run, "one-half of the town did not speak or associate with the other half." [49] William Ross, a one-time governor of the state from Seaford whose son had gone to enlist in the Confederate army, decided to live out the war abroad rather than face harassment and possible imprisonment as a traitor. In 1862, two companies of loyal Maryland troops appeared suddenly in Dover and disarmed the local al-

---

48. Hancock, *Delaware during the Civil War,* pp. 62–63.
49. Hancock, *Delaware during the Civil War,* p. 84.

legedly pro-Confederate militiamen. The threat of an intrastate insurrection was reduced, however, when the governor appointed a Republican, General Henry du Pont, a West Point graduate and president of his family's powder company, to be major general of the state militia. Du Pont saw to it that henceforth only loyal companies would receive arms.

In spite of the strong influence of the Democrats, most Delawareans who served in the war fought on the Union side, and the Blue Hen State provided more soldiers to the United States, in proportion to the state's total population, than any other state. Estimates of the number of Delawareans serving in the Confederate army vary greatly, but the number could not have exceeded a few hundred. Their route to the Confederacy was the reverse of Harriet Tubman's underground railroad for escaped slaves, via the Nanticoke River from Seaford to the Chesapeake Bay. Not only men, but large quantities of medical supplies, food, and other contraband traveled that route down the peninsular railroad to Seaford and then by water to the Virginia coast. Union officials captured a few of the small craft that practiced the trade, but most eluded them.

Elections during the war years were bitterly contested. In 1862, some Republican businessmen in Wilmington, who claimed that their rivals would steal the election by intimidating loyalist voters, called upon the federal government to send troops to maintain order at the polls. Two days before the election, Maryland and New York troops landed at Seaford and were dispatched to polling places throughout Kent and Sussex counties, while Delaware soldiers performed the same duty in New Castle County. Although no major incidents occurred on election day, Delaware voters faced naked bayonets as they went to the polls, and the Democrats were enraged. The voting was very close. The Democratic candidate won election to the House of Representatives by a mere thirty-seven votes out of more than sixteen thousand cast, but a Republican, William Cannon, a former Democrat from Sussex County, was elected governor. Afterwards, the Democrat-controlled state assembly conducted exhaustive hearings that proved to their satisfaction that the use of federal troops had been a tyrannical, unjustified attempt to frighten antiadministration voters.

From the floor of the United States Senate, Willard Saulsbury raised his invective against the president and his policies to new heights after the election by calling Lincoln "a despot, a man perfectly regardless of every constitutional right of the people," and contradictorily, "a weak and imbecile man." [50] Meanwhile, in Dover, the legislature studiously ignored the will of Governor Cannon, spurned his appeals to support the war effort, and passed bills whereby the state would assist drafted men in paying their way out of the commitment to serve their country.

Although Delaware escaped becoming a battlefield, the state does boast one authentic remnant of the Civil War in Fort Delaware, an imposing stone fortress that commands the Delaware River from tiny, swampy Pea Patch Island opposite Delaware City. The federal government built the fort in the 1850s to guard against potential foreign naval invasion. When it became clear that the Confederates were not a threat to the river, the fort was converted into a prisoner-of-war camp. Thousands of Rebel soldiers and a few disaffected civilians rotted away in its musty corridors. Some hardy prisoners managed to escape by swimming to the shore, where they found willing accomplices to help spirit them back to the South. Thousands more died and were buried on the Jersey shore. The number of prisoners in the fort rose with each campaign and battle until they numbered nearly thirteen thousand after Gettysburg, spilling out of the fort itself and into temporary barracks throughout the island. In the South, the gloomy monster was a monument to federal tyranny, but it was certainly no worse than Libby Prison in Richmond or the horrors of Andersonville. The fort has since been somewhat altered by refurbishing during the Spanish-American War, when more modern artillery was installed, but its forbidding presence continues to remind Delawareans of the fratricidal war that once so disrupted their state.

The Civil War left Delaware with deep-seated hatreds. One

50. Hancock, *Delaware during the Civil War*, p. 129.

old survivor from Kent County told a Dover audience in 1902
that he had seen "bosom friends who differed . . . and went to
their graves, hating one another, leaving the old hatred to their
children, in many instances, their only legacy." [51] For years afterward, Republicans continued to vilify the Democrats as traitors, only to be called "nigger lovers" and "race amalgama-
tors" in return. The state legislature refused to ratify the
Thirteenth Amendment that finally freed the state's remaining
slaves and rejected the Fourteenth Amendment by a margin of
fifteen to six, the six being all from New Castle County.

The single most disturbing outcome of the war for white
Delawareans was Negro suffrage, which became law throughout
the United States in 1869 with the adoption of the Fifteenth
Amendment. Slavery had played a minor role in the state's
economy and could have been eliminated without trauma, but
the sudden enfranchisement of nearly 20 percent of the state's
people was another matter altogether. An overwhelming number
of whites shared the view that blacks were inherently inferior;
only a few agreed with black leaders and white abolitionists in
ascribing the Africans' poverty and ignorance to social conditions rather than genetics. Democrats had particularly strong
reasons for wanting to thwart the blacks' exercise of their Fifteenth Amendment rights, for they recognized that black voters
would flock to support the party of Lincoln, the Emancipator.
The very idea of blacks being in proximity to polling places had
always been abhorrent to many Delawareans. As early as 1798,
before the creation of local election districts, the legislature had
passed a law barring blacks, either slave or free, from entering a
county seat on election day unless a master could prove that
they were there on an urgent matter.[52] The postwar Democrats
were, therefore, acting in response to long-held custom as well
as partisan advantage when they adopted a new law in 1873
designed to prevent blacks from voting.

To understand how blacks were disenfranchised, it is neces-

---

51. Hancock, *Delaware during the Civil War,* p. 178.
52. Peltier, "Border State Democracy," p. 119.

sary to look more closely at Delaware's election practices. In 1870, the Republicans, counting on several thousand votes from the blacks, predicted their first victory in Delaware; but on election day, their hopes were dashed as the Democrats swept the state elections. In the aftermath of their defeat, the Republicans protested that their loss had been engineered through their opponents' flagrant abuses of the election laws. Delaware was then operating under a constitution written in 1831, which had preserved the 1792 requirement that voters be taxpayers. A constitutional convention in 1853 had sought to eliminate that voting prerequisite, which was becoming out of step with the practices of other states and had proven itself to be ripe for fraud. For reasons that had nothing to do with the voting provision, however, that constitution had failed to secure enough support to be adopted. In consequence, the state was left with a defective suffrage law. Under it, property owners were required to pay a special poll tax to a county tax collector in order to qualify. By the 1850s, politicians had discovered that many poor people failed to vote under that law and that one way to increase the voter turnout was to furnish such people with counterfeited tax receipts and ballots already thoughtfully filled out with the names of the party's candidates. The more honest politicians actually paid the poll taxes and handed out legitimate receipts along with the ballots.

In 1870, the tax collectors were all Democrats who used various means of evasion to prevent blacks from paying their taxes and securing the necessary receipt. The Republicans collected enough evidence against one of these officials to have him tried for wilfully evading his duties. At the trial, several blacks testified that the defendant had refused either to let them into his office or to take their money. The Republicans won their case, and there was mass consternation among the Democrats. In 1873, the overwhelmingly Democratic legislature passed laws that shifted responsibility for tax assessment and tax collection from the county officials to the taxpayers, thus, in effect, restoring their old system.

In the years that followed, election fraud became an even

more prevalent part of life in the First State than before. Constitutional guaranties were utterly ignored. Delaware's unsavory election practices attracted national attention from reform-minded, muckraking journalists. A writer for the *North American Review* complained in 1885 that "There seems to be no doubt that the old Commonwealth of Delaware is substantially in possession of a thoroughly organized band of political conspirators [the Democrats], who have taken it out of the hands of the people, and hold it under their own absolute dictation." Another magazine described Delaware as the only state "which maintains so composedly and so contentedly the usages and ideas of the medieval period of American politics." [53] Meanwhile, the Democrats continued to play upon the race issue to protect their control of state politics and to perpetuate conservative agrarian interests. But more than one could play the game of bribery and corruption, and the law of 1873 that piled up their majorities could also be manipulated to destroy them.

Enter onto the scene John Edward Charles O'Sullivan Addicks—"Gas" Addicks, the Napoleon of Gas, utility magnate, and would-be United States senator. Addicks, the son of a minor political figure in Philadelphia, showed a flare for speculative business dealings that won him control of several urban gas monopolies during the 1880s, including the Chicago Gas Trust and Boston's Bay State Gas Company. Although his business connections took him to all parts of the country, the gas king maintained a residence in Claymont, Delaware, from which he commuted by train to Philadelphia. Nevertheless, he was a complete unknown in Delaware when, in 1889, he suddenly appeared in Dover, nattily dressed in a tall silk hat and a sealskin coat and carrying a gold-headed cane, and announced his candidacy for the state's vacant seat in the U.S. Senate to the astonished Republican legislators.

It was through a fluke of politics that the Republicans had gained control of the legislature at all. In the elections of 1888,

53. Amy M. Hiller, "The Disfranchisement of Delaware Negroes," *Delaware History* 13 (October 1968):151–152.

two Democrats, Eli Saulsbury and James L. Wolcott, had so
divided the majority party that the GOP was for the first time in
possession of the legislature and in a position to choose one of
Delaware's senators. Addicks could not hope to be elected that
year, but even though another Republican was chosen, the gas
man was beginning to put together a following. The Delaware
Republican organization had been limited to New Castle
County, with a few minor outposts in downstate commercial
towns. Its supporters were mostly men in the business community who were attracted to the party because of its stand for high
tariffs and other favors to manufacturers. In 1894, the Republicans suddenly won victories all over the state, in areas where
they had never shown strength before, especially in Sussex
County. The surprised politicians discovered that Mr. Addicks
had advanced the party a large sum of money to pay delinquent
county taxes downstate. Addicks's presence and tactics split the
GOP. While some jubilant Republicans saw Addicks's money
as manna from heaven and flocked to support his senatorial
campaign, others, particularly among the old party men of the
northern county, regarded him as a self-seeking carpetbag-
ger.

   In 1895, when another U.S. Senate seat became vacant, the
state legislature was paralyzed into a single-issue battle over
who was to be elected. Although the Republicans held the majority, some of them joined with the Democrats to deny Addicks
the seat. After an exhausting 210 ballots, the legislators adjourned, leaving Delaware still shy one seat in the U.S. Senate.
At this point, Addicks thought that he had found the formula for
success, even though his quest was as yet unfulfilled. While his
lieutenants tried to persuade old-time Republicans to support
him on the grounds that he had saved the Republican party in
Delaware, he himself unwisely boasted of having paid for the
election in Sussex.[54] In 1896, friction within the party had
become so vituperative that the party split into two factions, and

54. Henry M. Canby, Jr., "J. Edward Addicks: A History of His Political Activities
in Delaware" (Senior Thesis, Princeton University, 1932), p. 13.

the Democrats temporarily won back control of the state assembly and named their own senator. Year after year, the three-sided battle went on. In 1899, Addicks allegedly spent $300,000 in Delaware, but still fell a few votes short in more than a hundred ballots taken at Dover. By that time, the new constitution of 1897 had eliminated the poll tax, so that dollars from the gas magnate went into direct bribes estimated to go as high as $50 per voter as well as toward such devices as paying off farm mortgages to buy support.

The National Republican party was acutely embarrassed by the bad publicity emanating from little Delaware, where journalists reported votes being sold as if at auction.[55] In 1901, Mark Hanna, the Cincinnati kingmaker who had secured the presidency for William McKinley, was appalled to discover that, although both Senate seats in Delaware were vacant and the Republicans controlled the state legislature, they could not agree on the selection of two senators. Not even the national chairman could persuade the warring factions to co-operate until 1903, when the regulars finally assented to the selection of one of Addicks's chief supporters, but not to Addicks himself. Colonel H. A. du Pont, a leader of the anti-Addicks "Regular" faction, said he would not consent to enter the Senate if Addicks were elected to serve there for as long as fifteen minutes.

By the time of the elections of 1904, even the perennially optimistic Addicks recognized that it was now or never for his senatorial aspirations. In a signed editorial in his own *Wilmington Sun,* he declared that there would be no more compromises. But the gas king's hold on Delaware politics was already in eclipse. That same year, his Bay State Gas Company was forced into receivership, and the flood of Addicks's money into campaign coffers was reduced to a trickle. Long-time supporters began deserting him and going over to the Regulars who, with Henry A. du Pont's money, were able to play politics Addicks-style.

In 1906, even Addicks knew he was finished, when the legislature chose as senator his implacable enemy, du Pont. A Dem-

55. Canby, "Addicks: A History," p. 70.

ocratic judge who had fought Addicks for years recalled that he had seen the fallen warrior on that day, leaving the State House to walk to a hotel on the Dover Green. Instead of the crowd that had always surrounded him before, Addicks was alone; instead of appearing dapper, as he had formerly been, he was shabbily dressed, and no follower carried his coat. The sight made even his old antagonist feel sorry for him.[56] The downhill slide for the former Napoleon of Gas did not end until 1919, when he died a pauper in a cheap flat in Brooklyn.

It has become something of a convention in writing about Delaware to consider the Addicks affair an aberration in the state's political history and to blame the gas man for instituting corruption in the First State. Such claims distort our view of Delaware's political development. Chicanery was a fixed part of the state's elections as early as the Revolution, when Caesar Rodney comments on it in his correspondence. In the nineteenth century, fraud became institutionalized. By the 1880s, both parties maintained funds to pay poll taxes and to bribe voters. Addicks merely did these things on a larger scale than had been done before. Nor did Delaware eliminate corruption when it got rid of Addicks. The Republican politicians who deserted his sinking ship merely switched their allegiance to the du Ponts, Henry A. and his nephew T. Coleman, who adopted the same style of vote-buying to establish and maintain their family's long reign as leaders of the state GOP. In 1932, a prominent Sussex County attorney, son of an Addicks lieutenant, wrote in defense of his father's political bedfellow that Addicks was neither the first nor the last to corrupt the state's politics with bribes, and that the practice was still prevalent. At the same time, another old Addicks supporter, playing the role of the pot calling the kettle black, claimed that the Addicks organization never bought Negro votes at the primaries, a practice, he noted, that the du Pont faction did follow.[57] Leaving aside these accusations, Addicks's most lasting influence on Delaware politics

56. Canby, "Addicks: A History," p. 96.
57. Canby, "Addicks: A History," p. 72.

was in promoting the growth of the Republican party from a hopelessly outnumbered handful to a position as the state's major party, ultimately under the control not of Gas Addicks, but of the far wealthier du Pont clan.

It was Delaware's small size that most attracted Addicks and gave him the false belief that he could convert its relatively few citizens to the cause of his advancement. The single-taxers, with their more altruistic motives, were also misled during the 1890s into thinking that they could convert such a small state. They, too, failed, but they left behind as a remembrance of their campaign the town of Arden, a unique community overflowing with rustic charm, north of Wilmington, that perpetuates the single-tax ideal to this day. The single-tax panacea was the creation of Henry George, America's first popular economic philosopher. His book *Progress and Poverty* was a sensation in the 1870s. George grappled with a question that confounded his age: Why, in the midst of such economic progress, should there be so much poverty in America? In the manner of other nineteenth-century economists, George assumed that there were immutable laws governing the economy and that, if things were out of kilter, the reason must lie in society's ignorant trampling on those unseen laws. He concluded that America's troubles resulted from the fact that landowners received enormous unearned benefits when the labor of the whole community raised the value of land. His plan for rectifying that disproportionate income was a single tax on land value that would replace all other taxation.

Some urban reformers embraced the George thesis with religious zeal and concluded that, if they could convert just one state to the single tax, their skeptics would be satisfied. Having chosen Delaware as the object of their campaign, reformers from Philadelphia and New York invaded the tiny state in 1895 and deluged it with propaganda in the hope of winning control of the state government in the 1896 elections. Their showing, far more hopelessly disappointing than that of Mr. Addicks, was only 3 percent of the total vote cast. Henry Seidel Canby, author and literary critic, wrote in a nostalgic recollection of his upper-class Quaker boyhood in Wilmington that the Georgeites marched upon Delaware, a blue-coated army of propagandists, speaking at street corners, dropping handbills at our doors, arguing even with the peach farmer on his lonely plantation. Never was effort so completely wasted. We were so uneconomic in our thinking, and so confident of the essential rightness of our order, that not even a scratch was made upon the complacency of our comfortable society. No one listened, or at least no one was effectively moved, not even among the workmen on strike, or the vegetable growers strangling under the grip of the one railroad that gave them access to market.'' [58]

The reformers did not give up, but they did reduce the scale of their prospective model from a state to a single community. By 1900, when Arden was founded, Henry George, who had doubted that the single tax could be fairly tested in only one town, was dead. Delaware's single-tax town was the brainchild of two versatile Philadelphia artists, Frank Stephens and Will Price, who were followers not only of Henry George but also of the crafts-revival ideals popularized in England by William Morris and John Ruskin. Stephens and Price were also devotees of the theater, especially of Shakespeare, and the name *Arden* came from the forest retreat for exiles in *As You Like It*. As a retreat from the pressures of city life and as a fulcrum for the arts, Arden, with its theater, guild hall, and quaint Elizabethan architecture, has attracted not only artists and writers such as Upton Sinclair but also many more prosaic people. Outside interferences, such as the income tax, have hampered the community's efforts to prove the validity of the single tax, just as Henry George feared; but the experimental single-tax town, now surrounded by conventional suburban developments, still retains its unique personality as a place where the arts are a part of life itself.

Another crusade that was shaking Delaware's politics at the turn of the century was woman suffrage. Suffrage agitation, which began in Delaware in the wake of the Civil War, attracted the support of such former abolitionists as Thomas Garrett and

---

58. Henry Seidel Canby, *The Age of Confidence* (New York: Farrar and Rinehart, 1934), pp. 230–231.

of women who had been engaged in wartime service work. Initially, the reformers had reason to predict rapid public acceptance for female suffrage. Wilmington's most widely read newspaper editorialized that "the next generation of ladies will, doubtless, receive possession of their right to vote. . . . Like the old anti-slavery work, it [woman suffrage] moves slowly, and finds its difficulties more in the apathy and indifference of the people, than in the real strength of its opponents." [59] Apathy and indifference abounded. For many years, the most active suffragist in Delaware was Mary Ann Stuart, a widow from a prominent family in Greenwood, who seemed to be battling all alone. During the 1870s, she appeared regularly at each session of the state legislature to lobby for the proposed suffrage amendment, and each year she paid her taxes under protest. Mrs. Stuart had some success in getting the legislature to modify laws that had given husbands control over their wives' property and earnings, but her arguments could not win their support for the suffrage.

The seventies and eighties were a time of slow beginnings for woman suffrage in Delaware. The Women's Christian Temperance Union, which attracted many members in this predominantly Methodist state, was a major factor in bringing socially conservative, middle-class women into the suffrage movement. Well-to-do women learned from their work in such organizations as the women's clubs and the Associated Charities that they needed political power in order to enact reforms in education and at prisons and similar public institutions. In 1895, a group of women involved in Wilmington's New Century Club and in local social work organized a Wilmington Equal Suffrage Club, which soon expanded to include statewide membership. In 1897, the suffragists were allowed to present a petition with the signatures of 1,592 men and 1,228 women, together with oral arguments, at a hearing of the state constitutional convention. When the convention later voted down an equal-suffrage resolution by a vote of seventeen to seven, a Wilmington newspaper declared apologetically that most women still opposed the

59. *Wilmington Daily Commercial,* November 12, 1869.

franchise, but that "when the women of Delaware unitedly ask
for the privilege of voting . . . it may be granted them." [60]
That setback must have seemed particularly demoralizing, because the amendment process under the new constitution was
very cumbersome, requiring a two-thirds vote of two successive
legislatures.

During the next two decades, the suffragists worked persis-
tently at the task of altering public opinion. A few Delaware
women became important suffrage leaders at the national level.
Mrs. Florence Bayard Hilles, daughter of Thomas F. Bayard, a
former Delaware senator and secretary of state in the first Cleveland administration, and Mabel Vernon, a Wilmington-born
graduate of Swarthmore College, were active in Alice Paul's
dynamic Congressional Union, which worked to convert the
federal government to equality of the sexes. As a young professional suffrage organizer, Mabel Vernon gained notoriety when
she interrupted President Woodrow Wilson's speech at the dedication of the Labor Temple in Washington with cries of "What
are you going to do about votes for women?" Both she and
Mrs. Hilles were later arrested and jailed for their participation
in a march on the White House in 1917. As charter members of
the Women's party, which grew out of the Congressional
Union, they were among the initial champions of the Equal
Rights Amendment during the 1920s.

It was not until 1918 that the suffragists could see the possibility of victory in sight. That year, the United States Congress
was expected to vote for the Nineteenth Amendment preparatory
to the amendment's submission to the states for final ratification. A delegation of suffragists met with the Delaware senators, Josiah O. Wolcott and Willard Saulsbury, but failed to persuade either of them to support the amendment. By May of that
year, however, a prosuffragist had replaced Saulsbury, and so
Delaware's delegation was split on the final vote in the Senate,
while in the House the state's lone representative voted for the
amendment.

60. *Wilmington Every Evening*, February 17, 1897.

Attention then turned to the states, since acceptance by thirty-six was necessary for ratification. Because many states had already accepted the amendment, the suffragists concentrated on those uncommitted states, including Delaware, where they thought they stood a good chance of swaying legislatures. The suffragists had powerful allies in Delaware. T. Coleman du Pont and Alfred I. du Pont, rivals for state Republican leadership, and Governor John Townsend, Jr., actively supported the amendment, as did both major party organizations and an array of other groups, ranging from the Methodist Church to the State Federation of Labor. But the women, taking no chances, toured the state giving speeches and holding rallies to increase their support. When the Delaware legislators convened in January of 1920, those women who had worked so long and so hard for the vote felt confident that their final victory was near.

As other states accepted the amendment, excitement mounted when it appeared that Delaware, the first state to ratify the Constitution, might be the decisive thirty-sixth state to bring into the Constitution the Nineteenth Amendment that belatedly promised the rights of citizenship to half the nation's people. But, contrary to their earlier sanguine expectations, the suffragists discovered that many legislators in Dover were backing away from the amendment. The Pennsylvania Railroad, then a powerful influence in the legislature, was lobbying against ratification, and some assemblymen identified votes for women with such controversial issues as prohibition and P. S. du Pont's school code. In March and April, the suffragists put on a massive effort to secure a favorable vote, but their work was countered by that of the women in the increasingly effective antisuffrage campaign. At the Delaware General Assembly's hearing on ratification, both sides fought to achieve propaganda victories. According to one of the "pros," the "antis" brought to Dover "every farmer and small politician they could secure and . . . pinned a red rose [their symbol] in his buttonhole." [61] Their opponents,

61. Mary R. de Vou, "The Woman-Suffrage Movement in Delaware," in *Delaware, A History of the First State*, 1:364.

meanwhile, installed behind the speaker's chair a yellow banner that read "Votes For Women" and handed out yellow jonquils to the many suffrage supporters who had flocked to the little town. Mrs. Carrie Chapman Catt, president of the Woman's National American Suffrage Association, made one of her many trips to Delaware to address the combined houses of the General Assembly on behalf of the amendment. Telegrams poured in from President Wilson, members of his cabinet, and other prominent national figures, urging the legislature to adopt the amendment.

With the eyes of the nation fastened upon them, the legislators refused to be pressured into accepting the amendment. Defying their national party leadership, a group of assemblymen telegraphed the Speaker of the Mississippi House of Representatives, "Stand firm against ratification. Delaware Legislature still firm for state's rights and will not ratify." [62] Governor Townsend, an untiring supporter of equal suffrage, saw that Delaware might refuse its opportunity to be the decisive state and went to New York to persuade T. Coleman du Pont to use his great influence for ratification. Du Pont had some luck with New Castle County politicians, but even he could not win over "anti" votes from downstate.

In April, when the Republicans met in their state convention at Dover, the suffragists staged their greatest demonstration extravaganza yet. "Every road was ablaze with decorated automobiles and hundreds of suffragists arrived on every train." [63] The town was treated to an orgy of decorations as American flags and suffrage banners hung everywhere. The massive display culminated in the presentation of petitions for the amendment signed by more than twenty thousand Delaware women and a parade of suffragists' children. Whether in response to that mighty outpouring or not, the Republicans unanimously adopted a resolution calling for ratification. Most Democrats had by this time moved into the "anti" camp, however, in

62. De Vou, "The Woman-Suffrage Movement," p. 365.
63. De Vou, "The Woman-Suffrage Movement," p. 366.

spite of the pleas of a Democratic president in the White House. Some may have been influenced by railroad lobbyists, but the biggest issues for them seem to have been their stands against prohibition and against the new school law that threatened to raise taxes. After all the intense excitement, the actual vote in May was something of a let-down. The state senate accepted the amendment overwhelmingly, eleven to six; but in the House, the antis had secured enough votes to force an adjournment before a vote could be taken. Thus, rather anticlimactically, Delaware lost its chance to be the decisive state to Tennessee, which ratified in August 1920.

The struggle over woman suffrage demonstrated that the old, conservative, rural elements could still muster great power in Delaware, but their day was rapidly passing. The du Ponts, determined to bring Delaware into the twentieth century, would brook no obstacles. P. S. du Pont, head of the large clan and leader of a company that had done an astonishing total business of nearly a billion dollars in the recent war, would get his new school code and build his schools. T. Coleman could employ his wealth not only to finance the state's principal highway, but to control the Republican party. He used his political power to secure the necessary public support for his highway and ultimately to get himself elected to the U.S. Senate. Not all the political snares in the paths of the du Pont cousins came from downstate farmers, however, for their most powerful and bitter opposition came from within their own family.

Just before the outbreak of World War I, T. Coleman decided to sell his share of Du Pont Company stock. Through a series of misunderstandings that Alfred I. du Pont interpreted as double-dealing, the stock was not bought by the company, but, rather, went into a securities company created by Pierre to benefit his own immediate family and a few close associates. The outraged Alfred, along with a number of other du Pont relatives who had been left out of the deal, brought suit in the federal courts in 1915, just as gigantic wartime profits had begun to swell the value of the contested stock. The case of *du Pont* v. *du Pont* remained in litigation for four years, poisoning family relationships, until it was finally settled in Pierre's favor in 1919. The family rift was complicated by other factors that made it difficult to reconcile. Alfred, described as "the family rebel" by biographer Marquis James,[64] had earlier shocked his family's sense of propriety by divorcing his wife to marry a divorced cousin in 1907. When Alfred I. discovered that he and his second wife had become socially unacceptable within the family, he built himself a huge marble-and-limestone palace, surrounded by a high stone wall topped with multicolored bits of chopped glass to keep his relatives at bay. Perhaps more important to the rupture, certainly from a business point of view, were Alfred's old-fashioned attitudes toward the company. He retained strong emotional ties to the relatively small-scale black-powder yards of his youth, in a day when Pierre and T. Coleman were expanding the company from a family-run concern into a broad-based giant corporation in which explosives would have only a minor role. Alfred, who as a college boy had once traded punches with John L. Sullivan, would not be cast off without making a fight. Although he did not wish to hold public office, he retaliated by trying to deny it to his cousin Coly.

Alfred bought a bank, the Delaware Trust Company, to rival his cousins' Wilmington Trust, and he built a building for it that was taller than the Du Pont Building, just one block away. He bought a newspaper, the *Wilmington Morning News,* to attack Coleman's political machine, and in 1916 he managed to hurt the Republicans so much that Josiah Wolcott, the Democratic candidate for the U.S. Senate, got elected. A few years later, T. Coleman thought he had found a way around Alfred's machinations when the Republican governor offered Wolcott the post of chancellor in Delaware's Court of Chancery. Wolcott resigned from the Senate, and the governor appointed Coleman to fill out his term. Alfred so blasted his cousin with shrill cries about "Delaware's Dirty Deal" that the Democrats beat Coleman again in 1922, and it was not until 1924 that his ambition

64. Marquis James, *Alfred I. du Pont, the Family Rebel* (Indianapolis: The Bobbs-Merrill Co., 1941).

to be elected senator was finally realized. Two years later, Alfred relinquished his position as spoiler in Delaware's Republican politics and moved to Florida. When he did, he sold the *Morning News* to the Christiana Securities Co., Pierre's holding company for the Du Pont stock that had been at the center of the whole dispute. Christiana Securities thus acquired all the daily newspapers in Wilmington, in addition to ownership of a controlling share of the Du Pont Company and the state's best-financed bank, the Wilmington Trust Company.

By the 1930s, as the family split faded into insignificance, Pierre was the unquestioned leader of the du Ponts, and the du Ponts were the most powerful force in Delaware. Their largess was legendary, their wealth immense. Well-kept du Pont estates followed one after another along the gently rolling hills that led from Wilmington to Kennett Square, Pennsylvania, where Pierre had laid out his beautifully landscaped gardens at Longwood. Ordinary people in Wilmington regarded the du Ponts and their equally prestigious in-laws with awe. They were seldom criticized, most certainly not in the newspapers. It was a standing joke that if a du Pont did anything unflattering in public, it would appear only in the Philadelphia press. Wilmingtonians had many reasons to be grateful to them. The du Ponts had revived the city's faltering economy, had provided the city with a first-class hotel and theater, had endowed its hospitals, expanded the state college, and were the leaders in a variety of other public works and charities. But the people of Wilmington, and of Delaware as well, paid a price for these many benefits.

In 1934, *Fortune* magazine came to Delaware to study the relationship between the state and its leading family. The magazine's editors were interested in the workings of the nation's largest, most diverse, and most effectively organized chemical corporation "as an example of the concentration of power into the hands of one family, as a model of U.S. industrial management, and as an illustration of capitalistic influence upon social and political institutions." Although they coyly refrained from answering the question "Do the du Ponts own Delaware?", the magazine's writers did conclude that "the logical social result

of American capitalism—an aristocracy of great wealth—has
been more clearly achieved in Wilmington than anywhere else
in the U.S." Accustomed to writing about corporate leaders in
New York or Chicago, *Fortune* found the juxtaposition of an industrial giant in a pigmy state strange, if not slightly immoral.
They described the family as "self-righteous" and "self-satis-
fied," living "in a feudal atmosphere thoroughly inconsistent
with the contemporary science that supports them." As for the
du Ponts' political power, the magazine wrote, "Nobody seriously denies that Delaware politics stink. But the sad truth is
that nobody believes they can ever be reformed. Many people
believe that the du Pont influence is the best in the state. However they do it, the du Ponts have a reputation for exerting a
wholesome influence once they are in power." The du Ponts
showed a propensity for marrying into Delaware families that
had historically claimed great political power. Du Pont daughters married a Saulsbury and a Bayard. At the time when the
Fortune articles appeared, Delaware's governor was C. Douglass
Buck, a great-nephew of John M. Clayton and son-in-law of the
late T. Coleman du Pont. As a former highway engineer on
Coleman's state road, Buck was a driving force behind badly
needed improvements for Delaware's secondary road system.
Even in the troubled thirties, Delawareans were inclined to accept du Pont power, as long as it brought du Pont money and
expertise.[65]

By the end of World War II, democracy in Delaware faced a
challenge at least as great as du Pont dominance in the failure of
the rural counties to permit a much-needed redistribution of the
state's legislative districts. The 1950 census showed that 70 percent of Delaware's population lived in New Castle County,
which elected only 40 percent of the members of the legislature.
Unequal representation had been the prime reason for the Constitutional Convention of 1897, which had broken, albeit only
slightly, from the tradition of equality among the counties.

65. *Fortune,* November 1934, p. 65; January 1935, p. 140; December 1934, p. 193;
January 1935, p. 126.

Under the 1897 organic law, each county was divided into five senatorial and ten representative districts. In addition, the city of Wilmington, which in 1900 accounted for 41 percent of the state's population, was awarded two additional senatorial and five representative districts, which boosted New Castle County's total to seven senators and fifteen representatives. That meager concession to the most populous area of the state was further weakened by a clause requiring the vote of two-thirds of two successive legislatures to alter the number of districts in each county. The unfair distribution of legislative power persisted into the 1960s, when the Supreme Court of the United States declared such practices to be an unconstitutional denial of the franchise. Immediately, power in the Delaware General Assembly swung around from the rural counties to the suburbs of Wilmington. Another important step in the direction of greater democracy was the abandonment of the much-abused election system that had permitted the circulation of printed ballots before election day. The new voting machines installed in Delaware during the 1960s have eliminated a lot of the old-time election fraud.

Two other important changes made in the 1897 constitution removed the legislature's responsibility in granting divorces and chartering corporations. Until then, Delaware was decidedly antiquated in requiring special acts of the legislature for these purposes. Under the new constitution, however, the courts assumed control over divorces, and the ground was laid for a general incorporation law. In 1889, New Jersey had adopted a highly liberal law that had encouraged businesses to incorporate and pay chartering fees in that state. Delaware's lawmakers, eager to raise revenue in such an easy fashion and to give the state an image favorable to business, emulated New Jersey's law in 1899. The Delaware law did not require companies chartered in the state to do business in Delaware or to keep more than the most meager office staff there. A Delaware corporation could hold stockholders' meetings wherever it chose and was not restrained from acquiring other companies or creating holding companies. Time was to prove that the law, by its very liberality, could not, by itself, bring new industry to Delaware, but it could and did support many lawyers and bring in sizable revenues. In the first thirty years of operation under that law, 84,146 firms incorporated in Delaware, which brought the state government between 20 percent and 40 percent of its annual revenues.[66] In recent years, a number of other states have enacted similar laws with the same hope of attracting easy revenue. That Delaware has continued to be a popular state for incorporation rests in part on its Court of Chancery, which over the years has built up considerable experience in handling stockholders' suits and other legal problems common to big corporations. The Court of Chancery originated in England during the Middle Ages to decide cases that could not be settled according to the common law on the basis of fairness or equity. In most states, other courts have absorbed equity jurisdiction, but Delaware still retains this specialized court, which now is concerned largely with family and corporate squabbles.

In spite of the state's small over-all size, its counties have retained a great deal of the autonomy that they exercised in colonial times. Creation of the state highway department, a statewide school system, and health and welfare agencies have diminished county power, but Delawareans continue to hold tenaciously to their local loyalties and identifications. Traditionally, county government revolved around the Levy Court, a small elected body that assessed and collected the county property taxes. The dramatic growth that engulfed New Castle County in the post-World War II years demonstrated the ineffectuality of the old system in dealing with modern problems. The usual horrors of suburban sprawl were exaggerated by lack of a county zoning ordinance, inadequate planning, and the inability of the Levy Court to exercise executive authority. In 1952, the state legislature adopted a constitutional amendment to permit counties to enact zoning ordinances, but initially only New Castle took advantage of the new law. Kent, which was

66. Donald A. Grinde, Jr., "Business Concentration and Delaware Incorporation Law" (M.A. thesis, University of Delaware, 1968), pp. 51–52.

experiencing many of the same problems in the wake of the construction of the Dover Air Base, postponed action until the sad results of inaction had become painfully manifest. In 1965, New Castle County finally abandoned the Levy Court in favor of a county executive-council plan of government, which has greatly expanded local government services, especially in the areas of police protection and land-use planning. Subsequently, Sussex has done likewise, but Kent still retains the old system.

The doctrine of one man, one vote demands more than reform in the mechanics of elections and office-holding. In 1971, a research crew of Ralph Nader's "raiders" spent a summer in Delaware and reported, in a book entitled *The Company State,* that the power and wealth held by the du Pont family and the Du Pont Company were seriously inhibiting the full realization of democracy in the First State. Nader's blast recalled the earlier articles by *Fortune* written during the depression. The theme of a giant corporation's impact on a small state has remained fascinating, because the du Ponts have personalized big business for Delawareans in a way that is unique to this state.

In the 1930s, when *Fortune* came to Delaware, the Du Pont Company was not a major employer in the state. In addition to its corporate headquarters, the company owned only one relatively small plant in Delaware, located on the banks of the Christina at Newport. Within the next decade, however, the company built two larger plants in Delaware, the huge nylon manufactory at Seaford in Sussex County and a pigments plant on the Delaware River north of Wilmington at Edge Moor. As the number of Du Pont employees increased, the nature of the company's influence on the state shifted away from dominance by a few individuals toward the creation of a large independent but loyal bloc of company employees.

The location of the world's first nylon plant at Seaford was a perceptive move designed, at least in part, to win friends for the company in an area of the state that had long been hostile to Du Pont influence. Overnight, the Seaford plant became the largest single employer and biggest payroll in that heretofore agricultural county. In the more metropolitan Wilmington area, the company's impact was equally great. Du Pont selected the employees for its home base from among the best scientists, engineers, and administrators in the country and supplied them with a rich array of benefits, including two country clubs in New Castle County alone. Meanwhile, the company's employee magazines never ceased praising the capitalist system and the advantages of bigness in industry. Du Ponters were, as a rule, able, faithful, and politically conservative. By 1971, when Nader's Raiders came to Delaware, the company employed 25,000 Delawareans, comprising 11 percent of the state's work force.

The Nader group mustered a variety of facts in support of their contention that Du Pont influence was too powerful for a small state to absorb. They noted that Russell W. Peterson, then governor, had come to Delaware from the Midwest as a Du Pont chemist, while the mayor of Wilmington, Harry G. Haskell, Jr., was the wealthy relative of a former Du Pont executive. The leader of the Republican forces in the state senate was Reynolds du Pont, and the state's lone representative in Congress was Pierre S. du Pont IV. In addition, the Naderites could point to the great power that the du Pont family exercised over communications and banking in the state through the Christiana Securities Company and to the presence of du Ponts or company employees on the boards of the University of Delaware, the United Way, the Wilmington Medical Center, and various other statewide charitable and educational foundations. In terms of names and numbers alone, the Nader indictment of Du Pont power was obviously not unwarranted.

"DuPont dominates Delaware as does no single company in any other state," said Ralph Nader in the introduction to *The Company State*. His researchers went on to conclude, somewhat inconsistently, that the relationship between the First State and its leading corporation was not unique but rather "the prototype of the large corporation in an American community." The Raiders censured the company for its apathetic attitude toward major social problems, especially in the racially troubled and decaying city of Wilmington, yet claimed that, when the businessmen did become involved and try to help, they were insensitive and expected dramatic results too quickly. The mere acceptance of responsibility was not enough. "The question is not whether any mammoth firm will make an impact on its political unit; DuPont affects the community even by its inaction. The question is: in what ways and by which methods should large companies like DuPont relate to the local community? The criteria must be: a large corporation should act so as to provide the community with a maximum of benefits and a minimum of domination." [67] Only an astute political tightrope-walker could hope to approach such an ideal.

Many Delawareans were willing to grant that the Raiders had correctly described the mammoth power of the du Ponts—both company and family. Typically, First Staters believed, however, that the study team had come with many preconceived ideas and had spent too little time in the state to reach valid conclusions about the du Ponts' use of that power. By exaggerating the woes that du Ponts brought upon Delaware, the team had ended only by alienating most thinking and concerned people in the state and thereby diminished the impact of their recommendations. From the earliest years of the twentieth century, when Pierre, T. Coleman, and Alfred I. du Pont forced Delaware to modernize its schools, highways, and welfare programs, various members of the du Pont family have used their family's wealth and prestige to interfere in state affairs, but generally such interference has been to the benefit of Delawareans. Not surprisingly, du Pont benefactors are sometimes blamed for demanding a commanding voice in the operation of the organizations they have underwritten. A great part of the problem of control has not been their fault, however, because other Delawareans, brought up in the habit of mind to "Let the du Ponts do it," have too often forfeited their own responsibilities for community betterment. In recent years, as the federal government has become more involved in every aspect of the state's life, the national bureaucracy has undoubtedly outspent and outmanaged the du Ponts, whose diffused fortunes are no longer

67. Phelan and Pozen, *The Company State,* p. ix, p. 409, p. 409.

gigantic. Today, no one family can compare with the federal government's funds or power in state policy-making. Furthermore, the Nader group erred in assuming that the members of so diverse a family, together with the top management and minor employees of so large a company, are capable of acting as a monolothic unit.

The debates surrounding the Coastal Zone Act demonstrate the last point most effectively. In 1970, when former Du Pont chemist Russell Peterson was inaugurated governor, he told the General Assembly, "I am convinced that Delaware has the potential to become a Model State. The state that started a Nation can also lead a nation." [68] Among the dynamic new governor's high-priority tasks was pollution reduction. To prevent a thirteen-company oil consortium from building a major refinery on the Delaware coast, Peterson proposed and carried through the Coastal Zone Act, which outlaws any heavy industrialization of the state's coastal area. Of all his accomplishments as governor, Peterson was most proud of that act, which brought good publicity to Delaware and won him an award from the World Wild-Life Fund. The Nader team interpreted the act as an effort by the wealthy to retain their favorite sporting grounds and simultaneously to block unwanted industrial competition in Delaware.[69] Peterson, on the other hand, claimed that the act had substantial support from blue-collar sportsmen who could not travel so far as the rich to enjoy hunting and fishing. More significant still was the reaction of Charles B. McCoy, a recent president of the Du Pont Company, who cautioned a Wilmington Rotary Club audience during the first stages of the energy crisis in January 1974 that the act was stifling Delaware's economy and must be modified. Peterson, by then head of the federal Council on Environmental Quality, reacted sharply, accusing his one-time boss of misusing statistics and doing "a disservice to the community." "It's not surprising," Peterson was quoted as saying, that the Du Pont Company would support

68. Russell W. Peterson, in the *Wilmington Evening Journal,* January 14, 1970.
69. Phelan and Pozan, *The Company State,* pp. 122–123.

"the oil companies and the petrochemical companies with whom [they] work so closely as a customer and a supplier." [70] The one thing that is clear in this complex situation is that the Du Pont Company and its employees, together with the du Pont family, may be very powerful, but they do not speak with one voice, as Nader had claimed.

Sherman Tribbitt, a Democrat who defeated Peterson in 1972, responded to the growing controversy over the coastal zone and other planning priorities by appointing the Delaware Tomorrow Commission. The thirty-two commissioners, who represent a broad spectrum of interest groups, are in the process of completing a plan based on their perceptions of the state's future needs. Their work is predicated upon a significant downturn that has occurred in Delaware's rate of growth since 1970. As recently as 1968, Governor Charles L. Terry, Jr., predicted that there would be 800,000 Delawareans by 1980, an increase of 252,000 over the 1970 census. Three years earlier, in a request for a capital-bond program to pay for more schools and highways, the governor had told the assembly that "Delaware is in the midst of a rapid population growth, no other period of our history has seen such vast and demanding change throughout the state. Business is excellent. New industries continue to seek locations in all parts of the state. The economy is booming and every indication is that it will continue to grow at an unprecedented rate." [71]

Now that rate of growth has been reversed, and the chairman of the Tomorrow Commission told a Wilmington audience in February 1976 that "the party is over." [72] In place of the earlier estimate of 800,000 by 1980, the commissioners' projections have been scaled down to a more modest estimate of 700,000 in population by 1985. Throughout the 1960s, when Delaware's growth rate was twice the national average, unem-

70. *Wilmington Evening Journal,* January 24, 1974.

71. Charles L. Terry, May 25, 1965, "Messages of the Governors," Morris Library, University of Delaware, Newark, Delaware.

72. Statement by O. Francis Biondi, February 10, 1976, First and Central Presbyterian Church, Wilmington, Delaware.

ployment in the First State was very low. By 1975, however, the state's economy had so deteriorated that 10 percent of Delaware's work force was jobless, a percentage that is slightly higher than the national average. In their recommendations, the commissioners are trying to find a middle passage between the unbridled courting of industry and the desirability of implementing pollution standards and planning. They recommend that the Coastal Zone Act be replaced by a more flexible statewide land-use planning act which environmentalists fear may undermine the law's purpose and effect. On the other hand, they advocate selected industrial growth that will put a premium on employment of the low-skilled workers who have been most affected by the recession. The commissioners urge that new industries be located in or near major population centers like Wilmington, where most of the unemployed live, where the cost of extending utilities will be minimized, and where industry will do the least damage to the environment. Their effort to save land and money also calls for a halt to suburban sprawl by concentrating housing in or close to cities. They also recommend the consolidation of many functions of local, county, and state government.

Small size has been both a curse and a blessing to Delaware. It has insured that the state's people feel very close to their elected officials, including their United States senators and congressman. On the other hand, the smallness of the state has permitted interest groups—such as the eighteenth- and nineteenth-century country gentry and, more recently, the du Pont family—to become more powerful than they might be in a larger and more diverse state. A few state leaders, notably Pierre du Pont and Russell Peterson, have used the state's small size to advantage in securing landmark legislation and reform. More commonly, however, Delawareans have been slower to accept the need for change than have their neighbors in more populous states. Conservatism has, no doubt, preserved much of Delaware's charm, but it also preserved slavery, the whipping post, and the almshouse far beyond their time.

Ironically, it now appears that we Delawareans are going to have to accept more change in the form of systematic planning if we are to preserve what is best in our state's heritage. A balanced economy, including a strong agricultural sector and improved fisheries, as well as industrial development may not lie in our future unless we insist upon it; neither will the continued mutilation of our landscape by ill-conceived housing developments cease automatically.

Whether or not any of the Tomorrow Commission's plans for the future will be taken seriously by the state legislature depends, of course, on the reaction of the people of Delaware, who must inform themselves and join in the inevitable debate. Delawareans have grown more sophisticated over the years. They are no longer so deeply divided between upstate and downstate, nor are they so inclined to vote straight party tickets or to look for leadership only to old, established families, even if the old, established family name is du Pont. Democracy has not only survived in Delaware, but it appears to be gaining ground continuously—if sometimes grudgingly—reviving the promise of 1776. Will Delawareans of 2176 look back upon this generation as one that planned conscientiously and intelligently for posterity, as the men of the Revolution did for us? It all depends on whether we can find ways to get along with one another, to husband our resources, to preserve liberty, promote political equality, and to meet the social and economic needs of our citizens. History is, after all, not a set of larger-than-life plaster characters preserved in a book; it is all of us.

Suggestions for Further Reading

Those interested in pursuing the study of Delaware history will find a wealth of printed material. Two comprehensive bibliographies are especially useful to Delaware historians: H. C. Reed and Marion B. Reed's *A Bibliography of Delaware through 1960* (Newark: University of Delaware Press, 1966) and Daniel M. Nelson's *A Checklist of Writings on the Economic History of the Greater Philadelphia-Wilmington Region* (Wilmington: Eleutherian Mills Historical Library, 1968). Among the multivolume state histories the best is still J. Thomas Scharf, *History of Delaware,* 2 vols. (Philadelphia: L. J. Richards, 1888), for which an index has recently been prepared by the Historical Society of Delaware. Other good comprehensive histories are Henry C. Conrad, *History of the State of Delaware,* 3 vols. (Wilmington: Published by the author, 1908) and *Delaware, A History of the First State,* edited by H. Clay Reed, 3 vols. (New York: Lewis Historical Publishing Company, 1947). In addition, a very fine introduction to the state including suggested tour routes can be found in *Delaware, A Guide to the First State* (1938; reprint edition, New York: Hastings House, 1955). *Delaware History,* the biannual journal of the Historical Society of Delaware, has, since its creation in 1946, published a great variety of high-quality articles and records dealing with all aspects of the state's history.

Among the many volumes on colonial Delaware, the most notable include a series of books by that productive student of Indian history, C. A. Weslager, including *The Delaware Indians, A History* (New Brunswick: Rutgers University Press, 1972); *Delaware's Forgotten Folk; The Story of the Moors and Nanticokes* (Philadelphia: University of Pennsylvania Press, 1943); *Delaware's Buried Past* (Philadelphia: University of Pennsylvania Press, 1944), and *The English on the Delaware, 1610–1687* (New Brunswick: Rutgers University Press, 1967).

212   *For Further Reading*

Amandus Johnson has explored the Swedish period extensively in a series of works including *The Swedish Settlements on the Delaware,* 2 vols. (New York: D. Appleton and Co., 1911), and, for less ambitious readers, his one-volume summary *The Swedes on the Delaware* (Philadelphia: International Printing Co., 1914). On the Dutch colonists, see David de Vries's account of his explorations, *Voyages from Holland to America* (New York: New York Historical Society, 1857) and C. A. Weslager, *Dutch Explorers, Traders and Settlers in the Delaware Valley, 1609–1664* (Philadelphia: University of Pennsylvania Press, 1961). Delaware's unique colonial experience has attracted some very capable local historians. Benjamin Ferris, a nineteenth-century Quaker gentleman's *A History of the Original Settlements on the Delaware . . .* (Wilmington: Wilson & Heald, Printers, 1846) and Christopher Ward's *The Dutch and Swedes on the Delaware* (Philadelphia: University of Pennsylvania Press, 1930) are both lively and accurate accounts. A valuable contemporary witness to mid-eighteenth-century life in Delaware may be found in Israel Acrelius, *A History of New Sweden; or, The Settlements on the River Delaware* (Philadelphia: The Historical Society of Pennsylvania, 1874). On Delaware's most interesting architecture, much of which comes from the colonial period, see Harold D. Eberlein and Cortlandt V. D. Hubbard, *Historic Houses and Buildings of Delaware* (Dover: Public Archives Commission, 1962); George Fletcher Bennett, *Early Architecture of Delaware* (Wilmington: Historical Press, Inc., 1932); and *Delaware State Historic Preservation Plan,* 2 vols. (Dover: State of Delaware, Division of Historical and Cultural Affairs, 1973, 1975).

Among other significant writings on colonial Delaware and the Revolutionary period are *The Collected Essays of Richard S. Rodney on Early Delaware,* edited by George H. Gibson (Wilmington: Society of Colonial Wars in the State of Delaware, 1975); Nelson W. Rightmyer, *The Anglican Church in Delaware* (Philadelphia: Church Historical Society, 1947); and Elizabeth Waterston, *Churches in Delaware during the Revolution* (Wilmington: Historical Society of Delaware, 1925). On the state's Revolutionary leaders, see John M. Coleman, *Thomas McKean, Forgotten Leader of the Revolution* (Rockaway, N.J.: American Faculty Press, 1975); Charles J. Stille, *The Life and Times of John Dickinson* (Philadelphia: The Historical Society of Pennsylvania, 1891); William T. Read, *Life and Correspondence of*

George Read (Philadelphia: J. B. Lippincott Co., 1870); and George H. Ryden, editor, *Letters To and From Caesar Rodney* (Philadelphia: University of Pennsylvania Press, 1933). The best books on how the war affected Delaware are Christopher L. Ward, *The Delaware Continentals, 1776–1783* (Wilmington: Historical Society of Delaware, 1941) and Harold B. Hancock, *The Delaware Loyalists* (Wilmington: Historical Society of Delaware, 1940). A book that covers both the war and postwar years is John A. Munroe's *Federalist Delaware, 1775–1815* (New Brunswick: Rutgers University Press, 1954).

There have been a number of studies of economic and transportation developments in the First State, such as Ralph Gray's *The National Waterway: A History of the Chesapeake and Delaware Canal, 1769–1965* (Urbana: University of Illinois Press, 1967); David Tyler's *The Bay and River Delaware, A Pictorial History* (Cambridge, Md.: Cornell Maritime Press, 1955); and Tyler's *The American Clyde: A History of Iron and Steel Shipbuilding on the Delaware from 1840 to World War I* (Newark: University of Delaware Press, 1958). On an important entrepreneur, see Bessie G. du Pont, *The Life of Eleuthère Irénée du Pont,* 11 vols. (Newark: University of Delaware, 1923–1927); and on the state's most famous inventor, Greville Bathe and Dorothy Bathe, *Oliver Evans; A Chronicle of Early American Engineering* (Philadelphia: The Historical Society of Pennsylvania, 1935). Carol E. Hoffecker's *Brandywine Village: The Story of a Milling Community* (Wilmington: Old Brandywine Village, Inc., 1974) and *Wilmington, Delaware: Portrait of an Industrial City* (Charlottesville: University of Virginia Press, 1974) also cover economic developments, while Elizabeth Montgomery's *Reminiscences of Wilmington* (Philadelphia: T. K. Collins, Jr., 1851) and Henry Seidel Canby's *The Age of Confidence; Life in the Nineties* (New York: Farrar & Rinehart, 1934) are outstanding first-hand accounts of nineteenth-century Wilmington. On more recent developments in the state's economy, dealing most particularly with the Du Pont Company, see the section on that company in Alfred D. Chandler, Jr.,'s *Strategy and Structure* (Cambridge: M.I.T. Press, 1962), as well as Alfred D. Chandler, Jr., and Stephen M. Salsbury, *Pierre S. du Pont and the Making of the Modern Corporation* (New York: Harper and Row, 1971) and Marquis James, *Alfred I. du Pont, the Family Rebel* (Indianapolis: The Bobbs-Merrill Co., 1941).

Various aspects of the state's political and social history can be found in Harold B. Hancock, *Delaware during the Civil War, A Political History* (Wilmington: Historical Society of Delaware, 1961); Lyman P. Powell, *History of Education in Delaware* (Washington: Government Printing Office, 1893); Robert Caldwell, *The Penitentiary Movement in Delaware, 1776–1829* (Wilmington: Historical Society of Delaware, 1946); and by the same author, *Red Hannah, Delaware's Whipping Post* (Philadelphia: University of Pennsylvania Press, 1947).

On race relations, see Charles Tilly, Wagner D. Jackson, and Barry Kay, *Race and Residence in Wilmington, Delaware* (New York: Teachers College, Columbia U., 1963). A very good ethnic history is Rabbi David Geffen et al., *Jewish Delaware* (Wilmington: Jewish Federation of Delaware, 1976). Paul Dolan's *The Government and Administration of Delaware* (New York: Crowell, 1956), the most comprehensive guide to the state's government, is currently undergoing revision to bring it up to date.

Index

Acrelius, Israel, 23–24, 75, 76, 103
Addicks, John Edward Charles O'Sullivan ("Gas" Addicks), 187–191
African Union Methodist Church (Wilmington), 97–98
Africans. *See* Blacks
Agriculture: in Swedish colony, 17–18; "by burning," 18, 23–24; before the Revolution, 23–24; in New Castle County, 26–27, 44–48; economic blight during 1830s, 43–44; sheepherding, 45; depressed state of, in twentieth century, 53, 122–125; farming, twentieth century, 59–60; land given over to, 60; gross income per farm, 60; one-crop failure, 90. *See also* Broiler industry; Peaches; Soybeans; Tobacco
Alison, Francis, 85, 86, 104, 112, 150
American Colonization Society, 98
Anti-Slavery Society, 96–97
Architecture, 15–16, 28–30. *See also* names of churches
Asbury, Francis, 87–89, 97
Asbury Church (Wilmington), 97
Associated Charities, 123, 128, 193

Baltimore, Cecilius Calvert, 2nd Baron. *See* Calvert, Cecil
Bancroft, Joseph: and textile milling, 35
Bancroft, William Poole, 35–36, 51
Bancroft Textile Mills, 34–35
Baptists, 79
Barratt's Chapel: and Methodism, 89
Bayard, James A., 173
Bayard, James A., Jr., 180, 182
Bayard, Thomas F., 180, 194
Belton, Ethel L., 129–130, 134
Beresford, John: at Lewes, 174

Bissell, Emily P.: early welfare worker, introduces Christmas seals, 123
Bjork, Eric, 74, 75
Black Anthony, 90
Blacks: slavery, 90–102, 160; in 1790, 93; in 1860, 93–94; presumed free unless proven otherwise, 94; in 1837, 96; lay preachers, 97; ties to Methodism, 97–98; population in Wilmington, 115, 132; integration, 131–132; special court for, 148; Negro suffrage, 185–186. *See also* Education; Race relations
"Blue Hen's Chickens," 168, 183
Boulevard Commission. *See* Highways
Brandywine Bridge, 29, 30, 31, 35
Brandywine River: disgorges into the Christina, 4; source of water supply, 28, 51; mills and factories, 30, 34; and industrial development, 51; and the du Ponts, 53–55 *passim*
Brandywine Village, 29, 30, 31
Broiler industry, 58–59
Broom, Jacob, 34, 36
Buck, C. Douglas (governor), 124, 200

Cadwalader, Gen. John, 162
Calvinists, 82–83, 85
Calvert, Cecil, 2nd Baron Baltimore, 20–22, 25, 112, 141
Campanius, Johan, 73
Canals, 39–40, 42–43, 113
Cannon, Patty, 99
Cannon, William (governor), 183, 184
Cape Henlopen, 4, 22, 28, 140, 163
Carriage-making, 49, 52
Chadds Ford, xiv, 164, 165
Cheswold group: Indians and mixed-bloods, 71

215